KU-538-693

'This is a warm and lyrical book about a tough trade in tough times'
Sara Wheeler, *Observer*

'Acutely observed and surprisingly moving... Clare's writing everywhere is of the highest order, assured, probing and alert. But it is his ability to convey the strange effect on the human spirit of being at sea that raises the book above the ordinary'
Spectator

'Clare has the two essential qualities of a good travel writer: a sharp observing eye and a generous spirit'
Scotsman

'Stupendous and extraordinarily exciting... What Clare demonstrates, even beyond his undoubted gifts as writer, is his basic humanity. I read his wonderful book with gratitude for his insight – but also with increased admiration for the men to whom we owe almost everything in our comfortable and secure lives'
Times Higher Education

'Rich and dense, full of old sea-dog stories, with barely a word wasted, it's a triumph of quiet artistry'
Daily Mail

'A fabulous account... There is Conradian insight in Clare's portrayal of the crews to which he is supernumerary, from the captain who hums as he negotiates narrow channels to the first mate constantly crunching carrots'
Giles Foden

'Clare's powers of plain description are tremendous'
The Times

'An epic and lyrical adventure in which Clare naturally recalls Melville, Conrad, Masefield and Coleridge to evoke a way of life that is so entwined with, yet alien to, our own'
Financial Times

DOWN TO THE SEA IN SHIPS

Horatio Clare is the bestselling author of two memoirs, *Running for the Hills* (Somerset Maugham Award) and *Truant*; the travel book *A Single Swallow* – which follows the birds' migration from South Africa to the UK – and a novella, *The Prince's Pen*, the retelling of a Mabinogion tale. An award-winning journalist, occasional teacher, former radio producer, sporadic broadcaster and Fellow in Creative Writing at the University of Liverpool, Horatio writes regularly on nature and travel for the *Daily Telegraph*, the *Financial Times* and various international publications. He and his family are currently based in Yorkshire.

ALSO BY HORATIO CLARE

Non-fiction

Running for the Hills
Truant: Notes from the Slippery Slope
Sicily: Through Writers' Eyes
A Single Swallow

Fiction

The Prince's Pen

HORATIO CLARE

Down to the Sea in Ships

Of Ageless Oceans and Modern Men

VINTAGE BOOKS
London

Published by Vintage 2015

6 8 10 9 7

Copyright © Horatio Clare 2014

Horatio Clare has asserted his right under the Copyright, Designs
and Patents Act 1988 to be identified as the author of this work

This book is sold subject to the condition that it shall not,
by way of trade or otherwise, be lent, resold, hired out, or
otherwise circulated without the publisher's prior consent in any
form of binding or cover other than that in which it is published
and without a similar condition, including this condition, being
imposed on the subsequent purchaser

This book is a work of non-fiction based on the experiences
and recollections of the author. In some limited cases names
have been changed solely to protect the privacy of others.

First published in Great Britain in 2014 by
Chatto & Windus

Vintage
20 Vauxhall Bridge Road,
London SW1V 2SA

www.vintage-books.co.uk

A Penguin Random House Company

Penguin
Random House
UK

global.penguinrandomhouse.com

A CIP catalogue record for this book
is available from the British Library

ISBN 9780099526292

MIX
Paper from
responsible sources
FSC® C018179

Penguin Random House is committed to a
sustainable future for our business, our readers
and our planet. This book is made from Forest
Stewardship Council® certified paper.

Typeset in Ehrhardt by Palimpsest Book Production Ltd, Falkirk, Stirlingshire
Printed and bound by CPI Group (UK) Ltd, Croydon CR0 4YY

For Rebecca, Robin
and Aubrey (the
First Sea Lord) – with love.

The rain continued to hammer the bridge. From time to time the thunder cracked, still violent. The storm united them. At sea storms weld the crew together. No sailor ever tells his family about times like that. Not in letters, not when he reaches home. So as not to worry them. Because they are indescribable, too. Storms don't exist. No more than sailors do, once they are at sea. Humanity's only reality is the land. So one does not know sailors, will never know them, even ashore. Unless one day you set sail aboard a cargo ship . . .

Jean-Claude Izzo, *The Lost Sailors*

The true peace of God begins at any spot a thousand miles from the nearest land.

Joseph Conrad

Contents

Author's Note

'Call me Ish . . .' – but Melville's third line is even better than the famous first. 'Whenever I find myself growing grim about the mouth; whenever it is a damp, drizzly November in my soul; whenever I find myself involuntarily pausing before coffin warehouses, and bringing up the rear of every funeral I meet; and especially whenever my hypos get such an upper hand of me that it requires a strong moral principle to prevent me from deliberately stepping into the street, and methodically knocking people's hats off – then, I account it high time to get to sea as soon as I can.'

It happened to be a drizzly November when I picked up *Moby-Dick* and began to read. I soon found myself walking by the river through a winter evening and vowing I too would go to sea. It was a vow born from a desire without a beginning (when does a boy first think of taking ship with pirates, or pirate hunters?) and, to this day, without an end. To leave the land, to know ships and sailors and their stories, to see the oceans in their vastness, to discover countries from their wharves inwards – what a dream!

I contacted a giant Danish shipping company, a mega-corporation which owns ports, aircraft, freight companies and oil rigs as well as ships, offering to be their writer-in-residence. The company accepted and foreswore censorship: that would make it pointless, said Michael Storgaard, the head of Maersk's public relations – write what you like. And so, with my partner's blessing and her son wishing me well and issuing me with selected pieces of Lego for my company on the voyages, I went to sea.

Many people, from children to the insane, from the devout to the philosophical, have supposed that the world is a charade. They imagine it a God game, an illusion that is extremely but not quite convincing. They speculate our existence is a shadow or speck in some great scheme which is far larger, more organised, more magnificent and perhaps more terrible than the life we know. They are right.

Just beyond the horizon there is another world. It runs in parallel with ours but it obeys different laws, accords with a different time and is populated by a people who are like us, but whose lives are not like ours. Without them, what we call normality would not exist. Were it not for the labours of this race we could not work, rest, eat, dress, communicate, learn, play, live or even die as we do. For a little while, for some months over two years, it has been my privilege to explore the sea in the company of its people.

Where the land ends certainty diminishes, modernity recedes and antique ways regather their power. Were we able to see the whole history of seafaring its accumulated impression might be akin to a borderless painting, a Turner worked over by Ernst, Pollock and Bosch. Flying wind and water are swirled about with breaking ropes. Here ships fight, founder and death-dive; here they are broken-backed. The scene flickers, incarnadine with fire and blood. Here it is dark as shoals and pale as corpses; here it recedes into the far distance, to a not-nothingness of wave-wastes and inconceivable weather. Around its corners there is longing love, people cheering and faces laughing, exhilarated. Here and there are flashes of passionate drinking, sex and Dionysian parties. In this picture's heights are drifting visions of wonder and unearthly beauty, empyrean skies and gulfs of paradise. Storms of money in ducats and dollars blow across this picture, and avalanches of cargo, jewelled tempests of every commodity and artefact humans ever needed or sought. The canvas is shot through with fear and endurance, and shaded, all over, in loneliness. It is not only that the nature of sea stories draws them to and from the dramatic. This picture is the consequence of a collision of two temperaments: the nature of men, and nature of the sea.

This book is an account of places beyond the coasts. It is partly the report of an observer and partly the story of a participant. You are designated, officially, a 'supernumerary', an addition who is part of the ship's company but not one of the crew. My deeper motives for going only became clear to me when I returned. I was fascinated by the idea of men at sea: shipping is still a man's world; quicker and more thoroughly than anywhere except perhaps a battlefield, the sea finds men out. I wanted to see men, their characters and their stories as if on a bare stage, away from women, children and the world. I was in love with the wonder, the rough romance and the potential horror of great ships: none of man's machines have more awe and character than they do. And I wanted, more than anything, to know something of the vastness of the oceans.

'They that go down to the sea in ships and do business in great waters, they see the workings of the Lord and His wonders in the deep.' The potency of the lines springs from the toppling inequality of the forces Psalm 107 describes. The human determination to be, to thrive, to 'do business' never seemed more puny or more admirable than in opposition to great waters – by far the most miraculous and dreadful of nature's manifestations. You may or may not see the workings of the Lord in a beetle climbing a blade of grass, but if you are going to see His wonders at all you will surely find them on the face of the deep.

PART ONE

To the East and West

CHAPTER 1

Spirits of Ships

The Captain is fierce with bulk like a small bear. His skin is pallid, his beard grizzled, his teeth are tinged with alloys and gold. We pay great attention to whatever he says; we watch him as if he were famous. He feels our scrutiny as he hums and mutters. He talks to himself in company but not when he is alone. The crew have not known him long but they are already fond of him. You can hear it in the way they relish his title:

'Yes, Captain!'

'Good evening, Captain . . .'

We never say his name.

Crew and captain are in a relationship with the vessel, a total entwinement that exists only on ships. It is something like a bee marriage, in which there are only two states, work and rest, and only one place, the workplace, and where there are almost no choices. In this sleepless hive the crew are the steel queen's workers, cleaning and tending to her, labouring in all her grim and dangerous places. High on the bridge above them, where the officers are suitors in order of rank, the Captain, the master, is the ship's betrothed. She is a hard mistress, interminably demanding. When she baulks, fusses, fails or sounds an alarm they call the Captain: he will know what to do. If there is a problem with the engine they call the chief engineer, but the engine is not the ship.

The engine is like a gigantic mad animal, howling in a cathedral of its own. Its decibels are dangerous. In certain latitudes the engine room is 80 per cent humidity, plus tropical heat, plus the fifty degrees radiating from the machinery. In swells this Hades pitches, rolls and rocks. There is no daylight, only constant vibration and the endless, terrifying roar. Four ladders up and two doors away from the noise you find the engine control room, a sickly yellow bunker lined with machines in cabinets and computer screens. Here are the chief engineer and his officers, coming and going on their sorties into the howling interior.

'I like the engine room!' Joel says, eyes shining.

Joel is the fourth engineer. He is small with a boy's smile, quick as a Thai boxer.

'I do – because I really like the engine.'

The ship is the limit of Joel's world for months on end. It is his hardest taskmaster, a job which is never finished, a danger, in great and small ways, his safety (you take to the lifeboats only in drills and nightmares) and, strangely, because it is ruthless in taking the shortest routes, and arriving and leaving on schedule, the ship is something to him beyond life and work combined.

'It's freedom!' Joel insists. 'Yes. It is freedom. It is!'

Joel is unusual, even by the standards of unusual men.

We are out far in the blue when another ship prepares to cut across our course. She ought to pass behind us because we are on her starboard side, but though there are conventions at sea, traditions and international agreements, and there is good seamanship and poor, really there are only three determinants in this world: how the weather changes, what ships can manage and what captains decide to do. This is why the sea is still the place where strange and worse things happen. The radar tells us what is going to happen now and the chief officer mutters:

'Where is she going?'

She is going to Long Beach, says the computer. Now she comes too close, too fast.

'What is he doing?' cries the chief, and curses, his irritation switching from the ship to her captain. Though there is little to choose between them – men and vessels being almost one out here – seafarers are quicker to blame men than ships. Bad captains, lousy helms and poor pilots are all facts of life. A bad ship, on the other hand, is a nightmare.

Bad ships might be old and slow, or run by crooks, or cantankerous to handle, or battered by thrift, poor maintenance and hard driving. There are truly terrible ships out there, ships abandoned by their owners, their crews unpaid, rotting at anchor off shores where the authorities want nothing to do with them. There are ships at sea which have seen stowaways thrown overboard, cadets raped, ships which have known murders and hijacks. There are once-powerful ships out there now, being flogged too hard, their machinery straining and deteriorating; there are ships being beaten through endless nights by harsh captains and miserable, desperate crews. Seafarers believe there are cursed ships, too.

In 1895 Walter Macarthur produced 'The Red Record', a list of cruelties and abuses on American Cape Horners. Cape Horners worked between the West Coast, principally San Francisco, and ports on the Atlantic. These were the dusk days of sail and wood, the dawn of iron and steam. Perhaps the worst reputation in the Cape Horn fleet belonged to a full-rigged sailer known as 'the bloody *Gatherer*':

'On one passage round the Horn to San Francisco two of her men were driven to suicide and a third was shot by the mate. This was too much even for San Francisco and the master, Sparks, had to relinquish the command while the mate, Watts, went to prison. The "bloody *Gatherer*" arrived in San Francisco after another of these hell-ship voyages and the mate had to be smuggled ashore to escape the consequences of having killed one of the crew . . .'

It is as though ships have spirits, good or ill, which are not merely the sum of their histories and the personalities of their crews. You feel that spirit late at night, when the corridors and the stairwell are silent but for the strum of the engine. You feel it in the deserted spaces of the poop, the low deck at the stern where the wake boils up below you, thrashed to white fury by the propeller. You feel it on the fo'c'sle, the foremost point, the quietest part of the ship, where the bow is a spear driven on and on into the hissing sea. You are quite alone in these places. The ship is alive to the swells and the wind and the beat of its diesel heart. The refrigerated containers, the reefers, moan and whirr. Steel boxes grate together, screaming and wincing. There are bangings and knockings from places in the stacks, as though ghosts or stowaways are imprisoned in the towering boxes. High above it all the bridge screens gaze forward, unblinking eyes staring down at the sea roads of the world, at the thousands of nautical miles and storms and calms to come.

CHAPTER 2

Signing On

Felixstowe on a late August day offers fish and chips and a beach hut called Larfalot. In a mini amusement park a tiny train goes round a tiny track. A pub caters for Events, Weddings and Funerals. Thirty-five pounds buys a room with a sea view at the Grafton B&B, and being a seafarer knocks a fiver off, since you will be gone by nightfall.

'Moving on, I at last came to a dim sort of out-hanging light not far from the docks, and heard a forlorn creaking in the air; and looking up, saw a swinging sign over the door with a white painting upon it, faintly representing a tall straight jet of misty spray, and these words underneath – "The Spouter-Inn: – Peter Coffin".'

Ishmael met Queequeg in the Spouter-Inn; Queequeg with his unearthly tattooings, lofty bearing, 'simple honest heart' and tall harpoon. There is no Queequeg in the Grafton, only the proprietor, his wife and a low-voiced couple who might be having an affair. There is a picture of the frigate HMS *Grafton* in the hall. The proprietor wrote to her captain, asking him if he would like to visit.

'He wrote back saying he couldn't, but he sent us the picture and his condolences.'

You can see why the captain of such a fine fighting ship might send condolences to his land-stranded namesake but perhaps they were premature. The frigate now belongs to the Chilean navy, according to the proprietor, along with twenty-five million pounds' worth of sonar gear.

'They'd only just fitted her with it!' he says, aggrieved.

The day you sign on to your first ship is special, one way or another. 'Signing on', British slang for receiving unemployment benefit, means the opposite at sea. The phrase descends from the beginning of the age of sail, through merchant ships, pirates, privateers and whalers, whose crews all signed contracts with their captains, known as the Ship's Articles, which specified shares of the profits of the voyage. Seafarers now enter into agreements with companies rather than captains, but when you sign on you still have your life in a bag and no idea of the friends or enemies you will make, no idea of the worlds you will see nor the adventures, and the boredoms, you will share. In Melville's time a whaling voyage could take three or four years, assuming you lived. Today the sentence is two or three months for a senior officer, who works half the year, and much longer as you go down the scale. For the poorest paid, often the youngest, signing on means nine months minimum, commonly a year and more. In all those months a man might reasonably expect to be off the ship a few times, for a few hours, but it may also be that he is not able to disembark at all. There is a tension between underpaid crewmen who beg for their contracts to be extended to thirteen months and beyond, and shipowners, who worry about the psychological costs of such endeavour, because of their effects on the men's efficiency.

So you say goodbye, hoist your bag and travel to the end of the land. This counts as an unusual departure not least because I am a Briton taking ship in a British port: most seafarers travel to work by aeroplane. A seaman from the Philippines, for example, commonly finds himself taking his first flight to his first foreign country in the days before he joins his first ship. By the time you reach your port of departure your ability to do anything about normal life has all but vanished, blocked out for months to come. You may be able to send emails from the ship. You may be able to make one phone call a month. You find out when you board.

There seems more happening at sea than on land in Felixstowe. The horizon is busy with wind turbines, a light-ship, buoys and towers – or are they ships? They look like broken blocks in loose clusters, sawn-off things, monster vessels belonging to the private Swiss company MSC and to COSCO, the Chinese government's shipping line. One in, one out all day, along a dog-leg channel which takes them to the north-east before they turn away. The sea is a mulling brown and the light changes towards teatime, grey showing it has as many shades as any other colour: black-grey, silver, blue-grey, white.

The *Gerd* comes in towards the beginning of evening. She moves quickly, her bow wave the only foam on all the sea. She is light: there are a couple of towers of containers but most of the deck bays are low or empty, revealing her lines. The *Gerd* looks like a ship that Hergé might have drawn for Captain Haddock, bonny in her red, yellow and blue, and a bit dirty, and very big. She does not seem to slow for the pilot boat which goes out to meet her. She turns in towards the cranes and the port, withdrawing around the corner behind the beach huts.

Graham, the agent, appears in a van. He wears an orange tabard and hard hat. We might be on our way to a building site.

'All right? It's been mad today. Hectic.' The agent is the ship's link to the port. He or she arranges crew accommodation, transfers, medical attention if necessary, the ship's mail and all the paperwork involved in arrival, departure, tugs and cargo. Graham casts an unimpressed eye over Felixstowe. 'It's all about the port,' he says. The port is divided into city blocks of containers. The cranes are gigantic; the new ones at the far end are the biggest in the world, ready for ever-larger Danish and Chinese ships. Seafarers say China owns Felixstowe. Hutchison Whampoa Limited owns it, along with forty other ports. HWL is controlled by Cheung Kong Holdings, a Hong Kong property developer, and you can see the connection. Felixstowe's Trinity Terminal is a little piece of Hong Kong on the Suffolk coast.

Along the quays the giant machines are moored, higher than castles, longer than villages. This close to them you cannot see any entire. Vast hulls loom like steel walls at the end of the world, their bows the axe-heads of titans. Mooring lines are tight and hard as beams. I crane my neck back to try to take them in, but there is no reducing ships like this to any kind of scale. No photographer could frame them. Way above, severe and straight-browed against the sky, are their bridges. The *Gerd Maersk* is just tying up. The ship is not officially here until her gangway touches the quay. The gangway is a sloping ladder running up, up – four – five storeys? My sense of scale is hopelessly overrun. The ladder bobs under me as I climb. Filipinos in hard hats and dark overalls smile uncertain welcome.

'Not scared of heights, are you?' Graham asks, at the top.

At first the ship is a cliff-edge of dark red steel. We hurry past stanchions, rails, up steel ladders, pass below a tremendous roaring from the engine air-intakes, step over sills through doors which wince behind us, sealing tight. Inside the passages are warm, yellowed by strip lighting. There is a smell of institutional cooking and diesel. Now we are in a steel lift. We rise eight floors to the Captain's deck, and prepare ourselves to meet the Old Man, as Graham calls him, 'But never to his face!'

What is the aura about a ship's captain? The word comes from the Latin *caput*, head. Though it is the highest rank and title on a merchant ship, it is still a title; the real prize is master, from the Latin *magister*, 'chief' or 'teacher'. This signifies a Master Mariner, a term dating from the 1200s in Britain, meaning someone as qualified and as expert as a seafarer can be. All captains must hold a 'master's ticket'. Should you receive a message from one, as I did, giving you permission to join his ship (no company, however large, can compel a captain to do this), he will not sign himself off 'Captain', but, in my case, 'Brgds/master/ Henrik Larsen'. (I had not seen the 'Brgds' before, either, and knew I would never be the kind of man whose work would allow him to make such an elision of 'Best regards' without seeming foolish.)

The image of the true sea dog, the old salt, has something of the ultimate man, the first and last about it – for man is or aspires to be a voyager, a returning Odysseus, though our Scyllas now come as monthly bills and Charybdises as traffic jams. We do not see sea captains these days, since the decline of the British merchant marine. He has become a story-book figure, the Old Man retired to land; pictured living like Captain Cat in a religiously ordered house where small trophies hold incommunicable memories and dreams of foreign shores drift like motes in the silence. You imagine he is much admired by his neighbours, who find him cheery and always immaculate, and mock him lightly for the way he walks.

You could not mock or mistake Captain Larsen. He is small and wide with narrow eyes, a short beard and thick grey-white hair. He would look like a child's idea of a sea captain if he were not wearing shorts, sandals and a sweat-shirt of uncertain colour. He smokes Marlboro Reds and scratches eczema on his leg. The scars and marks on his large hands and arms are not from eczema.

His greeting is warm, fierce with humour and assessment. He and Graham snap through their drills, exchanging paper-work. He shows me my accommodation.

'Your cabin, Clare. Clare?'

'Horatio, Captain.'

'We will try to remember that.'

'You need gloves if you're going out on deck,' says Sorin, the chief officer. He is a tall, fair-haired Romanian, rangy-tough, with friendly and searching eyes behind rimless octagonal specs. 'It's dirty out there. But it's good! Operational dirt.'

In the days of sail the mate, now known as the chief officer, was his captain's fists. The chief is still our Captain's hands: in an emergency the latter's place is on the bridge, while the mate deals with the problem. Sorin is all competence and strength; there is a compactness about his movements that makes you doubt he has ever dithered. It takes something to carry it off in a sky-blue overall like a romper suit, though his has three gold braids on each shoulder.

The Europeans look grey and tired. Their faces are pallid, their skin dry and flaked; everyone's eyes are reddened. Inside the ship there is no sea air, only the dry air conditioning and the diesel seep of the engine. No one is saying why they are late. Graham, the agent, mentioned fog in Bremerhaven, their last port of call, but he sounded uncertain.

Everyone works now. Only fog thick enough to blind crane operators, winds above sixty knots and Christmas Day stop the work at Felixstowe. Every minute of every other day and night cranes lift and lower, trucks line up to receive or deliver containers, stevedores fix and loosen lashing rods, agents arrive and depart, seafarers sign on and off, cargo planners board and disembark, officers supervise, crews from fifty countries work, dockers take or cast off lines, pilots climb or descend gangways and the big ships come and go. Under arc light, in the small hours, in summer dawns and winter darknesses, this never stops.

We will leave at 6 a.m.

'Four on the gangway,' the Captain says, over the top of his glasses.

Departure times are subject to change; the first version is chalked on a board near the gangway. While we are alongside a constant watch is kept there by a seaman with a clipboard which visitors must sign. For most of the crew this is as much as they see of the nations of the world, very occasional shore leaves excepted. Container ports look broadly the same. The main differences are climate and the languages of stevedores.

In his strip-lit office, the Captain prods his keyboard, muttering. He might be in a small meeting room in some chain motel were it not for the view. Beyond the portholes is the extraordinary. The body of the ship is a space station under a sky like a wet blue cloth, through which containers swing and float and fly. The cranes' claws, the 'spreaders', are yellow, the ship's holds red and the vista is lit by orange-pink floodlights, studded with white lamps in the hold. You can pick out ladders made miniature by the scale of the ship. The cranes are four-legged monsters, their necks thrust over us. Far up in the crown of each is a tiny human in his dark cabin. The dipping and winching is nearly silent. Sometimes a container booms hollow as it settles. The holds are deep, deep, dropping ten storeys down beneath hatch covers the size of barn ends. The hold looks like three demolished city blocks partitioned by giant circuit boards, gaunt and monumentally skeletal. When the holds are filled cargo is stacked another eight storeys high atop the hatches.

We are accustomed to miniaturised technology; to devices in the hand that talk to satellites. Seeing technology on this scale is hypnotic, awe-striking. This is how we will explore space and colonise planets, you realise, with giant machines operated by men made near-invisibly small by comparison. The eight winches stern and aft are three times the size of a car. They adjust automatically, tightening lines you would struggle to encircle with two hands. Every fifty seconds a container is deposited or removed by each of the four cranes working on the *Gerd*. A tug is pulling a huge COSCO ship out of her berth ahead of us. It seems impossible the little boat has any influence on the leviathan. Their relative sizes make it a match between a hedgehog and a horse.

Every passenger must have a tour. Prashant will conduct this one. He is a Dual Cadet, upright and alert in his immaculate overall. (The crew wear dark blue overalls with reflective seams and MAERSK across the back; the officers have Sorin's light blue version with braid on the epaulettes and the Captain has an immaculate white shirt with full gold insignia on the shoulders, which he produces on entry into ports, complete with fold lines.) 'Dual' means Prashant is being trained both as an engineering officer and a deck officer, one of the elite. He is from New Delhi, twenty-two years old. He has done ten months at sea: in another year, when he has passed his exams, he will be a junior officer.

'My instructors are real sea dogs,' he grins. His friends were becoming seafarers, and making good money, so he did it.

'The engine is something else,' he says.

The Captain says it has a problem that we are going to address in Le Havre. He waves a finger at Prashant.

'Give him the tour!' he says. 'Not less than one and a half hours.'

Prashant did not know the Captain before the Old Man took over the ship in Bremerhaven, but rank and procedure seem to simplify all relations. The Captain is the boss and uncle, Prashant the eager nephew.

We set off at a lick down the main deck, more than 360 metres of it. The *Gerd* is longer than the biggest US aircraft carrier. You cannot quite see the end of the deck, which is painted dark red and is almost flawless, with barely two spots of rust. Prashant points out hydrants for sea water and fresh water, ticks off their pressures (eight bar), lengths of containers (forty and twenty foot), the ship's capacity (she can carry the equivalent of nine thousand twenty-foot containers), and her deadweight tonnage, which is the total weight she can safely bear, including cargo, fuel, water, food and us: 115,700 tonnes. He points out bay numbers (twenty-footers in the odd bays), lashing rods (adjustable iron stays which are fixed criss-cross to the ends of the first two layers of containers), hatch covers, winches and anchor chains, lifeboats and life rafts.

When we are done I sign something and Prashant returns the paper to the Captain. Correctly signed papers, piles of them at every stage of every journey, are the price of the Captain's power.

On a ship in the age of sail the captain was among other things Master Sailmaker and ship's surgeon – 'the only such, in a dangerous life, too: her disciplinarian, accountant, keeper of the Official Log under the Merchant Shipping Act, magistrate, chief steward, legal guardian of his apprentices – not his but the ship's, which needed them: there were no extra hands – and instructor to them too, if anyone was. Above all he was the sailor, the driver, the squall-dodger, who made the best not only of fair winds but whatever winds might blow.'[1] With the exceptions of steward, sailmaker and surgeon, Captain Larsen is still all these.

The objective of the sailing ship's master was the same as Captain Larsen's: to bring cargo and crew safe to port in the minimum possible time. The sea cities of Britain then were twinned with the furthest reaches of the world. Swansea and Iquique were linked by copper ore, Liverpool was joined to San Francisco by gold and to Quebec by timber. Newcastle upon Tyne and Fremantle in Australia were brothers in coal. Famous runs were achieved, records set and broken. During the mass emigration of Portuguese to Hawaii in 1880 (11,000 made the journey) the British ship *Highflyer*, a former tea clipper, made the run from Portugal, around the Horn against the winds and up to the islands in ninety-nine days – no rival did it faster. Eight years later an iron sailing ship, *British Ambassador*, put up a record passage of twenty-nine days between San Francisco and Newcastle, New South Wales.

A fast ship, fair winds, good luck and a canny captain were all for nothing when you hit the doldrums or struck a patch of calms. One record from May 1897 describes fifty-four sailing ships becalmed in latitude 45 North, longitude 26 West, many short of food and water.

---

[1] Preface by Allan Villiers to Captain George Clark, *Four Captains*, Brown, Son and Ferguson, Glasgow, 1975.

In his journals Coleridge records seeing such a ship becalmed at sunset in the Bristol Channel:

> Idle as a painted ship
> Upon a painted ocean,

he rendered it, in his *Rime of the Ancient Mariner*. But imagine fifty-four of them together! Thirsty ghosts on a breathless sea: a glimpse of the measure of the age of sail.

With the coming of steam the ports of the world filled with unemployed sailing ships, trapped by plunging freight rates, made obsolete by technology which did not need the wind. Photographs of the port of Calcutta in 1898 show a dead forest of tall ships' masts. They could not use the Suez Canal (which opened in 1869) for a voyage to the East because of unfavourable winds in the Red Sea. Any sailing ship coming to Calcutta from the Atlantic would have made the Indian Ocean via the Cape of Good Hope, adding at least three thousand miles to a voyage, half of which was against the South Atlantic's southerly trade winds: you had to sail most of the way to Brazil, in a wide sidestep known as the volta, in order to circle back to Cape Town on the clockwise cyclonic winds. Steam changed captains' conceptions and maps of the oceans. Their world was still a bundled question of winds, currents and seasons, but the answers were far simpler calculations. The blue became inscribed with steamer tracks, the shortest safe passage between ports. We still use them. Voyage courses and times became predictable, more or less.

*   *   *

The *Gerd Maersk* is scheduled to cross the Channel tomorrow. She will leave Le Havre the day after that for Algeciras, the Suez Canal, Salalah in Oman, Tanjung Pelepas in Malaysia, Vung Tau in Vietnam, Nansha and Yantian in China, Hong Kong and finally Los Angeles. We have an arrival date in Los Angeles two months from now, 16 October, and a time: half past two in the afternoon.

The route we will travel is a main road on the map of a parallel world which sustains the one you inhabit. Rotterdam is the capital of the Netherlands and of Europe. Antwerp is the first city of Belgium. Felixstowe rules Britannia. Hamburg is the capital of Germany and Bremen its second city. New York still counts, thanks to Newark, but while the sea makes a place for Savannah in Georgia, Washington DC is nothing. Shanghai is the world's first city; Beijing does not figure. San Francisco was long ago surpassed by Oakland, on the other side of the bay, and both are dwarfed by Long Beach. The great Mediterranean capitals are Valencia, Algeciras and the gangster feasting-ground of the port of Gioia Tauro, the buckle on Italy's shoe.

'Hello, Mr Pilot!'

They shake hands.

'Good morning, Captain.'

'A grey dawn on the sea's face and a grey dawn breaking', John Masefield wrote, and it is running through my head not just because the view from the bridge is precisely that – a wash of non-colours between calm and dismal, and a rain falling which you would call dirty in a city – but because I am in a state of suppressed exultation. I had to recite 'Sea Fever' at school when I was ten and I longed to do this then. Now, at last, I am on a great ship going down to the lonely sea and the sky.

'Let go forward line,' Captain Larsen says. Three hundred metres away in the bow is Chris, the second officer, who repeats the order back over the radio.

'Let go forward spring lines . . . Let go aft line . . . Let go aft spring lines . . .' The spring lines are the ropes which run from the bow and stern of the ship back towards her centre, balancing the pull of the main mooring lines.

'There's a problem with the aft spring line,' says the radio.

'Well, it's quite urgent now,' the Captain says calmly, 'as we have left the berth.'

On the bridge are the Captain, humming to himself softly in between giving orders, Duncan, the pilot, who talks to the tug over his radio, and Sorin, checking the paper chart against the electronic chart, plotting, listening, double-checking, watching everything.

The Captain makes small adjustments to the little levers which control the bow and stern thrusters, then even smaller changes to the main engine telegraph. A long spear of green-brown water opens between us and the quay. The aft spring line rapidly behaves. Three men in the tug, six on the lines, and these three on the bridge – a dozen men are sending a giant machine, a chunk of steel cape, it seems, away to sea.

Now a helmsman appears and takes over the steering. The *Gerd*'s wheel is smaller than the kind which controls a Mini.

'Starboard ten.'

'Starboard ten!'

'Steer one oh six,' says Duncan.

'One oh six!' echoes the helmsman.

'Six knots.'

'Six knots,' the Captain confirms.

The pilot and the Captain confer about the wind and the current and the dredger ahead of us in the channel. The exchanges are brief, not quite laconic. The Captain's air is approving. Seafarers are quick judges of character and competence.

'You look for someone serious,' Sorin says.

As we move down the buoyed channel through rain nothing stirs in Felixstowe. The nape of a sullen night hunches away to the west as we turn northwards and increase speed.

'You can come up to eleven knots, Captain.'

'Eleven knots! Yes, yes . . . hum humm, di-dum dumm . . .'

With every yard we travel the atmosphere on the bridge lightens. Sea is safety, land is danger. Duncan readies himself for departure as the tiny pilot boat pitches towards us. Duncan will descend the gangway down our huge flank, transfer to a rope ladder, descend a few more metres almost to the water and step on to the little arrowhead of the pilot boat's nose.

'It's quite exciting in a gale,' he says mildly. 'You can tell how the economy is going by the height of the ship in the water. Since 2008 it's been a fair old climb . . . Oh aye it's all changed – especially the drinking,' he grins. 'In the old days we wouldn't have made it around the world unless we were half cut! That's all gone now.'

'There are many more *things* in the sea here,' the Captain says.

'Oh yes, the turbines, they're putting more up there. The winds are getting stronger. We get much more strong wind now than we used to . . . Right, Captain, I'll be off.'

'What speed would you like, Mr Pilot?'

'Ten knots should be fine.'

'Ten knots. Starboard side?'

'Starboard side. Thank you, Captain. Safe journey.'

'Yes, yes! Thank you, Mr Pilot, thank you.'

CHAPTER 3

Storms

'The worst?'

Sorin grins. It must be the question they are asked most often. Setting out with them, it is the first thing you want to know. Sorin's eyes take on a steady look as he sees the storm again. (His English is excellent, accented, and occasionally dispenses with articles.)

'I was on car carrier. Coming out of Portland into Gulf of Alaska. Winter of 2001.'

In the Bering Sea they ran into a violent storm, force eleven. The Beaufort scale only goes as high as force twelve, which is a hurricane. In force eleven large patches of foam driven by the wind cover much of the sea's surface, which is a maelstrom of exceptionally high waves, spray fills the air, winds are up to seventy miles an hour: above force ten you cannot stand up in them.

'No visibility. Freezing cold. Wave height ten metres . . . Yeah. It is really terrifying. On car carrier the bridge and accommodation is at the front so, every wave you go up – force maybe two Gs, then you come down – bang! I said if I get out of this alive I will never go to sea again. But . . .' Sorin laughs. Ten metres, though, almost thirty-three feet: most people never see that sort of wave, only fakes created by computers. This storm lasted, undiminished, for three days.

'We made maybe fifty miles. No one can sleep. You just hang on. We can't use the autopilot because if you go side-on to the sea you capsize. You're steering starboard, starboard, but you're being pushed to port. We just eat toast and cheese, feta, for three days, because obviously you cannot cook.'

'And if the engine fails?'

'That's what I kept thinking.'

You do not have to go to the Bering Sea in winter to find storms. The biggest wave Shubd ever saw was off Genoa. Shubd, also from New Delhi, is third officer on the *Gerd*. He was in the dining room on a previous ship when the wave hit them side-on. The ship rolled forty degrees.

'You can imagine if you are having lunch and you roll over like that. This was really something! Everything – the tables, the plates, all the chairs, cutlery, everything fell across the room. We were all piled up.'

Rohan, the second engineer, was with a new ship anchored off Hong Kong when they received a typhoon warning. Rohan is also Indian, his speech lilting.

'All the other ships pulled up their anchors and left. But my captain decided we would stay. This was not a very good decision because the typhoon was very bad and it moved so the ship was not in a good place, not in shelter.'

Rohan was also a Dual, like Prashant; now he is working his way up the ranks. He studied marine engineering and is partly in charge of our engine.

'It has more alarm points than a Boeing 747–800. It has many advanced systems – there is no engine more advanced. In terms of technology we are in space station territory here.'

He is not boasting. None of the seafarers are braggarts. Who is there to impress? Their only audiences are others like them, men who care for deeds. He is just trying to explain what he does. He is twenty-five years old.

'The thing I will not forget is the water in the storm. With the wind and the spray the rain was so hard it was also raining upwards, coming up off the sea and bouncing off the ship. The air was all water – I have never seen that again.'

The ferocity of typhoons in the eastern seas has led some nations to conclude that the Beaufort scale is inadequate to describe them. In China and Taiwan they measure on a scale of fifteen, with three levels more severe than the Beaufort's hurricane force twelve.

'The ship was anchored but the strength of the waves was too much. We were very close to the shore and the anchor was dragging. We had to pull up the anchor and ride it out. So the engine had to work perfectly – or . . .'

I imagine one of the *Gerd*'s gigantic sisters. (If you walk down from the bridge to the main deck and take a turn around the ship, by the time you return to the bridge you have pretty well walked a kilometre.) Picture her riding in the typhoon. It is night and she is all but helpless on her anchor chain. Each link of the chain is as thick as your thorax. The bridge is in darkness, the low glow from the computers and radar the only light. It is cool on the bridge,

air-conditioned, but the Captain is sweating. Astern of the
ship typhoon waves are exploding on rocks, just there in
the darkness. You cannot let go of the rails which are screwed
to every edge, not for a moment, or you will be thrown.
The whole ship is plunging like a thing insane, rearing and
plunging, rearing and plunging.

It is hard to do the simplest thing. Using the stairs takes
strength: first they lean under you, and your heavy legs
seem stuck to them, though you are trying to descend. Then
they topple forward as if trying to hurl you off.

'How I describe it is – it is not hard to screw a nut on
to a bolt. But when you have not slept for three days, and
the engine room is flying around in the swells, everything
is tilting twenty degrees one way and twenty degrees the
other, and you have not eaten properly, and if you don't
hold on you fall, and it is very dangerous in the engine
room, and now you must put a nut on to a bolt – this is
not so easy.'

Rohan is a young man with an infectious smile. Most of
the work in the engine room is much more difficult than
screwing a nut to a bolt.

'The engine worked,' he says.

An extraordinary story of a ship in a storm – so small were
the odds of it ever being told – is the tale of the *Indian
Empire*, which left Newcastle, New South Wales, on 18 July
1895 under the command of one Captain Johnson, with a
cargo of coal for Peru. August the tenth finds them in mid-
Pacific with a northerly gale worsening and the *Indian
Empire* awash. The sea is huge and terrifying, the tops of

the waves a white welter high above the deck. Just after midnight she is struck by a monster sea astern which rolls and pitches her so steeply down the sailors think she has begun her last dive. Her bows surface but the coal has moved, tumbling into a heap; the lee (sheltered) side of the deck is now twelve feet under the water. If the hatch covers fail she must sink in moments, but they hold. The hull, which is iron, is still sound.

Dawn came up to reveal three of her four lifeboats gone, the fo'c'sle and the deck house smashed, and the galley, lamp locker and paint store washed away. The lee side was badly damaged and all the navigational equipment was gone, along with all the men's clothes and belongings. By a miracle the carpenter's tools remained to them.

Captain George Clark heard this story from a survivor, who later became Captain Simpson, and was at the time third mate on the *Indian Empire*. In his account Captain Clark now writes: 'Then began a fight which was only won through sheer courage and tenacity.' Captain Clark published his story in 1975, but he used the understatement of another era.

First, all twenty-eight hands went below, via a ventilator cowl, to try to shovel the coal back to the weather side, but the ship was too far over and they failed. The storm returned on the night of 11 August and the ship was pushed further over. By the morning of 12 August the ship was lying on her side. The sailors set to work to cut away the masts. On the high side, the port side, this was accomplished with hacksaws. The trouble was that the lee shrouds and stays – the wires retaining the masts on the starboard side – were quite deep under water. As the ship rolled the shrouds would emerge briefly, or at least be pulled closer to the surface. Lowering themselves on ropes, the crew fought to cut them loose. Captain Johnson divided the men into two gangs. While one battled to cut the iron fastenings with their hacksaws, the other group continued to try to trim the coal, flinging spadefuls uphill in the hold. It is hard to picture the conditions below, the sliding mountains of coal lit by flickering lamps. It is only slightly easier to see the outside crew at work, dangling like spiders from the side of the ship, swinging against the near-vertical deck, tackling steel wires with saws as the waves rise and fall.

A third heavy gale on 15 August broke a spare spar off the deck and water began entering the hold, rising to a depth of eight feet. The battle down there seemed hopeless, with coal rolling back down the incline faster than it could be shifted. Captain Johnson sent Simpson to assess the situation in the aft (rearmost) hold. Simpson reported that water was pouring in through the broken deck bolts and that the ship's stern was leaking at every seam. Captain Johnson told him to say nothing of this to anyone.

The crew sighted another ship and Captain Johnson ordered the carpenter to make repairs to the sole remaining lifeboat, which was badly damaged. Before the boat could be made seaworthy the other ship vanished. Orders were given to put the boat in the water, ready to take off all hands should the *Indian Empire* founder, which seemed likely at any minute.

'There now occurred a sequence of events which had almost a miraculous quality about them,' Captain Clark writes. Seventeen of the crew, including Simpson, took to the boat, already half full of water despite the sailors' baling. As more men attempted to board the order was given to let go and lie close by on the sea anchor. No sooner was this done than the lifeboat drifted away from the ship. There seemed no way of getting back to her in the wind and sea. As night came down the men in the lifeboat thought they saw the *Indian Empire* go down. They were barely afloat, through constant baling. They had a little biscuit and some tinned beef but just as they were being issued drinking water a sea swamped the rowing boat, and that was the end of the water. Only two oars remained. The men were in rags. That night it blew a gale with hail in the wind. They did all they could to keep the little boat's nose to the sea.

At daybreak the wind relented. Rising high with a wave under them they saw their fallen ship. Captain Clark writes: 'Had she been anywhere but dead to leeward they could never have reached her with their two oars; and as it was, they were very apprehensive as to their reception, for more than one of those left aboard had gone out of their minds before the boat got adrift. However, a lifebuoy was thrown to them and they got back aboard. It is a good indication of the state of the boat that it was not considered worth keeping and was cast adrift.'

Those men worked twenty hours a day at the pumps, at cutting spars loose, and at dumping coal into the sea. They worked for many days, eventually getting their ship upright and a tattered sail rigged. At three knots they worked their way north into the south-east trade winds. They had no sextant, chart, chronometer or compass; they did not even have a watch. Judging that if they made their way eastwards they must eventually meet South America, they continued, and eventually encountered a German ship bound for Portland, Oregon. The Captain of this ship advised them to abandon the *Indian Empire*, 'but when Captain Johnson put it to the crew not a man would leave'.

The German gave them charts and navigational equipment.

'Three days later Easter Island was sighted and anyone who wished to do so was given permission to leave the ship there. But again not a man chose to go.'

The *Indian Empire* was on her side in the Pacific for twenty-two days, and it took another sixty days' sailing to make Callao, Peru. Only one man had been lost. Crews of other ships in the port made a collection of clothes for the gaunt, long-haired and ragged men who had brought her back from the sea.

The story of the *Indian Empire* is echoed in Joseph Conrad's novel *The Nigger of the 'Narcissus'*. The ship is blown on her side in the southern Indian Ocean, near the Cape. Chaos and destruction roar down on her, all but fracturing the sanity and discipline of the terrorised crew, as they dangle from her perpendicular deck. But Captain Allistoun is inflexible – the shrouds and stays will not be cut, he decrees; they will wait out the storm. Mr Baker, the mate, bullies, chides and enforces the order. The cook saves the company's morale with a miraculous brew of hot coffee, and a credo: 'As long as she swims I will cook!' The wind changes, the seas abate and the *Narcissus* rises again. Conrad's narrator says of the cook: 'His saying – the saying of his life – became proverbial in the mouth of men as are the sayings of conquerors or sages. Later, whenever one of us was puzzled by a task and advised to relinquish it, he would express his determination to persevere and to succeed by the words: – "As long as she swims I will cook!'"

Somewhere between the true story of the *Indian Empire*, whose men twice refused to abandon her wrecked shell, and the fable of the *Narcissus*, saved by her iron Captain, redoubtable cook and long-suffering crew, lies a tumultous, evasive but palpable spirit, some essence of the relationship between sailors and their craft. In these early days in which I begin to know the *Gerd* I cannot measure or explain this spirit, but I can feel it, even in the bare corridors. There is no superfluity in the ship, either in her construction, her atmosphere or the bearing of her men. She is so huge and they are so few (there are twenty-one of us aboard) that any emergency would put each character to the sternest test. It is as though the briskness and unsentimentality of the way the least thing is done, right down to making tea, leaving no drop, stain or spoon out of place, is a constant rehearsal for some not-quite-unthinkable disaster.

CHAPTER 4

World of Men

The day lightens as the English coast diminishes over our shoulder and the Channel turns holiday blue. It is highest summer; the wind whips light off the sea and whirls it round the funnel. There are vessels at every point of the compass. A lifeboat passes behind us, shepherding a yacht with a faulty engine towards Rye harbour, beyond the power station at Dungeness which is a tiny nub. The coast of Normandy solidifies as England fades. It is a seascape from a children's book, bereft of threat, and, almost, of children. The young now begin their travels at airports and stations, while many of their parents and most of their grandparents first left the country by ship. Mine was perhaps the last generation for whom Dover's cliffs were the end of Britain and Calais the beginning of the world. I first felt swells on a ferry from Portsmouth to St Malo. It was a night crossing, the moon made a lane on the water and the ship swayed as my brother and I tried to sleep, stretched out on seats. We were worried about the rolling, troubled with that uncertain, low-level fear like a pulse in the chest – the landlubber's first apprehension of the ungovernable. We had no idea how safe we were.

The Captain cannot count the storms he has seen and does not reminisce about the giant waves he has rolled over. His monsters are supertankers forging through seas of fond recollection.

'October the eighth 1973,' he says. 'You will never forget your first voyage.' He was an apprentice on a supertanker. They sailed her to the Persian Gulf in the middle of a war. 'Three hundred and thirty thousand tonnes of crude oil. A big bomb! We anchored by islands so we were harder to see – we travelled at night.

'We used to have to go in there,' he says, his finger on the chart some way north of Le Havre. 'But not on super-tankers. Too big! We had to anchor in Lyme Bay and pump the oil on to smaller ships.' (One of our Danish Captain's irresistible traits is his pronunciation of this crucial English word. He has risen to the heights of his profession as a master of 'sheeps'.)

Le Havre resolves through binoculars into towers, quays, steeples and cranes. Chris unclips the radio handset.

'Le Havre pilot, Le Havre pilot, this is *Gerd Maersk*, *Gerd Maersk* over . . .'

There is an answering crackle and a woman's voice, French-accented:

'*Gerd Maersk*, Le Havre pilot, good evening Captain, what is your ETA, over?'

'Le Havre pilot *Gerd Maersk*, good evening ma'am. Our ETA at the pilot station is 1915, repeat 1915 over . . .'

The language of the sea is English and its mode of

address is a charming courtesy. Men on the radio are 'sir'; women are 'ma'am'. When shores speak to ships they often pay the officer of the watch the compliment of calling him 'Captain'. On board, as well as good morning, afternoon and evening, there is 'Good watch!' which you say when you leave the bridge, and no meal passess without multiple wishes of 'Good appetite!' bestowed on diners by those entering or leaving the saloon. These formalities are of a piece with the swept and mopped corridors, the washed decks and the laundered overalls. No feminine touch, patience or perseverance, no matriarch nor stooping maid could make this ship cleaner, tidier or better ordered; no female presence could make her crew more polite or more gallant. The rules, roles and customs of the sea seem to have erased half the stereotypes of our gender.

A gannet dives for fish, its black wing-tips and lemon-coloured head emphasising its white plumage; the bird appears a plunge of luminous speed. We search the sky beyond it for our pilot. While most ports use pilot cutters, Le Havre uses a helicopter.

'You will see him on the radar,' the Captain says. 'There!'

In port after port he will be the first person to spot the buoy, the pilot boat, the hazard. He wears glasses but he always seems to know where to look. The helicopter is a smart green and silver thing which hurtles out to us, arcs round behind our funnel, stops dead above the bridge and lowers the harbour pilot. The pilot wears shades like a movie star. In moments he is off the roof, on to the bridge and shaking hands with the Captain. In we go.

A great port, which Le Havre once was, shows its best face to the sea. The city looks calm and philosophical this evening, gazing westward. Our pace up the buoyed channel affords a scrolling view of the fishing fleet and the docks. The Captain brings us alongside under the cranes of the container port so gently that arrival is imperceptible.

'The ship is so heavy you cannot bump at all or you will dent her. You cannot do that! No, no . . .'

The Captain deals only in absolutes.

The stasis of arrival generates a sort of panic, as though somehow you have fallen behind with work. The constant motion of the ship through every yard of sea, every nautical mile, is achievement; every wave shouldered aside is a victory. Now we are stopped everyone moves quickly as if to compensate. The first man up the gangway is the agent, tired-looking and carrying a black document case. Then come the stevedores, all swagger.

'They are hard men,' says the agent, 'the reservoir of tradition.'

The first two layers of containers are secured to the deck frames by steel lashing rods. The stevedores' job is to take these off containers which are being moved and to secure them to containers which are loaded. They are equipped for a night's work with food and cigarettes. They do not sign on or off the ship and they show little interest in the crew, barely nodding as they come aboard.

Work will go on all night in the engine room. The casing of one of the cylinders is cracked, so we have been proceeding on eleven, not twelve, giving us a maximum speed of seventeen knots, rather than twenty-three.

'We cannot leave Europe without full power,' the Captain explains.

The cylinder casing is an elongated steel funnel higher than a bungalow. It weighs nine tonnes. We carry two spares, stored in corners of the engine room.

The chief engineer is Carl-Johann. He will run the operation from the background, unobtrusively. The second and third engineers will take turns at directing the job and working in tiny hot spaces, full of peril and complexity, leading their crews. Carl-Johann is a pacific man with deep mournful eyes, his moustache black against pale skin. He has a little bi-plane on his desk, scarlet and decked with black crosses. It is a Fokker, he says. He made it himself. Carl-Johann is passionate about model planes. The Captain is equally passionate about model trains. Late at night sometimes they get together in the Captain's cabin and bid for rare engines or planes on the internet. When you know this it takes nothing to see them as they must have been as boys: standing in a corner of the playground – always the same, favoured corner, you feel, for young Henrik Larsen. A little tubby, peering up over the tops of his glasses at the interruptions of bigger children, he must have been as uncomprehending of their stark world, bizarrely bereft of any knowledge of the workings, colours, serial numbers and capacities of trains, as they were ignorant of his horizonless shunting yard of exactly known shapes and memorised numbers, his constellations of detail. Little boys are adorable for the endless accuracy of their devotions, the tables of goals and runs, the three hundred and twenty-fifth *Star Wars* figure known down to the calibre of its gun and the colour of its insignia. When certain of these boys grow up they are easily mocked for their undimmed passions, none more than the groups of anoraks at the ends of platforms or the solitaries huddled in hides, with their treasured note-books, their lists of Deltic locomotives or megatick birds.

But perhaps it is that little boy within each man at work on the *Gerd* tonight who shuffles one giant cylinder casing for another according to safe procedure, who will work through heat and fatigue and danger on hundreds of nuts, bolts and cables. It is that passionate precision which will be needed to disconnect a multitude of couplings in the correct sequence, and to reconnect and replace them in the right order. Perhaps it is the owlish engagement of little boys in love with certain and calculable things which builds machines as great as the *Gerd*, and greater.

Le Havre's container port is an unfinished jigsaw of fences, gates, towers of steel boxes and oil storage tanks. Along the quay yellow machines are levelling a hundred acres for new cranes and container yards, half for Maersk, half for China's COSCO. The men on the quay wear hard hats and hi-vis jackets, the uniform of the human cog. But one of the cogs, at least, is loose: a van pulls over and a man with a raffish grin makes a smoking gesture – do we have any contraband? We shake our heads.

The agent lifts shaggy Sam, his Shitsu, off the passenger seat. He accelerates around the container stacks, dodges the container lifters and stops at an office block. This is a flood-lit, mechanised and intensely masculine world of bare spaces, functionality, lights which go on and off by themselves, easy-clean surfaces, concrete and echoing acoustics. It is an architect's model precisely realised, complete with little men who can be picked up and set down and who leave no trace. Is this what earth would be like if there were no women? The trip to normality is a fast drive along deserted roads, through high gates and the reek of petrol from the storage tanks, over swing bridges and black water.

Not so long ago the quays of Le Havre would have been a jostle of sailors. They are gone but Le Havre has not forgotten its heritage, its oceanic cachet. It is there on the wall of the restaurant, Le Grignot: a grand poster advertising a liner of the thirties, Companie Générale Transatlantique – French line – Paris–Havre–New York. It is in the conversation at the bar where a couple shake their heads with the proprietor over the pacbos, the passenger boats, which come in the morning and only stay the day. It is there in Bar Belge, Le Trappist, in the enthusiasm of François, serving beer, who used to be at sea.

'I was on oil tankers,' he says proudly, with a shake of his head which seems to marvel that anyone should be so rash. He seems rueful, too. Perhaps he misses the order of seafaring, the routines which eat up the miles and months, and which are built around food. Breakfast is at eight, lunch at twelve and supper at five thirty.

Breakfast is boiled eggs, cereal and fruit salad.

'Morning, Captain, morning, Chief.'

'Good morning!'

'Good appetite!' says Sorin, cheerfully.

He has just completed the dog watch, four in the morning to eight. He will sleep before he is on the bridge again at four this afternoon, but he is not done yet. At lunch and at supper he will load his plate with four raw carrots. He will eat each of them like this:

'Crunch – crunch – crunch-crunch-crunch-crunch-crunch!'

We will share Sorin's pleasure of carrots twice a day for the next two months.

At meals I solicit stories from the officers. Usually the Captain will bark 'What?' when I begin a question, and furrow his expression like a Zeus with toothache. You can see him wondering what detail has caught my eye, what corner of the continent of my ignorance he is being asked to illuminate this time. His manner is not intended to be intimidating, I decide. A man of little small talk, he regards questions as problems to be solved. Mine must sometimes seem arbitrary.

'What's this picture –'

'*What?*'

The Captain looks like Beatrix Potter's owl, Old Brown, when the squirrel tickled him with a nettle.

'I was just wondering about this picture, Captain? Is it an actual place?'

On one wall of the dining saloon is a large blue and white fantasy of a rural, pre-industrial scene: a curving river, a church, a village, people on horseback.

'Yes yes yes that is Svendborg. It is supposed to be the home port of the ship but our home port is Dragoer. There was a mix-up – another ship has our picture and we have theirs. I had a chief officer who wanted to change them. She asks me if she can arrange for us to swap them over.

She said she will contact the other ship . . . I said are you sure you want to do it? Is it worth this trouble?'

We laugh. The Captain does mystification well.

'She says we will do it, we will leave ours in Algeciras and then they will leave theirs – but then she left the ship because she was pregnant. Maybe this is why she worries about these pictures . . .'

Sometimes the Captain will talk to the chief engineer in Danish. Often we will comment on the food, which can be rich in the pleasures of fat and salt but is otherwise reasonably healthy. Occasionally we will laugh at something, like the pregnant mate attempting to nest-build across the oceans. But often, very often, we will eat in a silence that stretches from moments to minutes to indeterminate longueurs, underscored with chewing and carrot-crunching. In these periods the Captain hums to himself and mutters half-whispered words and phrases, as though two tiny trolls are having a conversation not quite out of earshot. At such times I will dig away at my plate and think what strange men we are, in our companionship of self-consciousness, which we pretend we do not feel; and think about how gentle these big, tough figures are. Seafaring seems to attract more introverts than extroverts, for which we are grateful, in our shared shyness. And often I sit there, marvelling: women would never live like this! Then I miss them. We all do and we never say so.

Several decks below us, in the devil's cathedral of the engine room, Prashant is wedged into a tiny space, scalding-hot steel surfaces all around him, working non-stop with a spanner. The cracked casing has been lifted off; it is now a question of preparing the way for the new one. A Filipino, Roy, is in an even more cramped space behind Prashant. Roy is the youngest member of the crew and he looks shattered. Tools, nuts, washers and cables are scattered around the walkway. The job would be impossible in a swell. Everyone has luminous green plugs jammed in their ears, though these barely curb the roar. Even at rest the engine is terrible. As a neophyte you feel yourself trembling below the monstrous threat of its shake and howl.

The men down here do not know it is a bright day outside, the first of September. They only know that we are bunkering, taking on 6,400 cubic metres of heavy diesel fuel.

'It's a heavier grade than the stuff they use to make roads,' Chris says. Chris is already a master of the laconic, along with most aspects of seafaring.

The hazard-orange barge is alongside and everything smells of fumes: the lift, the corridors, the sky. Bunkering is danger, a perfectly ordinary thing in a world of ordinary danger. The merest mistake will cover decks with oil. If any were to escape into the water we would be responsible for an environmental crime. Fines would be levied, at the very least – captains are liable and have been jailed for spills.

Before the job began the crew held a meeting to agree who would be responsible for what. A crucial role is the watchman's: for hours he will do nothing but stare at the pipe and its fittings on the fuel barge and the ship. He is urged to eat properly first, to never take his eyes off the couplings and to shout for relief the moment he feels tired or his focus wanders. Everyone knows he will be tired, and his head will swim with the fumes, and he will have to force his concentration not to sway despite that, and he will almost certainly not call for help.

CHAPTER 5

Out with the Tide

A still evening and satisfactory: bunkering is complete, the piston casing replaced. The crew have eaten supper and retired to their cabins, apart from two men in the bow and two in the stern who will handle the lines. Shipping is the only industry in which schedules are devised not according to hours of work but, rather, by mandatory hours of rest, otherwise there would be no rest time at all. The pilot is aboard, the tugs are alongside and we have clearance to depart.

'Let go forward spring line,' the Captain says.

Chris echoes him on the walkie-talkie and the procedure rolls once more. Turning the ship to face the sea is a behemoth ballet. The breakwater south of us has a bulge in it, forming a semi-circular manoeuvring area. With one tug pulling the bow to port and the other tugging the stern to starboard, and the Captain's hand on the bow-thruster controls, they spin her in this space like a compass needle in its setting, rotating her perfectly, as if she were twirled slowly by a titan's fingertips. Dead slow ahead when she reaches her apex sets us in the channel and moving seaward. The mood on the bridge is both alert and easy, an atmosphere you begin to recognise, the professional calm of men who maintain the world, out of its sight.

In the voyage to come pilots will sometimes mistake me for an officer, and sometimes hesitate, realising I am not one.

'Writer,' the Captain will say, sometimes, as casually as if announcing that he has been asked to transport a Martian, and someone's got to do it. If I am recording he says 'Journalist', with the kind of nod which is one step away from a shrug. Sorin is entertained by my Rycote, the fluffy windshield which goes over the microphone. 'Ah, the chinchilla is back!'

Joel is the first of the Filipinos to ask what I am up to. I explain and he seems delighted by the idea. 'So you want to tell our story! Great! Come and spend time with us.'

I do, I try to, but it is difficult. When the watches are working they are in no position to talk. When they finish they disappear into their cabins. As the voyage goes on I catch them in the gym or the library, on their laptops, and we watch films together. We often meet late at night, and exchange smiles and greetings, but then I stay out of the way, because they tend to be absorbed in messaging home.

'Ships used to be much more social places,' the chief engineer says, 'but now everyone takes DVDs to their cabins.'

Fishing boats come out with us on the falling tide. It is an hour to low water. Little sailing boats are all but becalmed, save one optimist with his spinnaker out. Our tugs, unleashed, escort us between the breakwaters into a mellow and sleepy sea. The helicopter comes and takes the pilot away, his sunglasses still in place. The Captain talks to Shubd. Eight to twelve, morning and evening, is the third officer's watch. He is the most junior of the navigators, with the most to learn, and therefore the most likely to need the Captain. His shifts are matched to times when the Captain is most likely to be awake.

'It will be good to see this in future navigation,' the Captain says, showing Shubd something on the electronic chart. 'There's no ships now.'

The Captain rests his foot on the rail behind the bridge, briefly, as we leave Le Havre, and stares out. Cormorants in packs pass below us, heading in towards the estuary, and sailors in yachts stare up. Who knows what the Captain is thinking? Is leaving harbour always soul-stirring, on a great ship and the ebbing tide – even for the thousandth time?

We are steering thirty degrees north of the sunset. The western sky is turquoise, feathered with few clouds. There is no wind, only our turbulence, as we pick up speed to fifteen knots, then eighteen, and the leading lights of Le Havre, two dazzling white glares, slip out of line astern. We will head north-north-west into mid-Channel until we are nearly equidistant from Dorset and Cape Ouessant, then turn south and west for the Bay of Biscay.

'The Biscay can be a real pig,' Chris said, heavily, this morning. He has a deeply stolid manner but there were traces of enthusiasm, even hope about him, then.

The Captain goes below and a watchman comes up. Mike is from the Philippines. He will gaze at the darkness ahead of us for the four hours of the watch. Normally he and Shubd would have the bridge, the vista of the ship and the whole wide ocean to themselves. Radios chatter. Solent Coastguard and Jersey offer weather information and respond to vessels which have called them.

There is a lurch underneath us, suddenly: current, the North Sea draining vastly right to left. Night comes on and the stars are tremendous; the planets bright as leading lights. The Plough hangs off the starboard bow and the Milky Way is a sparkling arch above. Every half-hour Shubd marks our position, a little pencil cross on the ruled line of our course. The ship is steering herself now and she is vocal about it – every ten minutes a bridge alarm goes off, requiring that Shubd press a button to silence it, proving that he is still alive and awake.

'Oh yes,' he says, in his lilting Indian voice. 'You can be Mr Lonely up here.'

The bridge is dark, the screens turned right down. On either side of the funnel is a sliding door leading out to bare decks behind the bridge, each equipped with an ashtray and a hose. On the starboard side another ladder leads up to the monkey deck, the roof of the bridge. This highest point is studded with radar, satellite communications, aerials and an orange dome containing the voyage data recorder. On the topmost rail is a white box containing a float and a radio transmitter: if the ship goes down this will break free and broadcast signals, giving rescuers our last position.

Our container towers are all in darkness. The view is broken water surging away from the hull, the black sea and the sky. You descend a red-lit stair to J-deck, the Captain's deck, also red-lit. At the starboard end of the corridor is the Captain's suite of rooms, at the other end the chief engineer's. Between them is the library and the pilot's cabin – mine. The library has novels in Danish, a copy of *Daniel Deronda* in English, an anthology of three John Le Carré novels, a dozen American thrillers – police, slasher and historical – of varying quality, and a couple of lads' mags in Russian.

The pilot's cabin offers an Anglepoise lamp on a desk, a chair, an empty fridge, a sofa, a wardrobe and a shower cabinet. The window above the desk faces the foremast and the sea across the container tops. The bunk is a little wider than a standard single. With a faint sway on the ship's hips and the only sound the rumble of the engine, sleep is a deep wide sea. Shoals of dreams come bright and vivid.

At daybreak the view makes no sense. There must be something wrong with the window or my eyes: nothing – nothing – fog! Thick grey-blue vapour shrinks visibility to less than a hundred metres. You can barely see the stern of the boat, never mind the bow. Sorin is on watch.

'How can you see where you're going?'

'I can't!' he laughs. 'Everyone has to give way.'

We are in a Traffic Separation Scheme (TSS), a controlled shipping lane in which north- and south-bound vessels are separated into two streams, thirty-four miles from L'Île d'Ouessant, an island off the Brest peninsula notorious for the violence of its storms and currents. Coming in from the Atlantic and preparing to run up the Channel, with the south-westerlies behind you, Ouessant, Ushant to the British, makes a vicious lee shore – a sailors' grave. On the chart the TSS is a purple corridor, a checkpoint, a chicane in the sea. There are invisible ships all around us, coming north in the lane on our port side and going south in ours.

'It's worse in China,' Sorin says. 'So many fishing boats you can't see them.'

'What do you do – post a lookout in the bow?'

'No! He can't see them until it is too late and I can't do anything about it when he tells me. Reduce the radar to three miles and –' he shrugs. 'We go round them or they get out of the way.'

Sorin explains the different readings on the monitors. Speed over ground is eighteen knots, speed through the water is sixteen knots.

'So we are in counter-current. Two knots.'

The fog has shapes in it, wraiths. You think you see a ship but the radar paints nothing there. The fog hushes sounds and plays with distance. The waves seem doubly far below the bridge: these are our waves, the sea is flat. Leviathan rumbles on, steering herself, knowing like a clairvoyant where the other ships are. We see nothing; her computers know all, and she drives her vast cargo forward. The crew risk their lives to carry the cargo; for cargo they leave their homes and families for months, even years, and yet most of them have no idea what is in the containers. Even Sorin, the best informed, knows only a little about it. The cold-stored goods in the reefers – refrigerated containers – are known, because the reefers have to be kept at a certain temperature and checked. Ours contain meat, chocolate and fruit. The dangerous cargo is also listed because in the event of fire or accident we must know where the threats are. They are stored in the bow, as far away from the accommodation and control centres as possible.

We are carrying solid-state sodium hydroxide, paint materials, solvents and thinners. We have hazardous cargo belonging to Procter & Gamble. We have some small-bore sporting ammunition from Germany, destination Malaysia. The sailors say they are kept in ignorance of everything else deliberately, so that they are not tempted to steal. Informed guesswork suggests we will have flashy cars in some of the boxes – the kind no one wants to risk on a car carrier – and scrap metals for China's hungry markets, and paper and plastic waste for recycling or disposal. We are also carrying naphtha and perfumery products, marked flammable and polluting.

In 1925 Captain Clark sailed with a man who had made a voyage in a Nova Scotia barque at the turn of the century from New York to Rouen in the dead of winter; they too were carrying naphtha. This man told Captain Clark that the master of that wooden ship considered the cargo so dangerous 'no fires were allowed, even for cooking, despite the bitter conditions'.

With a yellowish light astern the sun rises and the sea hisses as our turbulence surfaces in translucent bubbles. Now the sun throws peculiar figures and different densities on the fog: above us is clear blue, aft all is pearly silver and gold-grey, while forward is a blind world. We add our own fumes to the sky, a trail like a foul banner, drifting behind us in a gaseous worm. This company carries 18 per cent of the world's container trade. It made a net profit last year of ten billion US dollars. It added as much carbon dioxide to the atmosphere in that time as did the entire nation of Denmark, where the company is based.

The giant exhaust worm is not as poisonous as it will be. We are burning low-sulphur fuel to comply with the emissions regulations of the English Channel. We will switch to high-sulphur when we are through the invisible gate at the end of Ushant's Traffic Separation Scheme, sixty-five nautical miles – about 130 kilometres – south of the Lizard. We pass Parson's Bank and leave Kaiser-I-Hind Bank to starboard.

'Pacific is also great place for fogs,' says Sorin, staring forward, where the foremast comes and goes.

We enter the Biscay and begin to roll in following swells. Swells are the memories of storms. We are crossing a sea like a failing memory; the fogbanks thicken and thin and thicken again. Now you can barely see a hundred feet, now the vapour falls back, forming opalescent curtains on all the horizons so that we sail in a barrel of sun.

Samuel Taylor Coleridge came this way on his voyage to Malta in 1804. He was not a good sailor and often beset by seasickness; the journey, as he records in his notebook, did not begin auspiciously: 'In weighing anchor the men grumbled aloud a sort of mutiny – not half our complement of men – Two pressed in the Downs, one ran away at Portsmouth, a rascal of a one-armed cook better gone than stayed. Now we are a Captain, Mate, 2 boys, 4 men, 3 passengers, one sheep, 3 pigs, several ducks and chickens, one dog, a cat and two kittens.'

He was sick and feverish at first. The Captain advised him to lie down, which he did, but when night came he slept 'diseasedly': 'In consequence partly of the build of the brig, & partly of its being so heavily laden at its bottom, the cabin rocks like a cradle when a cruel nurse rocks a screaming baby. On Monday night we travelled like a top bough on a larch tree in a high wind, pitching and rocking . . .'

By the time he reached our latitude, in the bight of the Bay of Biscay, the poet was much happier: 'Delightful weather, motion, relation of the convoy to each other, all exquisite – and I particularly watched the beautiful surface of the sea in the gentle breeze! – every form so transitory, so for the instant, & yet for that so substantial in all its sharp lines, steep surfaces, & hair-deep indentures, just as if it were cut glass, glass cut into ten thousand varieties / & then the network of the wavelets, & the rude circle hole network of the foam. And on the gliding vessel heaven and ocean smiled!'

A line later he writes suddenly, 'Why aren't you here?'

He gives no hint as to whom he is thinking of, but his marriage to Sara Coleridge was in dire trouble and he was partly in love with Sara Hutchinson. Though I sometimes share his wish to enjoy the excitement and beauty of this voyage with my partner, my family and certain friends, I feel none of the ache of that line – I am selfishly, absolutely enjoying the separation of this adventure. But then I am only at the beginning. I have no concept of what it would be to be parted from home for months and years, unlike N, who would prefer not to be named.

N has just finished sweeping and spraying the deck at the bow, beneath the hazardous cargo. He is small, barely up to my shoulder. He has a red kerchief around his neck and wears ear defenders perched on his head like the ears of Mickey Mouse. Like most of the Filipinos he has a sweet welcome of a grin.

'One child!' he smiles, then instantly frowns. 'Two, three not possible – cannot afford.'

You can see how much he wants more children but his wages are little more than a thousand dollars a month. Some years he is home for two months, but more often only one. These months are unpaid: though the officers are Maersk employees, with annual salaries and benefits, the crew are on Voyage Contracts. Like N, the crew are employed by a manning agency, which pays them and bills Maersk, thus relieving the company of responsibility for the great majority of its seafarers. N has signed a contract which entitles him to basic pay, overtime pay and 'hardship pay', a bonus he receives when the ship crosses the areas of pirate danger between the Red Sea and the Indian Ocean. His figure of a thousand dollars includes these extra payments.

If the ship were covered by an agreement between Maersk and the biggest seafarers' union, the International Transport Workers' Federation (ITF), N could expect to receive more than twice his basic pay, plus seven dollars per hour of weekday overtime, and thirteen dollars per hour of weekend overtime. (Until recently rest times were regulated but not enforced, so you worked all hours and as many as a man could stand.) There would have been no point N researching the *Gerd* on the ITF website before he signed his contract with the manning agency. Shipowners have everything to gain by avoiding unions and they do so with impunity. Looking up the *Gerd* in the ITF's files returns a simple message: 'Vessel not covered by ITF agreement.'

As a newcomer to the sea I am confused by N's position. This company is supposed to be the industry leader. Filipino seafarers run, clean and maintain the world's cargo fleet: they make up over a quarter of its manpower. (Their nearest rivals are Chinese sailors, who endure worse conditions.) Their tireless work ethic, positive disposition and sea-going tradition make Filipinos indispensable. Barely a shipping company in the world could survive without them.

'You need a union, don't you?'

'Union is no good! Weak! Good for themselves . . . You make story!' N cries, as a farewell, and returns to work.

When the Filipinos reach home they are 'one-day million-aires' in their own phrase, rich for the time it takes for family, friends and relatives to pile in with their needs and wants. Manila is the centre of a global trade in the skills and endurance of Filipino seafarers, symbolised by the open-air market at Luneta Park where manning agencies run recruitment stalls which offer seafaring jobs on boards. These stalls are famously unregulated, operating in the absence of certification, licence, taxation or oversight, and were recently declared illegal. In an ironic parallel, the park has been officially named Rizal, not Luneta, since the 1950s – but both the illegal stalls and the old name endure.

Because of their country's low cost of living it is undoubtedly true that one dollar spent in the Philippines goes further than a dollar spent in Denmark. The shipowners argue that this redresses the massive imbalance in wages paid to

Filipinos compared to the money Indians and Europeans receive. The shipowners are apparently content that in the engine room there are two officers of the same rank, possessed of the same skills, performing the same task, one of whom is receiving less than a third of the wage of the other merely because he holds a different passport. The ten-billion-dollar profit is the excuse for this disparity. Filipinos accept the situation with a shrugging fatalism: this is just the way it is. It is identical to the way it was under apartheid in South Africa – it was 'fair' to pay blacks much less than whites because money went further in the tribal areas, the authorities said. Our world then was revolted by this formula. Our world now relies upon it.

CHAPTER 6

Bay Life in the Biscay

Albatross! It flies the length of the ship and veers off west, huge wings never stirring. The bird that brought the fog and mist, wrote Coleridge, and this one does too: a rain-grey bank, dark behind the brown and white bird, now swallows us.

Dolphins! Common dolphins, *Delphinus delphis*, break out of the water in a hectic chasing pair off the port bow. More appear to starboard, charging the ship. They come right at us, disappearing beneath the bridge. Did they dive under the hull? We watch them playing in the wake waves, huge in the water they seem and so fast. There is such thrill and unity in the way they fly in pairs together, then six in a pod, torpedoing under then breaching in a volley. One turns in a wave and leaps back, reversing its course in an instant.

Whales! A pair blowing just off the starboard bow, moving slowly to dead ahead. The blow looks V-shaped, so they are baleen whales. They stop on a perfect collision course and float there until they disappear under our line of sight. Move!

Move out of the way! Should I ask Sorin to change course? But I do not know where the whales are going, and it takes too long to turn . . .

They are gone; the spray of their blows hangs in the sunlight. I scan the sides and the wake, praying for no red. Long minutes. Then – there! One blows, port side, away aft, and now the other. They were just playing with us.

'Phew! I thought we'd hit them.'

Sorin laughs. 'We would have felt it.'

'We can't go round the world running down whales, Sorin! Imagine the publicity!'

He is from the Danube delta: 'I was always around boats. I first went to sea as a motorman–electrician but I don't like the engine room.' He prefers the northern latitudes because of the climate. 'Malaysia and Hong Kong just kill me in three days.'

He says China and Hong Kong smell distinctive from the sea. For colour only the Caribbean comes close to the Mediterranean's intensity of blue.

'New Zealand is green. The land is green, the sea is green, the air is green . . .'

Two more whales surface, one briefly close to the ship before it vanishes, and another. Humpbacks, I think at first: they are like two humpbacks I saw once, but how alike? Just as whaley, certainly. At least twenty different species have been seen in these waters. Humpback sightings are not common. They could be fin whales, they have that great length, and give an impression of U-boat-like narrowness, and we saw swept dorsal fins. But they are the eighth and ninth whales I have ever seen, not counting the blue in the

Natural History Museum. I could be quite confident of iden-
tifying that. These beasts surface seventy miles south of La
Chapelle Bank as we head south-west across the Biscay
Abyssal Plain, with four kilometres of water below the keel.
The sun puts out its flare path and dusk comes on.

Another whale passes us in a whale-coloured sea, ominous
and dark grey. Its singularity recalls Shakespeare's sketch
of a crocodile in *Antony and Cleopatra*. Antony has been
drinking when he mocks Lepidus with a description which
would certainly go for this whale:

'It is shaped, sir, like itself; and it is as broad as it hath
breadth. It is just so high as it is, and moves with its own
organs. It lives by that which nourishes it, and the elements
once out of it, it transmigrates.'

'What colour is it?'

'Of its own colour, too.'

All we see is one long heave of the great beast's back,
heading north. The sight brings two planets into overlap.
Only when you see a whale do you catch a glimpse of theirs,
given scale by an inhabitant, a huge native; only then does
its full wilderness, its wide desolation, strike.

It is Shubd's watch. He agrees with Sorin: of all the
countries he has visited (excluding India, naturally) New
Zealand is the best, for three excellent reasons: 'It is
extremely nice and extremely beautiful and the people there
are most friendly, yes, they are extremely helpful, very kind,
you know.'

We look at the moon through binoculars. The seas of
tranquillity, the craters and the ridges beyond the shadow
line are no stranger than this world we cross. The whole

orb of it hangs there, not far above the horizon and huge, so close. Yesterday the crescent was gold; tonight silver-white.

'Do you like cricket?' Shubd asks, hopefully.

Shubd would like to be a District Administrator. He says this is a very good job. He looks as though he would make a wonderful District Administrator, too; round-faced, hair neatly parted, his expression open, ready smiling and fair. We talk about women, about love, about ports, stars and ghosts. Shubd tells tales of thousand-kilometre train rides to see his girl, and of his brother's encounter with a haunted house where a spectral party was in progress.

Tonight's action includes the overtaking of the *African River*. We can see her lights one point (ten degrees) off the starboard bow. The computer gives her course, speed and destination – Abidjan, Ivory Coast. Our next waypoint, the next point at which we will change course, is 260 nautical miles away, off Finisterre.

We wake to a morning of rains. You see each squall coming a long way away, a lump of darkness like a giant mushroom, black water at its base. As the gloom reaches us Sorin appears suddenly on a walkway below the bridge, checking the reefers. The ship sways; the rain rags down; Sorin concentrates, acknowledging the conditions with the slightest frown as the water streams down his specs. Every other chief officer and bo'sun and first mate who ever crossed this sea looked the same way, you realise, as he stared straight through whatever it threw at him, at whatever had to be done.

After the rain comes a blue clear and a bright-skied afternoon. Marlon makes tea in the crew mess. Marlon was chased by a pirate. He was on the *Albert Maersk* doing twenty-two knots across the Gulf of Aden.

'The pirate came up behind so the Captain increase speed – twenty-seven knots. The pirate can't keep up. He come on the radio and say "Fuck you fuck you!"'

'You see many in the Gulf of Aden,' says the Captain. 'Sometimes they are fishing but they are towing skiffs. They have a dual role.'

Chris says the skiffs are no good, unstable in swell and frail beside our great mass moving at speed:

'The lowest part of the ship is the poop but the hull curves inward so they wouldn't be able to come alongside.'

'But what if they come over the rail?'

'We would put the hoses on them and bash them,' he says, confidently. 'A Russian ship caught some pirates. He put them in a zodiac and cast them off. Without a motor.'

You can imagine that Chris, Sorin or the Captain bashing anyone would leave that person insensible, but it is hard to see what use sea-water hoses would be against Kalashnikovs. Besides, my tough shipmates are not fighters in the conventional sense. It is much easier to fight someone else than it is to combat your own desires, whether you crave booze, sex, recognition or advancement. The ship offers none of these. For the duration of the voyage all you have is your job and your bunk – battlegrounds a monk would recognise.

We ride swells from astern all day as we run south round Finisterre and parallel the Portuguese coast. It is Saturday

so there is 'Special Tea': a tradition on merchant ships. At
the head of the table are the King and Queen of Denmark.
They look slightly pained, perhaps at the necessity of wearing
traditional ornamentation over contemporary evening dress.
The awkward and dutiful air emanating from the portraits
is echoed along the table they survey. At Special Tea everyone
eats together: officers and cadets at the Captain's table, and
crew at the other, normally unused, table in the same room.
There is much less life and noise than when they are in their
own mess, round the corner. Avocado and prawns are followed
by steak and chips. Everyone plugs away at the food with
enthusiasm but there is a definite feeling that many of us
would rather be next door, jammed in, forced to accom-
modate elbows and meet requests for the salt.

We do our best.

'Steak, chips, green beans!'

(For all that I am the company's official writer in residence,
taking no money from them, and working industriously with
notebook and microphone, I am a beneficiary of these men's
work, and feel at mealtimes like a guest in an extremely
unusual hotel, and find myself praising the meal as one would
at a host's table.)

Rohan raises an eyebrow, grins.

'All we need is a good glass of red . . .'

There is a deal of feeling in the faces responding to this.
The Captain was not joking about his plan to go out for a
'nice fish and a glass of water' in Algeciras. For the duration
of your voyage you cannot even drink on shore.

'When they brought in the no-alcohol policy they had
to put some of the captains and mates through rehab,' Chris

says. 'They couldn't afford to lose them but they had to dry them out.'

We see whales after supper. The Captain hums and says, suddenly: 'I want to get that whale and take him home to my wife.'

He offers no further explanation.

CAPTAIN IS SLEEPING says the sign on his door, the following afternoon. We are arrowing across a glittering paradise of sea. Our wake is the only flaw on its flashing surfaces, our smoke the only stain in the air's pavilions above. A sailing ship, now that would be the thing! But it is such a day, such a hot afternoon, with the sun bright beyond every doorway, that you imagine we might just be forgiven our pounding diesel. You can believe it as long as you do not look at the long banner, like a burned belch, stretching away behind our funnel.

Carl-Johann is sleeping too. He is leaving us tomorrow; perhaps he is dreaming of his first meal at home, which he has already planned: crab. His wife will prepare it and they will sit down with their two daughters.

'One wants to be a navigator,' he says, proudly. 'And the other a journalist.' Because officers may have wives or family on board for up to two months of the year, given a certain length of service, Carl-Johann reckons his daughters have had twenty-four months of sea time.

'More than most first officers!' the Captain puts in.

Cadiz passes somewhere to the north of us; we should see land in an hour and a half if it stays clear. Noon to four is

Chris's watch. I suggest we take a right and go down to Casablanca for some fun.

'I don't think I have quite enough credit in the company for that,' he says.

Chris is as round as a buoy and he does a fine line in deadpan. He has a not-quite-concealed love of the life. His baggy shorts reveal a tattoo on his calf. In red, green and blue it shows a ship in sail, an anchor, a telescope and the legend 'Sailors Grave'. The sailing ship means he has crossed the Atlantic, he explains. He could have a red dragon, denoting a stop in a Chinese port, 'But that's not so cool any more.'

He has also earned many gold dragons, for crossing the date line.

'You could read an old sailor's whole life in his tattoos. A leatherback turtle for crossing the equator, a blue star for going round the Cape of Good Hope. A swallow is five thousand miles at sea.'

'I could get one when we reach LA,' I speculate.

'I'm thinking about a piece of work,' he admits.

'How will your mother feel about that, Chris?'

'Ahh, my mum doesn't mind, she's cool about it. My dad won't be too impressed.'

Visibility is twenty-five nautical miles – fifty kilometres – to the horizon, which is notched by the smoke of a ship. It is about the limit of vision on the water, from the bridge of a ship this size (we are forty metres up), though you might see land further off.

'But we don't see land too often,' says Chris.

We saw the lights of Capo St Vincente last night and this morning at dawn the low hills of Capo di Faro. Day

broke ethereal, the hills sandy against a lemon sky. The
light began in a rainbow across the dark horizon, a carmine
band against the sea. It was Sorin's watch and he was
using the time to study, listening to a training CD about
stowaways.

'Stowaways will use great ingenuity to trick you. They
will lie to you and deceive you. Stowaways will attempt to
befriend you and manipulate your emotions. Stay professional, stay detached. Stowaways cost the company money.
Be on your guard. Prevention is better than cure.'

This is all recited by an American woman with a voice a
shade more humane than the speaking clock. It is quite
chilling to picture the world's law enforcement authorities
being programmed with this stuff.

'I had stowaways,' Sorin said. 'In Hong Kong. Seventeen
Chinese guys. They come aboard dressed as stevedores –
they had help from a crew member. Hid in the bo'sun's
hatch. Hong Kong police came on, dogs and guns, took
them all off. But they miss four guys – so many places
to hide in a ship. But we were going to China next, so they
got them there. Took them away for . . . interrogation.
They had jackets with food and water in pockets. Not
much, they knew they would be looked after.'

He remarks that stowaways who choose the wrong ship
are thrown overboard.

'It happens, sure. In northern latitudes you're dead in
ten minutes and no one will ever find the body.'

No one ever did find the bodies of three Romanian stowaways, Petre Sangeorzan, Radu Danciu and Gheorghe
Mihoc, who were discovered on a ship in these waters in

1996. The vessel, the *Maersk Dubai*, was owned by the Taiwanese Yang Ming company: ship and crew were on charter to Maersk. On 12 March 1996 they were approximately where we are now, fifty miles off Cape Trafalgar, on their regular run from Algeciras to Halifax, Nova Scotia, when the three stowaways were discovered. The men's pleas for their lives seem to have had no effect on the Taiwanese officers of the *Maersk Dubai*, Captain Cheng-Shiou, First Officer Wu Chung-Chih, Second Officer Kuo Chin-Chiu, Radio Operator Jang Che-Min, Chief Cook Wang Ko-Lung and Chief Engineer Ni Yung-Lai.

The ship was heading north-west into the deep ocean when Sangeorzan and Danciu were found. They had crept aboard in Algeciras in the hope of a passage to Canada. A third would-be stowaway who failed to board had watched the ship leave with the two men on it. One of the ship's Filipino crew, Rudolfo Miguel, told CBC Radio in Canada what happened when the stowaways were caught.

'They have a passport, and picture for their family and children. The master, he said, "throw overboard". And now these people: "No, no, no – please, please, please, please captain, no, no, please." Crying. They understand that they will throw overboard . . .'

Another Filipino member of the crew, Juanito Ilagan, said, 'One of them are kneeling on the floor, I think begging for somebody to spare their lives. And he's kissing one of the boots of the crew.'

Ilagan said the captain had 'devil's eyes, fuming mad'.

Captain Cheng-Shiou was adamant that the two Romanians should be thrown off the ship. The Filipinos asked to be allowed to construct a raft for them. The first they made broke up on hitting the water; a second held together. Taiwanese officers then forced the two men down the pilot ladder. When Sangeorzan and Danciu were last seen, one had climbed on to the raft and the other was in the sea. They had no means of propulsion, no food or water, and no one was looking for them.

Extraordinarily, the same ship, carrying the same crew and controlled by the same officers, was making the same run two months later when the same thing happened. On 18 May the *Maersk Dubai* was a night and a morning's journey out of Algeciras, well into the eastern Atlantic, when Gheorghe Mihoc was discovered. Rudolfo Miguel told CBC: 'I saw the captain, the chief officer, the second mate, chief engineer, the chief cook holding knife grab this person.'

'The second cook, who is a Filipino, knocked on my door when I was having a nap,' Juanito Ilagan recalled, 'and he said they're gonna get rid of him. I said I don't think they'll kill him. He said they were carrying knives. I said who – who was carrying knives. Well, them, the Taiwanese officers.'

Miguel heard screaming – 'No, he said, no' – and watched from a hatchway as Mihoc was forced over the side at knifepoint. When the crew discovered a fourth stowaway, Nicolae Pasca, they hid him and fed him. In Halifax the ship was stormed by the Royal Canadian Mounted Police, alerted by a letter the crew had sent to a port chaplain in Houston, Texas, in which they detailed the first incident. Arrests and court cases followed.

The upshot, years later, says much about the lawlessness of the sea. Four Filipinos, including Ilagan and Miguel, agreed to remain in Canada to testify. They were accused by the officers' defence lawyers of inventing the whole story in order to emigrate to Canada. Their families in the Philippines were threatened. It took two years before they were allowed to work minimum wage jobs in Canada, the sea for ever closed to them. (Manning agencies and shipowners continue to deny the existence of blacklists, but the men had no illusions about their chances of new contracts.)

The court ruled that Canada could not extradite the accused for trial. They were returned to Taiwan. Captain Cheng-Shiou was tried there for negligence, but his case was dismissed for lack of evidence that the victims were dead. His motive for the murders seems to lie in Canadian regulations which fine ships seven thousand dollars for every stowaway who arrives in Canada, and Yang Ming company policy which punishes captains of ships where stowaways are found 'according to their degree of fault'. Yang Ming paid off the families of the deceased in an out-of-court settlement. The *Maersk Dubai* now sails in the livery of her owners, renamed the *YM Fortune*.

Entering the Strait of Gibraltar the seaways are flecked with fishing boats, ferries and freighters. As we track between the Pillars of Hercules I dash around the bridge with binoculars, gazing hungrily in all directions. The atmosphere of the Strait is charged, as if by an approaching storm, with the tense proximity of two mightily distinct cultures, as though planets have swum too close together. The weathers here change with squally speed. Below us are at least seven major currents, dominated on the surface by the Atlantic inflow, and near the seabed by the saline Mediterranean outflow. When Coleridge first saw the two continents simultaneously he recorded his exhilaration in his notebook, and the sense that must strike every traveller through the Strait, that man has made a lunatic division of existences out of a small gap of water.

I [am] sitting at the rudder case, my desk on the duck coop, my seat, have Spain, the Coast of Cadiz to wit, on my left hand, & Africa, the Barbary Coast, on my right. I am right abreast of a high bank, black brown heath with interspaces & large & small scarifications of light red clay – beyond this mountain islands, alongside & in file resembling canoes and boats with their keels upward. We have a breeze that promises to let us laugh at Privateers & Corsairs that in a calm will run out, as a fox will a fowl when the wolf dog that guards the poultry yard can only bark at him from his chain. This is Spain! – That is Africa! Now, then, I have seen Africa! Power of names to give interest! When I first sate down, with Europe on my left and Africa on my right, both distinctly visible, I felt a quickening of the movements in the Blood . . . This is Africa! That is Europe! – There is division, sharp boundary, abrupt Change! – and what are they in Nature – two Mountain Banks, they make a noble river of the interfluent sea, existing & acting with distinctness and manifoldness indeed, but at once & as one – no division, no change, no antithesis!

Tangier reclines on its hillside, all temptation, like a magus leaning on a bar. Jebel Musa in Morocco wears a magnificent hat of cloud while the sun shines on the Rock of Gibraltar. We slide into Algeciras towards evening. Dolphins play between us and the pilot boat as it comes alongside. The Captain pretty well guides us into the harbour; the pilot has little to do. Some communication problem with Chris on the fo'c'sle provokes a deep blast from the horn. The Captain tells a story of an infamous Algeciras brothel, Los Lagos, which was closed down because of drugs, crime and fighting.

'Then the authorities in Gibraltar begged them to reopen it because all the crime went there. So they reopen. New beds and clean sheets! The seaman's priest told me this so I know it is true.'

Everyone likes Algeciras because the port is at the foot of the town. The containers, fishing boats, quays, lorry-slalom and the Spanish evening you expect, but you walk through a Moroccan village first.

There is that smell, halfway between meat and spice, and women in djellabas, men smoking, teleboutiques, mosques and Allah Akbar is chanted softly from a window. Two obese prostitutes in bad moods mark the fringe of the settlement. The upper town is *cervezas* and pigs' legs, people eating tapas and seafood. There are ships and cranes at the end of the streets. On the basis that tomorrow is my birthday – and though I am in solidarity with the crew I am not actually an employee – I have a gin and tonic at a swanky bar, conscious that my hi-vis jacket sends a confusing signal. Slightly lost and slightly thirsty, I console myself that I must look a bit like a seafarer. On the way back to the ship Rohan and Prashant disabuse me of this illusion.

The first time I have seen them out of uniform, and they are strolling along the *calle* in their T-shirts and shorts like the cooler sort of tourist. They look well off, alert, as ever, healthy and contented: strikingly different from the old image of the merchant seaman, raddled with drink and vice. They want to know if I know where the action is. I wish I could tell them. It is the first time we have met in my environment, or at least one where I am not awed and innocent. Rohan and Prashant look at me eagerly, hoping for the inside take on Algeciras. These wonderful, terrifying young Indians! They are so kind and encouraging on the ship that I could hug them: they seem almost to sympathise with a plight you did not know you were in before you met them. When we talk I cannot help feeling that their civilisation knows mine for a foppish, effete and idle abstraction which cannot even look up its own train timetables without Indian help. There must be twenty-five-year-old Britons who could match Rohan's knowledge of one of the most sophisticated machines on earth, who are already married, who have children and a series of ten-year plans which are actually going to be realised, but I suspect there are very few.

'So do you know where is good to go?' Prashant asks. Spanish girls, tapas, flamenco and a roiling atmosphere of sensuous vivacity would evidently be welcome.

'Things tend to start very late in Spain . . . I found a nice cocktail bar,' I say, lamely, 'where you could have some – lemonade?'

They go on their way, laughing. The route back to the ship is lined with fishing boats, some of whose crews have not finished, and queues of silent lorries, their curtains drawn: another strange, still glimpse of the numberless tribe of men far from home, from company, from family, working to the regulations of a concrete world.

All night, in clunks and booms, we take on cargo: we are now lower in the water by a metre and it takes 120 tonnes to sink us an inch. Stevedores and deliveries come and go, two technicians fiddle with one of the radars, calibrating it, and fail to work out what is wrong with the other. Carl-Johann has gone; the new chief engineer, Andreas, looks stoically resigned. Like captains, senior officers work 'back to back' – three months on, three off, handing over to their relief quickly, because they know each other and the ships they maintain. But many officers hide from their phones on leave, especially over Christmas. If they can be reached they can be asked to work, which means being flown anywhere in the world at no notice.

We depart in thudding sun. In the bow two crew work the lines, feeding them on to the drums of six huge winches. Chris is at the winch controls, on a raised walkway which runs around the gunwales above the deck space where the two men work, separated from the peril by railings. Something goes wrong.

'Captain, the ship is moving forward!' Chris yelps, and dives for the controls. The winches pay out. They are still on automatic, so nothing snaps.

'The lines are designed to break backwards,' Chris says. 'But in some ports you still find steel – they whiplash. Cut you in half.'

It turns out a throttle on one of the slave stations, a sub-control on the bridge wing, was not quite at 'Stop'. When power was switched to it our monster moved.

'I always like this bay. I like that mountain,' the Captain says, as we turn out across the afternoon glare. He and Sorin mock Tarifa Traffic Control when it fails to ask the standard question.

'How many persons on board?' Sorin prompts the radio, not transmitting.

'Nineteen point three!' jokes the Captain. 'My first mate is pregnant.'

The pilot soon departs; the gangway and ladder are raised and secured.

'We are free!' says the Captain. 'Free as a bird!'

He and Sorin are in high spirits, as excited to be leaving as they were to arrive. Deep water comes quickly and dolphins with it – a large pod, including babies, flinging themselves at our bow waves. We progress past tankers, container ships, ferries, a cruise liner, fishing boats, the Guardia Civil in a rib, yachts under sail and catamarans. Gibraltar is a fortress-fist, watching us go.

Afternoon gives way to rose-orange evening, the coasts of Europe and Africa darken. Slow falling stars are planes descending into Malaga. Two strange beasts appear at sunset as we enter the Alboran Sea. They are very big with no blow, their dorsal and tail fins show as they surf in our wake – are they basking sharks? A Kraken's kittens?

Another sleep, another breakfast, another shimmering day, another Captain-humming, Sorin-carrot-crunching lunch. It is like being in a rolling dream, conscious but unable to wake until the next promised event, Suez, days away. It is as though we are in a benign daze as we cross this slumbering blue, but the sea turns time into distance in a way that could make you insane. Imagine seeing the months and years of your life surging from horizon to horizon as you age, and everything on land changes, while the sea remains exactly the same. We converse about anything to pass the time. The Captain talks about two passions: golfing holidays with his wife, and model trains. He has just landed a beauty, a particularly special locomotive, a rare thing.

'Twice the size of a normal engine! I remember seeing him when I was young . . .'

The model did not come cheap. The Captain takes precautions against over-indulgence. 'My wife looks after it for me when it arrives,' he says, before confiding, 'when I buy another one I send it to my friend's house.'

In mid-afternoon the bridge telephone rings. Chris turns the ship into a light sea from the north-west and pulls the telegraph back. All stop.

'What's happening, Chris?'

'Exhaust gas leak.'

We drift, our transponder sending the signal 'NOC' to passing ships: 'Not Under Command'.

Forty-five minutes later the phone rings again.

'OK, we are fixed,' Chris says. 'The Captain is letting me start her up, which is cool. Most captains like to do this themselves.'

He looks pleased. He nudges the control centimetre by centimetre, as gently as if he were afraid to break it, as if the telegraph were linked to some intricacy of glassware, rather than the steel citadels of the engine. He carefully plays the rudder control.

'If you turn the rudder too early it is like having a house blocking the water off the propeller – no thrust.'

It is touching how delicately a big man directs such a big ship. They all have this capacity for gentleness, for precision. It reminds me of my father repairing a bicycle or overseeing the assembly of a toy – 'Don't force it,' he always said. 'Gently, gently . . .' You can see someone like Chris being very good with children. The men's conversations about the solid world are not unlike those of boys at boarding school, minus the sex. They touch on food (food a lot), families sometimes, films now and again, airlines, airports and escape routes, often. With no audience, little praise, little status and almost no public understanding of what they do, these men achieve something that land life frequently fails to supply. You notice it in all of them, however junior; a kind of quiet self-possession. Paradoxically, the isolation of seafarers from the fullness of the world, and the confines of the mould they must fill, seem to make of them men in full.

This fullness was attained by previous generations through a tradition stretching back centuries. Many of today's older captains began their sea lives with a year's separation from all they knew. Of all the practical, technological and theoretical understanding a cadet acquired in that time, perhaps the most fundamental was philosophical: you are no longer what you were. You are not of the land. You are not of your family; you are barely of your nation: you belong to your ship, your crew.

With only an echo of the hierarchies of naval discipline, merchant shipping relies on precedent, routine and procedure. There are so many ways to do a thing wrong, and so few to do it right, and generally one which is the way it is expected to be done. Improvisation and resourcefulness are principally reserved for the captain and the chief engineer, extending occasionally to the senior officers. These qualities make good sailors but they are only required from the crew in exceptional circumstances. The history of professional seafaring is a story of man's attempts to minimise exceptional circumstances, in the environment most likely to produce them.

A cadet learns that his place on ships and the fate of his career, perhaps his life, will depend on fixed and unified purpose: the extent to which he can close the gap between his sense of himself and the nature of his role. The rank, the work and the ship must pre-empt the self, its feelings and desires. This is what Sorin means when he says he looks for someone who is 'strong with himself'. Joseph Conrad explores the point in *The Nigger of the 'Narcissus'* through the characters of Singleton, the old sailor, and the rebel, Donkin. Singleton sees no distinction between himself and his work. Thrashed to exhaustion by the storm, Singleton perceives 'an immensity tormented and blind, moaning and furious, that claimed all the days of his tenacious life, and, when life was over, would claim the worn-out body of its slave . . .'

Singleton contemplates this prospect with equanimity: he understands and does not baulk at his fate. Donkin, failing to incite a revolt, and being thwarted in an inarticulate attempt to assert ego over rank and role, becomes submerged in himself and is ostracised, a petty thief who steals from a dying man.

Captains, crews and the life itself are ruthless in scouring out those who do not fit or are not ready for the sea.

'If I find out someone has a problem at home,' a captain said, 'I want him off. If a man's father dies I want him off the ship – he can't work and he infects the others. But supposing you are married, so your father is not your next of kin, then you pay for your own flight. You think, where is the compassion?'

That captain winced but he shrugged, too. You do not look for much mercy at sea.

We pass the island of Pantelleria at sunset, known to seafarers as 'Telephone Island': though we are nearer Tunisia than Italy, Pantelleria is Italian and grants a European-tariff phone signal. Mussolini called Pantelleria 'the only unsinkable aircraft carrier in the Mediterranean'. Its airfield and radar station threatened their planned invasion of Sicily, so in June 1943 the Allies dropped over four thousand tonnes of bombs on Pantelleria's garrison, which surrendered as the invaders' landing craft drew near. Churchill claims in his memoirs that the only British casualty was a man bitten by a mule.

This one-sided affair is of a piece with the island's first entry into English letters, and British propaganda, in 1589, with 'The true report of a worthy fight, performed in the voyage from Turkey by five ships of London, against eleven galleys and two frigates of the King of Spain's, at Pantalarea, within the straight, anno 1586'. The writer was Philip Jones, the publisher Richard Hakluyt, evangelist of North American colonisation, confidant of Raleigh and collector of Elizabethan voyage accounts, who included it in his *Principall Navigations, Voiages, and Discoveries of the English Nation*. The 'worthy fight' Philip Jones describes is a striking piece of Elizabethan derring-do in which honourable English merchant-adventurers are waylaid by the squadron of one Don Pedro di Lieva, who bids them yield and show obedience to the King of Spain. Naturally the English refuse.

'The Spaniards hewed off the noses of the galleys, that nothing might hinder the level of the shot; and the English, on the other side, courageously prepared themselves to the combat, every man, according to his room, bent to perform his office with alacrity and diligence. In the meantime a cannon was discharged from out the Admiral of the galleys, which, being the onset of the fight, was presently answered by the English Admiral with a culverin; so the skirmish began, and grew hot and terrible.'

Though greatly outnumbered and very busy with the battle, the English, so Jones says, 'ceased not in the midst of their business to make prayer to Almighty God, the revenger of all evils and the giver of victories, that it would please Him to assist them in this good quarrel of theirs, in defending themselves against so proud a tyrant. Contrarily, the foolish Spaniards, they cried out, according to their manner, not to God, but to our Lady . . .'

After a five-hour fight 'furious and sharp', three of the galleys drew away, 'ready by the force of English shot they had received to perish in the seas'. The victors could not tell how many Spaniards they had slaughtered, and conjectured that their opponents had lost so many men that they lacked hands to reload their guns. On the English side Jones reports 'the loss of only two men slain amongst them all, and another hurt in his arm, whom Master Wilkinson, with his good words and friendly promises, did so comfort that he nothing esteemed the smart of his wound, in respect of the honour of the victory and the shameful repulse of the enemy'.

The interventions of an English-leaning God notwithstanding, the encounter records the death of an old technology, the Mediterranean galley, at the hands of a new one, the English full-rigged sailing ship, which was far more manoeuvrable and able to discharge broadsides of cannon fire. The poor Spanish, desperately sawing off the prows of their galleys so that their few, forward-facing cannons might have a better field of fire, clearly knew what was coming to them.

'You will see a lighthouse,' the Captain says, as darkness falls.

'Yes! There! How did you navigate before GPS when you could not see lights or stars?'

He makes an eel-like wriggling motion with his hands.

'We feel our way.'

CHAPTER 7

Madness, Superstition and Death

At dawn on 8 September we are south of Sicily's Capo
Passero, 'Sparrow Cape'; the island is a yellow-blue
line on the horizon, rumpled up at the eastern end where
the volcano, Etna, is a smoking egg. An antique-looking oil
rig works the Vega field, spindly with legs and flares. There
is a bee aboard today, and a swallow. The Captain has a piece
of advice regarding sea lions.

'You don't want to swim with them – they are in their
element. And you will see why they are called lions!'

Shubd says he saw them in Chile. Shubd is keener on
sport than wildlife, and particularly partial to table tennis.
We agree to a competition.

'My last captain loved TT,' Shubd says, leading the way
down the stairs. 'Every day, four o'clock, he was down here.
He is dead now. It is very sad.'

'What happened?'

'They were in port, the agent was aboard and he died.
His head went on his desk – like that. It was a heart attack.'

'How old was he?'

'He was very young. This was a good guy you know, a really good guy.'

Until recently the diet, the danger and the sedentary routine shortened the life expectancy of seafarers by up to six years, compared to men living on land. The diet has improved and many ships are equipped with gymnasiums, though it tends to be the same few who use them. It is also common for the weights and exercise bikes to be eschewed altogether because the noise of using them disturbs sleepers in adjacent cabins. There is almost always someone asleep on a ship.

The *Gerd* has two void decks, one of which is equipped for sport. They are eerie places, windowless steel ghost-spaces, added into the ship's design only to give the bridge more height, so that two more layers of containers could be accommodated on deck without obscuring the view forward. The echoing, grey-painted rooms do not lend themselves to the gaiety of leisure but we do our best. We use the rowing machine and the table football, but Shubd is not so good at the football so we return to table tennis. Shubd smashes the ball like a champion. He is a very gracious and patient winner.

Sorin fills the swimming pool, a container-sized cavity behind the superstructure. It is warm, salty and thick-spotted with paint flakes and black matter from the funnel. Our Captain loves his pool.

'This is another world,' he says, gravely. 'It is the best place to clear your head.'

'There was a ship in the Pacific, the Captain went mad,' Shubd confides. 'He had to be kept in his room, guarded by two cadets.'

'This must be alcohol,' snorts the Captain.

Sorin drains the pool at night because on another ship a sailor sleepwalked in and drowned.

'What do we do if someone goes mad or gets hurt, Chris?'

'We have a number for a hospital in Denmark where there is always a consultant standing by,' he says. 'If we can't handle it then we will get help.'

'How?'

'There was one ship in the Pacific, somebody got hurt and they needed to evacuate him, so they got orders to go to a certain position. They got there and there was nothing. Then a submarine comes up right alongside them. Pretty cool.'

We are contemplating this when the alert box spits out a message: an empty five-metre white lifeboat is adrift in the Sicilian Channel. There is no other information.

We are in the Eastern Mediterranean Basin, heading for the Ionian Abyssal Plain. Last night, after leaving Pantelleria and Cape Bon to the south of us, we passed Terrible Bank to the north.

In Italy I spoke to a man who should have died on Terrible Bank. Originally from Benin City in Nigeria, Charles was working in a garage in Tripoli until the war came. He bought a place on a boat which aimed to make the run to Italy, fully loaded with refugees. The first boat turned over in the harbour. Sixty passengers were drowned. Charles, on the upper deck, survived to try again with the second boat. Its engine stopped in the vicinity of Terrible Bank. The captain was able to broadcast one call for help before his radio battery died.

'The sea was very strange,' Charles said. 'It was a white sea, all white, the waves were big. Everybody was sick. I was sick a lot, so sick, and there was no water. One boy said his spirit had drunk all the diesel for the engine. He was crying. Everyone started to pray to their own gods.'

An Italian Coastguard cutter found them. The first Europeans Charles spoke with were two Italian navy divers. 'They were very tired. They said the place where we were found is somewhere no one survives. They call it the dead zone. I will never forget all that white, the white sea . . .'

As all seas, this one is a soup of bodies. The Strait of Gibraltar alone is believed to swallow a thousand would-be human migrants every year; no one knows how many perish attempting to cross the wider Mediterranean. It is migration season in the natural world, now: a billion birds are adding their mortality rates to the waves. Two warblers rest on the containers astern. The seafarers are doleful about their chances – any non-seabird seen on board is reported, once my enthusiasm is known, with a regretful shrug.

'These small ones die,' says Sorin, but it is not necessarily so. Ornithologists believe that birds like warblers migrate via memory maps, making regular stops at the same places. Why would a ship not count? There is not a day of the year when many ships our size do not pass this way. We carry a small population of insects, and sometimes rainwater. The *Gerd* might well be a link in a chain of predictable, accommodating stopovers.

A yellow wagtail appears next, and a ragged line towing itself through the morning resolves into a flight of fifteen purple herons, followed by a yellow-billed stork and more swallows, all going south.

In these waters Coleridge's ship also attracted migrating birds: he travelled through the spring, nature's other season of changeover. His ship, the *Speedwell*, was one of a convoy escorted by men-of-war, as a defence against French privateers and Barbary pirates:

> Hawk with ruffled feathers resting on the Bowsprit – now shot at, & yet did not move – how fatigued – a third time it made a gyre, a short circuit, & returned again. Five times it was shot at, left the vessel, flew to another & I heard firing, now here now there & nobody shot it but probably it perished from fatigue, & the attempt to rest upon the wave! Poor Hawk! O Strange Lust of Murder in Man! – It is not cruelty it is mere non-feeling from non-thinking.

Quarters of the blue world still host populations of pirates: the Arabian Sea, the Strait of Malacca, the South China Sea and in the Bight of Benin particularly. Their combined activities cost around seven billion dollars a year, most of it spent on prevention measures and patrols, rather than ransoms. But the sum is a mere mote compared to the spectacular economic and geo-political changes effected by Aruj, Ishak and Khizr, the Barbarossa brothers, born in the 1470s on Lesbos, then under control of the Ottomans. Their father was a warrior-turned-potter who had a small boat which he used to trade his goods; his sons must have become proficient sailors when still very young. They rapidly graduated to privateering: early reversals saw Ishak killed, their boat seized and Aruj imprisoned for three years. Khizr sprung his brother from captivity and the two began an astonishing campaign. In the early sixteenth century, when the Mediterranean was the Barbarossas' hunting ground, the ships of their prey – Spanish, French, Genoese and Venetian merchantmen – were rowed by slaves, often Turkish or other Muslim captives. When the Barbarossas boarded the Muslims were freed and Christians took their places, shackled to the rowing benches. They were not unchained for any reason. The downwind stench of galleys was infamous.

The success of the Barbarossas was partly due to man-management. Their preferred attack craft were galiots, small boats with two masts which could also be rowed by volunteer crews with a stake in the expedition. Part of the ferocity that achieved their victories came from the morale of these unchained men, who leapt from their oars to join the battle. Starting with two galiots, the Barbarossas fought, boarded, captured, raided and traded their way to extraordinary power, enslaving tens of thousands along the way. Aruj besieged and took Algiers, proclaiming himself Sultan, before shrewdly relinquishing the title and joining his domain to the Ottoman Empire. He was killed in a battle with 10,000 Spanish soldiers under Charles V. By the time Khizr died in 1546 the younger brother had become Hayreddin Barbarossa, master of the North African littoral and Grand Admiral of the fleet of the Turkish Sultan.

Two and a half centuries later, when Coleridge sailed this way in April 1804, the threat of the Corsairs was still not extinguished. Only two months before Coleridge watched the hawk a desperate action had been fought in the harbour of Tripoli by men of the nascent United States Navy and Marine Corps, who lost, retook and set fire to an American ship that was being used as a gun battery to repel American attacks on the Tripolitan fleet. It was the United States' first foreign war. Another two centuries on, America has been again engaged in military action in Tripoli, assisting the overthrow of Colonel Gaddafi. Bizarrely, this part of the Mediterranean currently smells as dreadful as ever it did in the days of the Corsairs.

'God's teeth – that smell!'

(My rather BBC English amuses Shubd, who remarks, 'You speak very well!' I am now experimenting with antique exclamations in place of the traditional Anglo–Saxon expressions with which my shipmates are well acquainted.)

You cannot but complain about the stink. You step out of the cool bridge into North African heat and a sickening reek issuing from Bay 26.

'Animal skins in brine,' Sorin says. 'Not nice, eh?'

The stink falls halfway between rotting meat and rotting fish; it becomes stronger by the hour. 'The brine overflows and washes around the decks,' Sorin says, darkly relishing. So this is what you walk through if you are idle enough to be taking morning and evening strolls. As the voyage goes on and the stench increases, and more foul water sloshes about the decks, Sorin requests more information about these skins.

'They are cow heads,' he reveals.

'What!'

'Cattle heads in brine. From Algericas to Malaysia. We are going to need to hire some people to clean the bays . . .'

We make faces as we imagine every wave that rocks us setting all the cattle heads bobbing and nodding in their dark tank.

We pass the Archimedes Seamount and push out over the Abyssal Plain. The clouds at sunset are puffy flotillas and you feel you can see for ever – the sinking light effects a sudden widening and deepening of the space on the horizon. All at once what appeared fixed, the range of vision, is revealed to be an illusion. There is more distance there, now, much more, gulfs of coloured sky and burnished water diminish to a new limit of sight. For a few moments you seem to glimpse the impossible, some mythological West over the curve of the world.

Hotter, hotter, this must be an Egyptian heat. Sorin talked to his family last night, as he tries to every night, on Skype or Messenger. He shows me a photograph of his wife and son.

'How beautiful they are!'

'Yes,' he says. 'Thank you very much.'

We talk about superstitions.

'No whistling on the bridge.'

'Why not?'

'It brings storms. In fact no whistling anywhere.'

'OK, anything else?'

'Don't turn your back on the sea. No harming any birds on the ship.'

'Why not?'

'This Turkish bo'sun told me about a guy who found a bird on the fo'c'sle, shitting everywhere – bird was sick. So he killed it – broke its neck – and throw it over the side. Within one week he lost his whole arm in an accident.'

'Whoa!'

Sorin is not smiling. 'If it had been a Russian, a Romanian or a Bulgarian I would not believe – but these Turkish guys don't lie.'

Shubd holds the same belief, about birds rather than Turks.

In superstitious vein we discuss women on ships. It seems that this taboo – still held by the skippers of certain Scottish fishing vessels – left the merchant world a long time ago.

'In the old days the agent in Bangkok couldn't get on board the ship for all the girls on the gangway,' says the Captain, and chuckles.

Boogie Street, he said, was the place to go. Singapore was also held to be special: 'Beautiful girls,' says the Captain.

'South America,' says Shubd, dreamily. 'Brazil.'

As often, mention of the Old Days brings further reminiscence of their glories. When they broke down in the Old Days everyone started fishing off the boat. They don't break down so much now, and the fish are harder to find. In South American ports, Shubd says, you can be besieged by fishermen offering catches, and also peddlers of very high grade marijuana, he hears.

It is very hard not to whistle. Nobody else does. Coming out of the crew mess with a cup of coffee, heading for the saloon where we eat, a few notes escape – barely notes, more like a pursed prelude to more tuneless humming (semi-tuneful humming is one of the commonest sounds of the ship). In the saloon the Captain, Andreas the chief engineer and Sorin all raise their gazes from their plates. Their faces are expressionless: alarm and disapproval is conveyed psychically, with considerable force. I hum and 'sing' louder, as if trying to drown out the memory. There is the smallest pause before Sorin chomps a chunk of melon. Breakfast continues.

Lifeboat, fire and man overboard drills are all publicised in advance. When the alarm goes at ten thirty I hurtle as carefully as possible down to the ship's control room on the main deck to find everyone lounging around waiting for their name to be called. This achieved, Sorin informs the Captain, now alone on the bridge, that all are present.

'Very good, carry on,' says the radio.

We divide to our assigned lifeboat stations, port or starboard, where we don life jackets. I have seen more pathetic buoyancy aids but cannot remember where.

'This is a piece of shit!' I pronounce over the four blocks of foam held together by a scrap of orange plastic, pleased to be able to demonstrate something like expertise, having spent time on lifeboats.

'Well,' Shubd says, 'it is very economical.'

We check that the lights switch on and that the whistles blow, then we file into the lifeboat. An orange capsule like a suppository with a little turret, the lifeboat is painted pistachio-green inside. No one can see out except for the helm, who would be Shubd or the Captain – Sorin and Chris are on the port boat. We strap in. Every face betrays the same feeling: this is ghastly.

'The first thing that happens is we issue seasick pills,' says Andreas, 'otherwise someone will puke and then everyone will puke.'

There is no doubt about that. Strapped in, facing each other, blind to the sea, acting as a kind of meat ballast in the bottom of a capsule which would be upside down half the time, in any sort of storm, you would certainly puke.

Shubd starts the engine. It runs first time, the only piece of good news, as far as I can tell. The engine is capable of five knots – five! You would be lucky to keep the boat's head to the wind.

We are all relieved to conclude lifeboat drill, but now the horn blasts and bells sound again: fire alarm. The 'fire' is in a container. Two of the crew, 'smoke-jumpers', pull on breathing apparatus and flame-retardant suits. They mime attacking the fire. Moving urgently, one holds a spike against the container while the other pretends to strike it with a sledgehammer. Others connect hoses and pretend to cool down nearby containers. A perforated nozzle is then held over the 'hole' in the burning container and a hose connected to it. It is easier to imagine the smoke-jumpers being horribly injured than it is to picture them suppressing the blaze, but everyone knows what they are supposed to do and everyone takes it seriously. The Captain would turn the ship so as to create a lee between the fire and the wind. Sorin would be his eyes, and to a great extent his judgement: the Captain remains on the bridge, the chief commands the fight. The Filipinos, led in this case by Ray and Mike, would do the fighting.

* * *

There are many more examples of conflagrations at sea which ate lives like air than there are stories of fires which were successfully fought. Wind to fan flames, toxic materials to poison smoke, distance and situation to cut off help and a demonic alternative of burning or drowning put fire first among the nightmares of the sea. Seafarers collect these stories almost in spite of themselves, horrors which do not bear close study, except perhaps by those whose business it is to prevent them.

One that might stand for many was the fate of the *General Slocum*, a paddle steamer which caught fire on an excursion up the East River of New York in 1904, approximately where the Triborough Bridge is now. In full view of hundreds on shore, over a thousand people perished – a disproportionate number of them women and children. New York was shaken with an agony of grief, a foreshadowing of September 11th 2001, the only tragedy in that city to surpass the *General Slocum* in loss of life. Newspaper headlines tell of mourning crowds at the water's edge in the days following the disaster, of people so beset by anguish that they had to be prevented from throwing themselves into the river.

Captain H. Van Schaick remained at the helm, while the wheelhouse burned, until he got the *General Slocum* aground. He left the bridge, he said, only when his cap caught fire. Though he seems to have done everything possible to save lives he was criticised for spurning an opportunity to ground the ship earlier, at a wharf he believed was imperilled by warehouses and oil tanks. He spent three and a half years in jail and was not pardoned until eight years after the tragedy.

If ships are models of their times in miniature, the *General Slocum*'s was a shadowy era. Fire hoses burst. Life jackets were rotten: some were found to have been freighted with metal by the manufacturer to make them up to the required weight. Lifeboats could not be launched: there are reports that they had been wired and painted into place. Many of the passengers could not swim. A man in a white yacht is said to have stood off the scene, watched, and made no attempt to help.

The launching of rescue boats is next. Rohan gives the briefing. It is like listening to a young captain; Rohan has the gift of commanding attention.

'The rescue boat is gravity-dropped and control is from the deck,' he says. 'The important thing is that the deck crew really drop it. You want a big splash. If not, the boat is hanging over the waves by the hook. I have been in this situation in training and it is very complicated and very dangerous.'

Noel, our cook, is picked on to talk us through launching the life rafts. He recites the procedure at top volume. Noel lacks Rohan's ability to transmit solemnity but his words are followed closely.

If we are a model of our time in miniature then the *Gerd* is proof of progress. There are plans, there is adequate equipment (at least the life jackets are not weighted with metal) and the drills are practised. The last time this company was faced with the real thing, dangerous cargo in the forward holds of the *Charlotte Maersk* caught fire in the Strait of Malacca. The crew were on their way to attack the fire within seven minutes of the alarm. They fought the blaze for twenty-four hours before help reached them, saving the ship and themselves. It took a further ten days to kill the fire, which engulfed more than 150 containers and burned at over a thousand degrees. One man was treated for smoke inhalation.

The incident report is terrifying reading. Flames, detonations and palls of chemical fumes did not daunt the men cooling adjacent containers, retarding the spread of the blaze. (The intense heat of the fire meant they were prevented from a direct assault, at first.) This was brave enough on its own, but the report includes a reference to a tank of liquefied petroleum gas. The *Charlotte*'s captain, Dick Danielsen, decided that this tank would rule their efforts: if the flames came too close to it the ship would be abandoned. The men fought with the knowledge that the consequences of an LPG explosion would surely be lethal for some of them.

What formidable courage it required of the smoke-jumpers: as they suited up for our drill and peered out through their visors I imagined Mike and Ray hurrying forward along the narrow deck, vision constricted by their masks, their breathing loud in their ears as they make their ungainly charge into danger, knowing that if anyone is going to die they will surely be the first.

There is a photograph of the crew of the *Charlotte* taken after their victory. They are an almost perfect analogy of the men of the *Gerd*: four Europeans and three Indians wear the insignia of officers; squatting at their feet is the Filipino crew. Every man is smiling. Captain Danielsen, in particular, looks euphoric.

It is not unusual for captains to serve their periods at sea knowing little of most of their men. The ship sails on an understanding of combined strength, not certainty. The expressions on the men of the *Charlotte* are triumphant not merely in achievement, but in unity: the fire put them to the question and they answered. The different scales of pay, the racial divisions in treatment and privilege, the differ-ence between company-employed officers and voyage-contracted seafarers undermines the traditional language of the enterprise. 'Crew' in the *Gerd*'s case actually refers to a collection of entirely different classes, experiences, grades, cultures and sets of expectations which happen to be in the same boat. (It would not be strange or out of place for Captain Larsen to go halfway around the world without sharing anything but the briefest exchanges with Roy, the youngest of our crew.) But Captain Danielsen's expression is alight with pride and relief. At the moment the shutter clicked there was no captain anywhere who knew his crew better, who had endured as much with them, who had worried about them more, or achieved more with them. Of all the thousands of photographs generated and published by the company, this photograph is the only one I have seen of a complete crew.

We approach Egypt as night falls, passing south of Crete and beating on through spectral waters. The moon's broad path is cut with shadows like phantom ships. The air is milky and hot. The sea lies right down, darkest silver-blue and alive, flowing past us like a snake.

CHAPTER 8

Bitter Water, Bloody Sand

I wake early and the sun is already up: our clocks remain on Central European Time but we have been steaming towards morning. As we pass Tobruk and El Alamein a helicopter comes over from the north and soon after twenty-one turtle doves descend out of the same sky, settle on a pink container and fall asleep. They have the air of having done this before. The noon horn test blasts them awake. Oil rigs appear like traffic cones, serviced by strange-shaped ships, their silhouettes stretched, crushed and platformed. Sun stars sparkle on the blue in an infinite, strobing shimmer.

At breakfast there is discussion of a ferry which turned over in the Zanzibar Channel last night. 'And it is dark there then,' says the Captain. The ferry was overloaded. 'And there are many sharks there,' the Captain adds, 'great whites. Six metres. It was Christmas Eve for them.'

For hours we parallel the width of the Nile delta, which remains out of sight until an oil refinery rises over the southern horizon, the first sight of Egypt. Two flying fish skip out of a flat sea, bright silver. They change direction in the air, dipping and diving between waves, their wing-like fins extended. A pair of dolphins, bigger and jumping higher than the Biscay and western Mediterranean animals, rush up to take advantage of our wake. Huge and wild, they buck out of the water with such force that they fall head-first, their tails high in semi-somersault. Their play seems an assertion of joy or madness, the overexcitement of children disordered by wind, sugar or the moon.

It is still very hot at 5 p.m. At five thirty we eat the traditional Saturday steak and chips, with prawns in avocado halves to start. There is a general and contented chewing as we put these delicacies away, and a conversation about cars with Rohan. I despair: Nelson, Churchill, *Clarkson*? Can a professional irritant really be the blue world's most famous Briton? It is between him and Beckham. Most of those present are less keen on football than cars, because cars translate well to DVD, but seafarers have little opportunity to watch football. In place of Nelson, the greatest naval tactician in history, a man of surpassing courage who loved duty and country above all, a pantomime TV bigot is now Britain's foremost man at sea.

On the radar clots of vessels can be seen forming ahead of us, some anchoring, some exiting the canal. Container ships harlequinned with boxes follow car carriers in procession. It will cost us half a million dollars to transit to Suez, plus fees for the weight of our cargo, plus cigarettes.

'Do you know what Egypt is called?' Sorin asks.

'Umm – Egypt?'

'Marlboro Country!'

Displayed in the lift is the company corruption policy. If someone tries to corrupt us we are to have nothing to do with him or her; we must report the attempt immediately. Fortunately, no one regards the cigarette price of the Suez Canal (otherwise known as 'the Marlboro channel') as corruption. The giving of cigarettes is more like a traditional local custom.

If we arrive late at the assembly point we will forfeit half a million dollars. This eventuality falls in the Captain's broad field of impossible things which will not be permitted to happen. We make the arrival line at 1830 precisely. We lower our twenty-tonne anchor and are assigned a convoy number. We will be third.

'Do you worry about anchoring like this?'

Lights prickle the hulls of tethered giants around us.

'No no no I have stopped her so many times. At four knots I know I can stop her in one ship's length.'

The Captain is in a lively mood, humming to himself like a dynamo, circling the bridge, checking this and that, needling Shubd in the name of instruction.

'Have you plotted the course?'

Shubd hesitates.

'The COURSE!' roars the Captain.

'Two oh nine,' says Shubd, tentative.

'Two oh NINE,' says the Captain, decisively. 'Then one eight two.' His finger jabs the electronic chart. 'I will use the wind and the thrusters to swing around here, then fsshht! You see?'

With the fsshht! his finger streaks south into the mouth of the canal, as if we will be doing it at light speed.

There is an unfamiliar atmosphere in the ship. I cannot understand it at first and range around quizzically until it crystallises: peace. The anchor is down; nothing will happen for three hours; we have eaten well. Joel jumps about in the gym like a bantamweight boxer, smacking his gloved fists, messing with a skipping rope, talking more than exercising. I cannot persuade him to share my incredulity at the treatment of Filipinos by the shipping industry.

'They always say it's the market,' he shrugs.

In the engine control room Andreas is crawling around under Rohan's desk.

'What's up, Chief?'

'His music is not working. How can he work without his music?'

He makes an adjustment and the room fills with Robbie Williams announcing he just wants to feel real love and know it's for real . . . Rohan smiles and continues clicking through the graphic screens which report the status of all the mechanical systems.

Outside the saloon nine pairs of flip-flops are arranged on the mat. The door is closed and singing issues from within: a mewing, Americanised but clearly not American love song, soft rock. I very much want to go in but something prevents me: karaoke is a participant's pastime, not an observer's, and its place among Filipino seafarers is near-sacred. Filipino crews have the union-negotiated right to a karaoke machine and this one is being used with total commitment. A critic might not be kind about the voice of the singer but you could only applaud the sincerity of his song. He left his love behind, you see.

We haul anchor as the Captain turns us gently around it. Egypt is a sprinkle of lights in the dark. You can make out a minaret, oil flares and street lights, orange and white. A moon-sheen falls from a partly occluded sky, glimmering on the containers. Port Said Control is voluble on the radio. The Suez pilots are demanding that everyone lower the gangways and ladders on their starboard sides. The vessel in front of us, a big container carrier with a Russian captain, by the sound of him, objects that he has the other ladder down.

'Listen to this *Russian*,' Sorin says, with a withering emphasis.

'Put gangway down on starboard side,' Port Said Control insists.

'Repeat, gangway and ladder down on port side,' counters the Russian.

'Do you want to transit tonight or not?' snaps Port Said.

There is a pause. Every watch on every ship in the convoy is listening to this.

'Lowering starboard ladder,' concedes the Russian, wearily.

Our bridge roars with laughter.

The pilots then ignore the Russian's new ladder and board his ship on the port side.

As we cross the start line, marked by a winking yellow buoy, a fleet of pilot boats comes buffeting up to our flanks, searchlights jumping in the darkness. The first man aboard is a Suez pilot, Pharaonic with his white ducks, cap and prominent belly. He asks for a present: one carton of cigarettes. He asks for a second present but does not get it. Now the Maersk terminal at Port Fouad slips by on our left and three more pilot boats jostle for access to our ladder. They form a surging raft with men jumping between them. Two men appear on our bridge, present papers for signature and disappear, all in moments, and a small war breaks out on the starboard side.

Should our engine fail, the Suez crew will take our lines to buoys in the canal. Since they travel with us down the canal they need their boat hauled out of the water with them in it, and no stopping is permitted, so the operation takes place at twelve knots. In their little craft, far below, they can be seen gesticulating as our hook dangles above them. Tiny howls reach us on the bridge.

'What can I do?' Chris mutters, untroubled. 'I only have three men.' There is a degree of scepticism between the seafarers and the pilots. 'They think we're a five-star hotel,' someone says, scornfully. Chris is sceptical that the facilities on offer for emergency mooring in the canal – crumbling concrete cakes with inset iron rings – are good enough for us. 'That's what you get for a billion-krone ship?'

It is no little thing to hoist a little boat and three men up to the deck of a giant without stopping but the hook is attached, the boat and its crew lurch into the air and Chris reels them in. The men disappear to the Suez Lounge, a cabin containing bunks, a table and a bathroom. They slam the door, retreating into querulous Arabic and cigarette smoke, as we process past Port Fouad and lagoons of darkness, a line of giants steaming towards Ismalia.

Dawn treads over the Sinai as we prepare to anchor in the Great Bitter Lake. The air smells of dank ashes. The lake is highly saline; beneath the water salt deposits, sand and gypsum mix with decaying layers of organic matter and produce a tight hydrogen-sulphide smell. Hypersalinity in the Great and Little Bitter Lakes has steadily diminished with the passage of ships and the flow of currents, allowing the migration of Red Sea fish north into the Mediterranean. A man and two boys are trying to catch them. The man backs his oars as the boys haul in the net, hand over hand. They cannot be more than twelve or thirteen years old. The hauling takes an age and the boys do not wear gloves. They bring in about a dozen fish.

In the fo'c'sle the decks are ploughed with mud, residue of last night's anchoring. The lateen sails of feluccas shine whiter than the gulls and the lake is violent blue. The anchor goes down with a titanic rumble and a high singing-whine, as if the ship is a steel goblet, rubbed round by a giant's finger.

'One shackle up and down,' Sorin reports.

'Up and down' means the anchor is vertically below the ship. A shackle of chain is fifteen fathoms, each of which is six feet, so we have around twenty-seven metres of water below us.

'One up and down, very good,' says the radio, and the Captain slowly backs the ship. Three times more chain roars off the drum as the deck thrums, whines and vibrates under our feet. When they are satisfied Sorin locks the brake and the peace of being at anchor returns. We swing through a slow arc as the sun lights an escarpment to the west. There are sphinx shapes in the rocks and palms along the shore. The sun climbs higher, the light flattening and glaring as we wait for the north-bound convoy. It appears towards the end of the morning, led by a Spanish warship, the frigate *Santa Maria*.

Unfinished wars lie under all our horizons. The chart on which Chris plotted our approach to the canal shows Egypt, the Sinai, the southern end of Israel and Gaza. The refinery we saw last night was bombed by the British during the Suez crisis. During Suez, Port Fouad was the scene of one of the more dubious victories of the French Foreign Legion, which fought its way through the little town, taking no casualties while inflicting many. The lake we float on now was home to the 'Yellow Fleet': a convoy of merchant ships trapped by the closing of the canal in 1967 during the Six Day War. They remained at anchor, blown over with desert sand, until the canal reopened in 1975, when only two of them were able to leave under their own power. One of the Yellow Fleet, *African Glen*, was sunk during the battles of the Yom Kippur War in 1973. The crews trapped on the Great Bitter Lake had a terrifyingly good view of this war: the canal was one of the front lines and the counter-attack which eventually ended the conflict began with Israeli tanks crossing into Egypt at Deversoir, at the northern end of the lake.

The slow withdrawal of the *Santa Maria* into the north-bound channel is a paradoxically reassuring sight, visible confirmation that NATO warships are active in the Gulf of Suez and the Red Sea. Everyone on the *Gerd* hopes and believes we will not need those warships, but everyone wishes there were more of them.

In the dining room is Captain (Major Chief) Pilot Mohammed Roshdy, who is bald as a brown marble and wears elegant bifocals.

'In 1973 I was in the Egyptian navy. In the Red Sea. Our ship was attacked.'

'Attacked by whom?'

He gestures north-east. 'Israeli helicopters. I was hit in the back.'

'Does it still hurt?'

'No, it's OK now.'

'How do you feel about Israel?'

'Israel! Listen, I have met the whole world – all nationalities. In this job you meet everyone. Everyone. There is no difference at all. The only difference is nationality. Nationality – it is completely meaningless, it is our greatest mistake! It is all politics and business. It means nothing. I do not believe in nationality. I believe in humanity. The only real difference on ships is the food . . .'

'How does this compare?'

(We are eating chicken.)

'This is good. I do not like the Russian food! Or Korean.'

The canal clear, we weigh anchor and steam slowly south into the Little Bitter Lake. What looks like a river issuing from its southern end becomes a plumb line, straight and narrow. Mohammed Roshdy commentates as we bear south between crumbling sand walls: the Egyptians used them as strongpoints to fire on Israelis on the other side during the 1973 war.

'Around here, Ismalia, is OK now,' Roshdy says. 'This is a rich part of Egypt. In other places there is chaos. There is no law – no stability – the police are hiding. The dictator robbed us of political experience. I fear for Egypt. I fear.'

'What about the Muslim Brotherhood?'

'I fear fanatics, but I do not fear all the Muslim Brotherhood. Some of them are wise. They have political experience.'

For afternoon prayer Captain Roshdy unrolls his mat on the wing of the bridge, on a compass bearing to Mecca, and interrupts his worship only once: 'Steer one eight five!'

'One eight five,' echoes the helm.

When he has finished we withdraw to the deck behind the bridge for cigarettes, though Captain Roshdy never takes his eyes from the canal ahead. Suez and Panama are the two places where captains cede control and technical responsibility for their vessels to pilots (though it would not take much for our Captain to wrest it back). We are passing a hellish, dictator-chic palace on the Sinai side. You would have to be utterly corrupted to approve the aesthetics of its plans, never mind the practicalities. There is a parade ground in front; a kilometre behind is accommodation for the guards: tin huts. Nothing else disturbs the yellow horizontals of desert. Below the palace on the canal bank soldiers are filling sandbags, working very slowly in forty degrees of heat. Their stooped shapes and the lassitude of their movements make human grimaces of them; the platoon on the bank below us is a line of dark teeth clenched against the sun.

On the west bank are abandoned watchtowers. The sand walls are broken where Egyptian troops threw bridges across the canal. The Third Army crossed these during Yom Kippur, only to be cut off by the Israeli forces that had crossed the other way.

'If the revolution in Egypt succeeded you would see Saudi Arabia turn over one year later,' Roshdy says quietly. 'One year, I promise you.'

Again he gestures in the direction of his subject. Israel is just there, Saudi is over that way, here is Egypt, this is the Sinai. From the bridge of our mobile multi-nation you glimpse the terrible intimacy of the Middle East: so much glaring space, so little of it green, everyone simultaneously out of sight and just there, all wars fought and none quite finished.

'We must have no frontiers,' says Roshdy, 'but how many people think like this? Nought point one per cent?'

CHAPTER 9

Pirates, Soldiers, Thieves

The tenor of my messages to the company escalated from considered to desperate. I began with reasoned argument: the ship is safe, it is high in the water, it is fast, we will be travelling at twenty-three knots and there is no danger above eighteen.

Reasoned argument had no effect.

I will sign anything, I said, I will entirely absolve the company of . . .

The company was immovable. In desperation I offered to place a sum of money, all I could muster, in escrow, to be used as ransom in the event of . . .

The company's responses became terser. Its last communication contained a map of the Indian Ocean, including all the water between Suez to the north, Madagascar to the south and Sri Lanka to the east, with those three points joined by a thick red line. In this area, said the company, we carry only essential crew. You will disembark at Suez.

The Captain is consoling. 'In this area until recently we cannot even carry cadets.'

Chris is all mockery. 'I've worked it out. You are going to miss about half of the voyage.'

'No I am not! I'm not even missing a third!'

Noel, the cook, is hilarious. 'You go! You go? But you have not told my story!'

'I am coming back to get your story, Noel.'

'You come back? You come back OK! You tell my story! My story secret. No one ever hears!'

'If you'll tell it to me, I'll come back.'

Joel is the only man who does not shrug off the thought of pirates.

'Does it get frightening?'

'Only in the meeting,' he says, quietly. 'The meeting we have tonight when we talk about what can happen. Then you think about it and you feel a bit scared. But then you do your job, and you go on, and it's OK.'

The Captain gives me a version of the briefing.

'We show no lights and we double the watch. We are in contact with NATO. If something happens we report to them. I will go fast, if anyone tries to come close I will use the ship to stop them. If they come on board we send our position to NATO and we go to the engineers' passage and we lock ourselves in. But anyway they can't come up because we are too high and we go too fast. What?'

'It must be a very worrying time, Captain?'

'Worry? No no no . . .'

His demeanour is more phlegmatic than worried. It is as if conviction and by-the-book preparation have thrust the pirates beyond the realm of the possible.

'Are you worried, Sorin?'

Sorin shrugs. 'No. Not really. No. We are too big, too high in water, we go too fast.'

'Doesn't your wife worry?'

'No. I tell her is fine, she believes.'

Leaving is miserable. To be deserting my friends when they might actually be able to use another pair of eyes . . . I begged the company to let me back on at Salalah, in Oman, but no.

'You must be ready in fifteen minutes,' the Captain says.

Beyond the hard gold banks of the channel Suez Bay is broadening ahead and you can feel the officers relax, as if the constriction of the land had made them hold their breath. We curve out into widening blue and now we are saying goodbye. After lots of handshakes I go down to A-deck and out into the gulf afternoon.

Prashant is at the gangway controls. An electrician who has been fiddling with our radar goes down first. His boat comes to get him, there is a deal of gesticulation, Prashant adjusts the gangway, the electrician skips to safety, and it is my turn.

The gangway bobs beneath me, airily emphasising the fragility of the exercise. Chris appears, grinning.

'Safe journey, Chris!'

'Yeah. See you in TPP.'

'If Captain Prashant doesn't drop me.'

Bounce, bounce, down I go, bag balanced, one hand for the rail, no trouble. The ship is massive now, stacks of crates and the accommodation like a tower block atop the cliff of the hull. In comes the agent's boat, shoe-shaped with a little cab and a battling engine, making game way against the *Gerd*'s displacement wave, butting up to her vast shoulder. A man on the foredeck is signalling to Prashant to lower, then raise. I am hanging on and pretending to be confident. The foot of the elongated aluminium stepladder seems to be attached to Prashant's winch by two skipping ropes. Didn't Chris tell me the ladder is not designed to raise or lower more than its own weight? Didn't he see one collapse in training? How much does my bag weigh?

The water boils white-green between the little boat and the steel wall. You are suddenly aware of the *Gerd*'s speed.

'Have you got a passport?' shouts the agent.

'Yes!'

The water is hypnotic, just a couple of metres below. Prashant is a small head peering over the rail and Chris a blue blob. There will be a perfect moment to commit to the step across. I have watched many pilots do this, from high up on the bridge, and that instant, that just-so second, is always clear, even from up there. It is as though anyone attentive can sense it, the way a crowd watching sport all see as one – now . . . It's a step and a jump down to the little boat's deck on legs suddenly shaky. I wave madly at Chris and Prashant as we pull away.

The *Gerd*'s nation has changed again. They will anchor in the Bay of Suez this evening, change pilots and wait for clearance to move along the recommended safe transit corridor down the eastern side of the Red Sea. They will sail at midnight.

She looks so brave and resolute as she curves away. Chris and Prashant are absorbed into her size, the wide bridge high up reveals no tiny head: it is as though she has gathered her crew to her, and proceeds by her own laws. The scoop below the overhang of her poop deck is dramatic from down here. She is light, the top of the rudder two metres proud of the turquoise water. Now imagine she is moving three times faster than this, and the Captain is throwing her about, and the sea is not flat. It would take a brave pirate or a lunatic.

'We heard them attack,' says Khalid.

I nearly lost Khalid's trunk between the agent's boat and the *Kiel*, the ship behind us which Khalid was leaving. We clawed the trunk towards us, just. Seafarers are famous among themselves for the heroism of their airport transits: apocryphal Filipinos cross departure lounges with wide-screen TVs under one arm, towing suitcases and clutching a chainsaw. Khalid has six months of his life and a judicious selection of booty in his trunk, homeward bound to Bangladesh. We sit on the foredeck of the pilot boat in ruffling sun as our ships steam away and Suez chugs towards us.

'It was a ship behind us. A tanker, in the Gulf of Aden. We heard it on the radio.'

'What did you hear?'

'We heard them screaming. The pirates were shooting. They want to slow them down, confuse them, so they attack the bridge with machine guns and RPGs.'

The ship was taken. The crew, Khalid says, are still being held.

Khalid's ambition was to see the world. 'I wanted to be an airline pilot but in my country you must get into the air force first. But the air force refused to take me because my hands – they sweat.'

'I don't understand – your hands?'

'My hands sweat!'

'Your hands sweat?'

'You cannot join the air force if your hands sweat. This was terrible disappointment for me. I chose ships instead.'

'So you still travel the world?'

'Yes! But I am an engineering cadet! I travel the world in the engine room.'

The port of Suez at Bur Ibrahim is raucous with house crows and dusty. A man in a white uniform watches the afternoon from his deckchair in the shade. Dogs scatter past, hurried and glancing, as if chased by a pack of phantoms. Two more men in whites staff the immigration office, where there is a wooden chest of a hundred drawers left over from the 1930s. The halls of the passenger terminal echo our steps. A man X-rays our bags, and there is nobody, nobody else at all, it seems, here in Suez port. One of the gateways of the world is deserted.

The agent gives us a list of three telephone numbers to call if we have any trouble in Suez, though we will be here only for as long as it takes the driver to whisk us through the town and away to Cairo. Khalid, slouching insouciant behind his shades, gives the lead: we might as well be invisible; we are as invulnerable as ghosts. There may be no police, no effective government and no certainty in Egypt, but the links of the company's chain are unbroken, untouched, as it draws us smoothly away from the docks and up the town's main street. Our five-million-dollar convoy transited without a hitch; at either end of the canal two more are forming up. The tiny cogs which turn that mechanism, ships' crews, will not be inconvenienced by a mere revolution.

Concrete buildings, haphazard traffic and the zig-zag of rush hour does not quite betray the significance of the Cairo–Suez road, the town's main street, but the soldiers do. This is one of Egypt's exposed nerves: the last battle-ground of the 1973 war (Egypt claimed victory after an Israeli column, making a grab for pre-ceasefire advantage, was ambushed on this street), it also saw the first clashes of the 2011 revolution and its first fatality. The street mounts a fine display of Egypt's recent relationships with the world, thanks to the soldiers.

The knots of tense-faced boys grip rifles of Soviet origin, local copies manufactured under licence during the Russian-backed eras of Nasser and Anwar Sadat. They stand clustered around armoured vehicles behind semi-circles of wire, aggressively out of place among the commuters, who ignore them. Their vehicles are based on an American machine, adjusted and customised into an Egyptian version by BAE, the British arms manufacturer, during the thirty-year predation of Hosni Mubarak, when Egyptian military spending became a kind of collaborative international larceny.

Tides of money were diverted from the canal to the arms manufacturers of Britain and America, to the generals and to Mubarak's kind and kin. The floods of cash avoided the commuters of Suez, leaving them, and most Egyptians, a couple of dollars a day. In Suez, where the ships pass

ceaselessly, this injustice is particularly felt. You understand
why Mubarak never visited the town. You see why the ruling
army council feels the need to place combat troops every
hundred yards along the street, and a roadblock at the end.
You are surprised by the scale of the vast barracks just up
the road, an inland sea of pointless weapons, but not by its
existence. To travel from the canal, through Suez, across
the evening desert and into a Cairo sunset is to follow the
trail of one of modernity's great thefts. All along the way
the soldiers, conscripted accomplices, stand looking on.
They hold their rifles tight.

Khalid says farewell at the airport. We shake hands; his
palms are damp. I go into Cairo. The Nile's east bank is a
hot blizzard of pop music, scudding with grill smoke and
all a-dazzle with lights. Families on special treats take spinning disco boat rides on the river, watched by hundreds
along the quay. These are the people who brought down
Mubarak. They are excited, Saturday-night-feverish and
their faces are another Nile. Among them some must have
most to fear from the army, others from the Brotherhood,
and many must dread the counter-revolution, the canker of
the corrupt, Mubarak's thugs and conspirators. Some
among the leaning watchers must have been Mubarak's
men. Couples buy cups of tea, entitling them to chairs on
the rubbled embankments. The smoking steel rivers in
Tahrir Square are not entirely self-marshalling but the fact
that anything moves is a great tribute to a street-level sense
of justice. A taxi driver gestures with wild amazement and
fury which veers into laughter.

'He starts good! Mubarak! Good! And then – what? What? How can he do this? How? So many many houses! So much money money money . . .'

The driver is hammering on the wheel, squirming in his seat, battering the air with a frustration which has nothing to do with the infamous traffic.

CHAPTER 10

East

In another taxi, in Singapore, the driver cannot hold back.
'I'm just a smoky mountain boy!' he sings.

'She was just seventeen!' he yodels, grinning.

Clifton was eighteen years at sea and he loves karaoke.
We drive down boulevards of flowers. There is little traffic;
instead I catch the scent of hibiscus sometimes, and barely a
sniff of exhaust in the heat. When Clifton is not singing the
Beatles he is talking about his amours in ports around
the world.

'Japanese girl best! Eight dollars one hit.'

'One hit?'

'One hour one hit. Vietnamese girls best like Japanese!
Like get man hot and strong – hot and strong! I'm just a
smoky mountain boy . . . Brazilian girls best! Best tit best
ass! Vietnamese girls best, get man hot, hot –'

'Were you in Vietnam a lot, Clifton?'

'Vietnam 1967! On tanker. Two limpet mines in Vung
Tau, Vung Tau, Song Saigon.'

'Your tanker?'

'Yes yes my ship. No one killed. Tanker don't sink. Bless my soul what's wrong with me! Shaking like a bird on a funny tree . . .'

Clifton's erotomania is soon explained. There is the heat, first. Not the heat of deserts this, no sear nor fire, no sun: this is a vegetable, tropical heat, heavy and wet. You could lie down under it and sweat delirium with a lover. Then there is the commodification: you can be hanged for dealing in drugs here, but the malls sell live flesh, packaged in make-up and short skirts. Hotel lifts carry teen beauty queens up to the rooms of portly Europeans. Far below the hideous towers, the poor wear uniforms and clean while everyone else shops. Every brand and chain you have ever seen seems to have a lookout on Orchard Road. Order is so respected, and the law so feared, that enforcers do not have to show themselves. The only similarity between Cairo and Singapore is the invisibility of their police.

Seafarers love Singapore because food and drink and goods are cheap. Visitors and expats love Singapore because the money is good and food and drink and sex and shopping are cheap. Clifton likes Singapore because it is safe, and he says it is not corrupt, and the money he makes with his taxi is good. I absolutely loathe Singapore because if this is the triumph of order and money it is also the end of taste, the suffocation of soul, the death of feeling, the humiliation of spirit and the murder of freedom. Singapore is unutterably dreadful, a gussied-up nightmare, the dominion of emptiness. Sooner be anywhere, sooner be in a hot swamp . . .

Tanjung Pelepas, 'TPP' in sea speech, is a hot swamp. Perched almost as far south as Malaysia runs, just across the bridge from Singapore, the freight terminal of TPP is a cluster of cranes on a sluggish estuary, an operation designed to skim off a lucrative fraction of the container trade which pours through the city-state on the other side of the Johor Strait. At the end of an artificial peninsula, under smoggy mist, there is my ship, under cranes which are working, working.

They are loading the *Gerd* with nine hundred tonnes of clothes made in Indonesia which Americans will wear, seventy tonnes of edible fats and oils for the arteries of Peru and a dizzying, snapping, easily disposable five hundred tonnes of Malaysian rubber gloves for American doctors and nurses. Through the air swing four containers of car parts for Mexico and LA, tonnes of frozen crabs and fish fillets, Philippine pineapples, fourteen tonnes of polish, Indonesian coffee, Malaysian palm oil and frozen cake and the building blocks of Nicaragua, made in Thailand.

Three containers, not marked fragile (what would be the point?), carry sixty tonnes of glassware going to America from India, whence also five tonnes of perfume and make-up and twenty tonnes of plastic bags, for shoppers. Six tonnes of Cambodian-made trainers come aboard for Canadians. The holds are stacked with furniture for Chile and El Salvador, Cambodian clothes for Panama, eight hundred tonnes of shrimps and prawns, eight hundred tonnes of Thai rubber tyres, forty-two tonnes of Pakistani dates going to the United States and a hundred and forty tonnes of pet food.

Our dangerous cargo is augmented with one crate containing fourteen tonnes of Thai fireworks, destined to explode in American skies. The most intriguing addition to the manifest (which the company releases months after the voyage), below the thousand tonnes of new electronics for the Americas, are a further eight tonnes of electronic equipment, destination Jamaica, 'used'.

It is a joyful reunion for me but – back in the world of the deed, of the constant clock whose minutes measure thousands of dollars, where time is as tide, inexorable, where the ship will not be stayed, barring disaster, where the Captain rules with his absolutes and certainties – there is no sentiment. We exchange handshakes and grins and I distribute small presents: tea for Sorin, fizzy drinks for Chris, but I couldn't find a sufficiently specialist model train magazine for the Captain.

'So you came back!' they say, pleased. Flying across the world to rejoin them seems to be taken as a compliment, or at least a sign of serious purpose. If they did not exactly miss my questions, curiosities and enthusiasms for things which seem ordinary to them, they appear to welcome my return. I am more than pleased to see them. I craned at the window of the plane as we came into Singapore, looking for my ship.

Land, loved ones, family, friends, work, talks, books, meetings, the job and the quotidian burden of being are all very well, but who would not leave them behind for a while? The sea is simpler. There are no worries here about school and children and relationships and the logistics of the everyday. There are no shops and no bills.

Doing normal things in normal towns felt vaguely decadent, knowing that the men who supply them were crossing the Indian Ocean. Supermarkets never seemed more wasteful or more profligate. The names of countries which produced the food are written without meaning and read – if shoppers read them at all – without care. Shop windows are ludicrous agglomerations of the wretched, cumbersome lumber of stuff, of 'fast-moving consumer goods' (in which the 'good' seems questionable) and so-called 'consumer durables' of ever-diminishing durability. 'Throw it over- board!' urged Jerome K. Jerome. 'Let your boat of life be light . . .' It is a paradoxical thought on a ship with 50,000 tonnes of cargo space, and which depends, as all aboard depend, on people's appetites for stuff, on our inability to produce it where it is wanted, and the readiness with which we throw it away.

'How were the pirates, Captain?'

'No pirates, no, nothing like that . . .'

Later: 'How were the pirates, Shubd? See anything?'

'Oh yes. We saw helicopters and many warships. They were doing lots of checks.'

'Any pirates, Chris?'

'Every fishing boat looks like a pirate.'

The view from the bridge is muddy grey water and lowering cloud like boils of steam.

'When I was first coming here you would see sea snakes in the water,' the Captain says. He is limbering up for a bravura performance.

Just after sunset we leave the berth. The night is as black as the bottom of the sea, the air thick and languid. All three navigating officers are on the bridge because this a corner of the world in which you want as much practice as possible. The egress from TPP, which will take us out into the Singapore Strait, is akin to pulling out of a car park into the confluence of two eight-lane motorways. The first channel is tight, leaving very little room to move. A ship is coming up towards us. Ships under navigation show red light on their port side, and green on their starboard.

'Can you see his red?'

Naturally, in accord with the convention of the sea, we will pass port side to port side. That is not the problem.

'Can you see his red, Second Mate?'

Shubd is staring through binoculars, so is Sorin, but though we can all see the green on his starboard side with the naked eye, there is no red showing. This means he is angling across our bows.

'This is bullshit,' says the Captain suddenly, pointing at the electronic chart. The screen has the triangle representing the approaching ship neatly off our port bow, its course aligned in such a way that we could not possibly be blind to the red light on its port side unless the bulb had gone, the possibility of which is not even worth considering. The two hulls converge through darkness. The Captain's instruments are lying to him. There is very little time.

'Starboard ten!'

'Starboard ten.'

If we are where the automatic identification system (the AIS, an electronic chart that shows ships in real time) says we are this course could take us aground.

Sorin swears and jumps forward, pressing buttons on the radar console as the ship ahead shows red light, at last.

'The gyro! The slave station is not adjusted – . . .'

The electronic chart realigns. We are exactly where we should be and the radar screen is a nightmare, spattered with heavy gold rain, every drop a ship at anchor or charging under way. One monster shoots across us, doing twenty knots, showing three lights. The confusion is doubled because the anchored vessels are all lit up while the movers show only navigation lamps.

All the Captain's humming and muttering stop. Now he almost dances around the bridge, studying screens, spotting buoys and gruffly teaching Shubd.

'You see, Second Mate? Have they called you, Second Mate? Yes they have! You see here – . . .' He keeps talking, explaining where he is heading, where the hazards are, on which side we will pass them. We look out for certain buoys and certain depths as we turn north-east up the Strait.

'Now we will have some fun with the echo sounder! Look!'

He is navigating by paper chart, electronic chart, by lights, depths and buoys all at once. Singapore passes in a strobing, towering, silent glitter to the north; to the south the Indonesian shore is a twinkle of oranges in the dark. Above the hum of the engine and the sigh of the air conditioning there is the Captain's teaching, radio static and the voice of Straits Traffic Control, an alluring tone, both soft and clear.

'Could you do me a favour, Second Mate?'

'Yes?'

'Call that girl and ask her if she would like to have a baby with the Captain?'

We gust the over-hearty laughter of breaking tension. There is something quietly wonderful happening here, as the Captain teaches Shubd. The young man is receiving a lesson not just in what to do but in how to be, how to lead. In seafaring is the evolution – not of man, for there is little or no essential evolution of character between those dogged, brilliant men who first doubled the capes of West Africa, and those who found new oceans beyond the tips of continents, and men like Captain Simpson, who brought the *Indian Empire* home after she had lain on her side in the Pacific, and men like Captain Larsen – but of manhood: of what it is assumed and expected and required to be. Archaeologists now suspect that seafaring had a hand in the creation of manhood. Robert Van der Noort of Exeter University argues that in the Early Bronze Age the men who voyaged in sewn-plank boats (stitched together, in the absence of nails, by roots and willow twigs), the first men to go to sea as we do now, as a crew, with a captain, formed the kernels of their societies. 'The success of these journeys depended on a reliable crew, probably comprising a selected group of men, the retinue of the member of the elite who travelled to foreign soils. Through the shared experience a common identity of lasting importance would have been created,' Van der Noort writes, suggesting that crews offered their leaders something the land could not supply: 'the long-term support of a select but closely knit group of followers for many years after the overseas journey had been accomplished'.

The idea of retinues forged at sea, Van der Noort claims, 'has far-reaching implications for understanding the sources of social power and the reasons for rise to prominence of particular members of society in the Late Neolithic and Early Bronze age'.

Thus it may be that men who lived near the sea – who, like all men, imagine and create themselves according to role models, who naturally elevate and even deify certain among them – learned to measure themselves and their leaders against the most capricious, changeable and eternal element of all.

Outside the night is sweetly hot and utterly dark, a darkness like falling sleep, and the air is like a bathhouse, and the water far below is black, black and hissing.

On a Sunday morning where the Singapore Strait meets the South China Sea the waves are a metallic, lacquer-yellow and the sky a melancholy of greys. We hit current and you can feel the ship not quite check, and lurch a little, an effect as definite and sudden as stepping into a plash in a meadow. We are slow-steaming at eleven knots so as not to arrive in Vietnam too early. A wreath of swallows hunt around the containers. All day a stream of empty tankers comes down from the north-east, rushing west to refill with Gulf oil for China.

There are two new passengers. First comes a white egret with a short yellow bill and black legs; it stalks about, gripping the containers with long toes. And now there is a bird like a small goshawk, with an olive back and a creamy chest, barred brown. It catches something and feeds on it with savage leisure, having stuffed the bulk of its victim into the locking dock on the corner of a container.

'Yes, yes, once we had four oles in Korea.'

'Four owls, Captain?'

'Yes, yes the crew give them food. They disembark in Singapore.'

Writing in the afternoon I glance out of the window to see a small blue boat heading out of the wastes straight for us. There have been pirates in these waters for as long as there have been voyages. I charge up to the bridge.

'Fishing boat,' says Chris, patiently, as it ducks astern of us. An empty tanker that happens to be passing takes terrific fright, hauling ninety degrees off course and plunging away to the north.

We spend the next day and night steaming to Vietnam. Just before 3 a.m. I wake, exclaim at the view from my porthole and scramble to the bridge. We are 6 degrees North, 106 degrees East, south of the Scawfell and Charlotte banks. The dark sea is aflame with gold lights, they encircle us in floating bonfires.

'Amazing!'

'Yeah. Well. You think everything is amazing,' says the darkness, heavily.

'Evening, Chris!'

'Good evening.'

'What are they fishing for?'

'Squids. These are Vietnamese. There's going to be a whole lot more of them, and Chinese, and Japanese. The whole sea . . .'

I estimate there are eighty vessels in the gold armada. As we draw closer the lights change to pink-orange and glaring white blazes. The night is warm as smoke, with cloud clearing to reveal Orion and the Pleiades.

'How do you avoid the fishing boats?'

'You aim to miss them, then if they move, that's their problem.'

'Ouch.'

'Yeah, well. Haven't hit anyone so far. I don't think.'

Someone has, though. A barge has gone down in the bay of Vung Tau, our destination. The message reads:

> Barge was collided and sunk 05 persons on board 02 persons rescued 03 persons missing vessels in vicinity requested to keep a sharp look-out and assist immediately please report directly any related information.

The message repeats, unchanged, for the next two days. On the night of our arrival in Vietnam we are due to take Vung Tau pilots aboard at 0100, but the action starts around 2300. Up until this point the Captain dozes on the sofa on the bridge, more like a bear than ever, curled up in the darkness, listening to Shubd working us in towards the coast. More lights appear, and more: some fishing boats are anchored, some have nets down, others will set off from stationary to full ahead in a moment. Shubd threads our course between the fishermen to the tune of multiple alarms – every time she is taken away from her voyage plan *Gerd* squeals.

It is as though an admiral has set out a defence of Vietnam in layers of pickets: first fishing fleets, then oil rigs, tankers, anchored and moving ships, then invisible mudbanks, uncertain channels and scattered buoys. The *Grete*, our sister ship, made this approach recently with Vung Tao pilots aboard. They confused two sets of buoys and ran aground just off the town's waterfront.

'With pilots aboard!' the Captain repeats, horrified.

Dodgy pilots are a master's curse. Overrule them and you double your culpability in the event of mishap; fail to overrule them in time and you might as well have rammed the ship ashore yourself.

Sailors have made this approach for thousands of years: Chinese traders, Portuguese navigators, Malay pirates, French colonists and American and Australian warships have all done it, but by the staring and the tension on the dark-ened bridge we might be forging a new route, pushing back the chart.

'Actually the charts are very old,' Chris confides. 'They keep promising we'll get new ones.'

Somewhere in the utter obscurity to the west of us are the many mouths of the Mekong. Now, in the time of the south-east monsoon, the wet season, these mouths are pouring flotsam and current miles out to sea. We are bearing north into the outfall of the Song Saigon – the name of the river being the only remnant of former times left on our old chart. (Ho Chi Minh City is only a hundred kilometres upriver.) At the mouth of the Song Saigon is the little port city of Vung Tau. Its hills, peninsula and beach comprise the first landing place in hundreds of miles of mangrove deltas and estuaries. For the Portuguese it was a trading post, for the Malays a pirate base, for the French a strong-hold and for the Americans and Australians a rest and recreation area during the Vietnam War. The bay of Vung Tau then was strewn with anchored vessels, aircraft carriers, supply and hospital ships. The Song Saigon in this season gave American and Australian naval captains nightmares. The monsoon flotsam provided perfect cover for Viet Cong saboteurs, like those who mined Clifton's tanker.

Vung Tau is three humps of black against a faintly street-lit sky. The Mekong delta is a great darkness to the west. The night is hot, clouds squat low and heavy on the hills. There is an eeriness here, in the unknowable immensity of littoral, in the silent coast, a mangroved intermingling which refuses to be land or water, in the sound of our horn, lowing a long deep boom like the moans of a mourning giant, in the thought of '03 persons missing' whose bodies, turning and tattering, are somewhere in the water below us; there is eeriness in all the slab-black sea and in the heavy air. They are wrong who say the sea has no memory. The sea is all memory, and every captain who ever brought his vessel in here could feel it, almost read it.

We draw up-channel past the town, where people in dark bedrooms, their dreams disturbed by our lowing, must be drifting back to sleep. We angle in towards our berth.

'We need that tug now!' barks the Captain, as the stern crew struggle to make it fast. The pilot is talking to the tug, the tug is squawking back over the radio, there is some problem with the line and the Captain takes the thrusters, ignores everything else and brings his ship alongside himself. Cranes roll, stevedores board. It is half past two in the morning when work begins.

Vietnam is exporting rubber goods to Colombia and Venezuela, furniture to Trinidad and tinned vegetables to Mexico. Refrigerated containers full of frozen fish, four for

America and one each for Costa Rica, the Dominican Republic and Puerto Rico come booming down on the hatch covers. Another two hundred and fifty tonnes of frozen fish fillets join us, mostly for America, which is also importing forty tonnes of Vietnamese sticky tape, fifteen tonnes of carpets and textiles, fifteen tonnes of hats and caps, ten tonnes of luggage to put them in, fifty tonnes of sports equipment to play with, seventy tonnes of candles (seven forty-foot containers full of candles for lovers, diners and powercuts!), three containers of ceramics and stoneware, twenty tonnes of aluminium and almost three hundred tonnes of coffee, neither roasted nor frozen. There is half a container's worth of copper for Panama and four more carrying car and bicycle parts for Canada.

Funnels and superstructures hover through the morning rain as tankers and container carriers slide upriver, cut off below their bridges by the mangrove forest. The dock displays the usual stacks of containers, here surrounded by mud, puddled water and oil tanks. Behind the optimistic scrapes and semi-structures of expansion the green realm of the mangroves rolls back to a white horizon. The Can Gio forest is a biosphere reserve now, with UN designation. Its two millennia of growth was stunted relatively recently, when American aircraft sprayed it with defoliant. Along with tigers and crocodiles the mangroves sheltered Vietnamese fighters, giving them cover all the way to the centre of Saigon. The mangroves are being 'rehabilitated', in the UN's pleasing phrase.

A mix-up with the crew list means no going ashore. This will be a seafarer's visit to Vietnam. I feel I need to stand

on it, at least. Shubd, guarding the gangway, is exhausted
– everyone is exhausted.

Little trading boats approach us, offering fresh vegetables,
potted plants and soft drinks. There are no takers. It is not
clear how we would deal if we wanted to, from forty metres
up. The craft are shaped like upturned bird skulls, with eyes
painted on their beaks. The water is the colour of French
mustard. Sorin sees blue and yellow fish in it. By lunchtime
we are turning out of our berth.

'Did anyone actually see a Vietnamese woman?'

'No.'

'No.'

'I can see a woman. She is with a child,' the Captain
announces, studying Vung Tau's statue of the Virgin Mary
through his binoculars.

The weather breaks open behind us, high washed blue
over hills, and the mangroves are vivid now. The French
called the town Cap St Jacques; behind the hills, in
the distance, tiny figures are spotted over a beach. At this
distance they could easily be Australians, or young
Americans, running mad along the sand, having their R &
R. No one else is gazing backwards now: they are craning
forward, hungry to be off.

'The Captain is bored,' Sorin chuckles, as the pilot calls
the course changes and we head down-channel. The boat
comes to take the pilot away, and dithers. 'Let's hit the
fucking road,' Sorin growls. He wants to turn the ocean
under the hull and winch on the day and haul in the night
and arrive at the next port so we can leave it and arrive and
leave and sail and sail until he is home again. This is a man

who says he has salt water in his veins, and he can tell you to the hour how long it will be before he is flying home. He escorts the pilot down to his boat and returns, grinning.

'This guy asks for cigarettes for his boss, his brother, his uncle, his mother . . .'

Conversation turns to preparations we will need to make for China. They are very strict about bilge and ballast water, and, Sorin adds, wooden pallets. China fears pests and alien insects from the West.

'Wooden pallets?' the Captain frowns.

'Yes. Because they may contain keratin.'

'But the whole country is *infested with everything shit!*' the Captain roars.

Our mirth does not mollify him. He is still livid about an incident in which the details of a crew list did not quite tally with the numbers on the passports: one or two were smudged and hard to read.

'They stop loading for two hours!'

(I have been wondering what would happen if impossible things which cannot be allowed to happen were to happen. Now I know. The Captain looks like an outraged owl, mantling over a grievance he will never forget.)

'They stop loading for two hours! And I had to write an apology to the authorities! And if it happened again I would be banned from Chinese ports . . . ?'

He tells this story twice, with increasing incredulity.

The notion of China being infested with everything shit leads to infestation issues in general. The cockroaches in Mexico are the biggest cockroaches there are, according to the Captain. Savannah, Georgia, is infested with alligators, he notes. Sorin and Andreas nod agreement: very big alligators.

'Don't take your dog for a walk there, or your girlfriend, they are bigger every time,' says the Captain. 'And they are angry, like crocodiles. And sharks also. Sharks are born angry. Once we have a shark in the pool, I don't know how, someone catch him in. This shark was a baby but it was angry! It was *very angry*.'

We head into the deep water with light hearts. China is three days distant and there is a typhoon called Nesat in the way. Nesat is generating seventy-five-knot winds – over a hundred miles an hour – and fourteen-metre waves. It is composed of a hurricane sixty nautical miles wide, a storm surrounding it with ten-metre waves, and gales around the pair of them covering an area 360 nautical miles across where waves are over six metres. The whole heaving fried egg of low pressure is moving at a stately eleven knots.

'Let's run over a buoy and smash it up with the propeller, just to complete the party,' says the Captain, in holiday mood.

Day retreats quickly but the light rekindles in the same quarter: the west is lit by a huge flare of burning gas, a billowing, wallowing inferno in the sky which paints the sea flickering orange and ruddies the lower clouds. At its base is a tiny city lit up: the rig. It is an unearthly sight, an alien normality. Who knew this was here? What world is this, where they burn the night above the water?

We navigate north-west then north into four-metre waves, barely big enough to put a sway on us. There are squalls of rain; hot, dark and quick. Our usual course to China would take us up between the Macclesfield Bank to the east and the Paracel Islands to the west; in certain seasons, Chris says, the currents favour a more westerly course between Vietnam and the Paracels. But because of the typhoon we are swinging far out to the east, east of the Macclesfield Bank. The Captain plans to go around behind Typhoon Nesat and chase it up to China.

Although almost a third of all cargo shipping passes through the South China Sea the radar shows nothing but wave-echoes. We carry many birds; we still have a signature egret and there was a flight of nine, earlier, which seemed undecided, and went away. On the deck there is a wagtail, and a russet sort of wheatear. There was a falcon too, I think a peregrine, which paused for a perch, then flew, and there is our most endearing figure, a squat sort of heron with a broad bill which hunches on a container and endures and endures the wind and the rain. The wind is thirty-four knots now, almost seventy kilometres an hour, and the sea is the colour of a shark's back under the short and purplish dusk.

Under dim navigation bulbs on the bridge the charts are palimpsests of pasts and futures. The South China Sea is the shape of a dinosaur's head, craning over the top of the Philippines to graze on the coast of Borneo. British navigators marked its neck with Scarborough reef and Truro shoal – though the British were latecomers to these waters, Admiralty charts still map the seas for much of the world's fleet. Flora Temple reef – part of the Spratly Islands group which speck the dinosaur's jaws – was named by tragedy. Flora Temple was a famous American racehorse.

Her namesake ship was a clipper carrying coolies, Chinese slave labourers, from Macao to Havana in 1859. She struck the reef and began to break up. The forty-nine crew escaped, explaining to the subsequent inquiry that they had not sufficient lifeboats for the coolies. The crew also said the coolies had terrified them the day before the wreck in an attempted mutiny during which one of the crew was killed. The inquiry heard that the Chinese were locked below decks while the ship foundered. All 850 died.

Their grave, the Spratly Islands, is a constellation of reefs, sandbanks and islets claimed by Taiwan, Malaysia, Brunei, Vietnam, the Philippines (which they are closest to) and, most firmly, by China, from which they are furthest away. These little curves of sand and chips of reef offer nothing but access to the fossil layers at the bottom of the South China Sea. Over two hundred trillion cubic feet of natural gas and a billion barrels of oil are believed to lie beneath us, which may be why China recently included the Spratlys on maps in Chinese passports. Meanwhile the Philippines builds a pier on one forlorn sandbank with American help and other claimants say it will be a US base. Vietnam sends monks to an islet, to minister to the spiritual needs of a military garrison. China 'detains' Vietnamese fishermen and asserts its title to the entire chain, as well as the Paracel Islands, around the dinosaur's eye. If you did not know humans for an equitable, rational race, and nations for just and trusting collectives, you would predict a bloody future for the Surging Sea, the Boiling Sea, as Chinese navigators called it. The US Secretary of State referred to part of it off our starboard bow as the West Philippine Sea recently, which brought growls and rattles from all around its rim.

Around one in the morning we hit bigger waves; at two they are bigger still. By five, off the Macclesfield, we are rolling and yawing in the tail of the storm. We sail through the colours of a typhoon dawn. The vapours thicken so that daybreak seems to hesitate and retreat before coming on. Swirls of mist darken to bruised magenta, then thin claws of light appear and the sea turns from grey-black to black-green.

The conversation at breakfast is all about the barbecue. There have been rumours about it for days.

'Coming to the barbecue?' we ask one another, almost anxiously.

The ship's motion is the reach, turn and pull of a giant scoop, as though we are raking the scum of some elixir from the surface of a boiling tub. Typhoon-sent swells are marching down out of the north-west, six-metre monsters in fat ranks, arrogant with power. We lurch across them until we hit one square: the bow slides aside in a thump of spray and bucks upward in a tottering rise. At the same time wind-driven waves chase up behind us from the south-west. The swells and waves intersect in lumpen water sculptures of alps and pyramids, periodically exploding. In among them the boobies and albatrosses fight over flying fish. The fish fire out of the water in silver volleys and twist out of trajectory suddenly, skewing away between the wave tops as the birds come hurtling down. The boobies in particular are ferocious fliers. They are scruffy gannets skiing inches above the turmoil of the waters, screwing and skidding in pursuit. A snatch brings faster, unburdened hunters; as often as not a pirate steals the catcher's fish.

Every few minutes our headlong pitch brings the propeller out of the water. The governor reins it in, then, as the bow rises and the propeller submerges, the governor releases the power again and the deck judders as if the engine has just started. A great shake runs through the ship.

'So. We are rolling ten degrees. I know ten because my glasses fall off the table,' the Captain smiles. Ten degrees off vertical means we are yawing through twenty with each roll. The Captain is enjoying himself.

'The day you got your first command, Captain –'

He breaks in with a bark of pleasure.

'You need to be old to get it! Chief officers are always hungry! Of course it is a life's ambition. But you need to be calm. You need to have sharp eyes which know when to blind. You can't be like Captain Bligh, no no!'

The barbecue takes place on D-deck, in a rectangle of space near the base of the accommodation block, on the leeward side. A disco light is hung above two picnic tables. Two braziers char chops, steaks, mussels and squid. The music is lovers' elevator rock, a Filipino speciality. Everyone smiles at everyone else but conversation is stilted to stillborn. We grill our own suppers. Everyone enjoys that bit. Then we rush our food: we hurry partly out of shyness, partly because the music is too loud and partly because here, relatively near the water, the speed of the ship is keenly felt. The waves rush by as we plunge tilting on. Being on deck is not relaxing. It is vital and stimulating: you feel yourself alert and you breathe deeply, but the pace of the water passing is infectious. We cut and chew, everyone thinking of other braziers, shared with family and women, when there was beer to drink and friends to tease and grass or sand to sit on.

'You can't have a conversation because of the music!' shouts Andreas, the chief engineer, with a mournful satisfaction.

It is not his music or his stereo, nor is this the place for an officer to impose his taste on the crew. Someone has turned the volume up to encourage a party feeling and no one dares turn it down. Perhaps we fear that no bubble of conversation will rise to fill the sudden quiet. We load the grill again and concentrate on the spitting flesh, turning our choices over and over. We are not fooling ourselves now. There is no drowned-out laughter; there are no conversations waiting to erupt. This is a sad scene, brave and pointless as the disco light. We swap smiles, the grills smoke in the hot grey air and everything is wet with spray.

Night comes in under grim veils. The waves increase with the darkness; Shubd logs them at seven metres before the weather shifts and the swells realign, from fifteen degrees off the port bow at midnight to beam-on in the small hours. The cargo bangs and creaks as if steel beasts have woken up in the containers. By two in the morning I know we are rolling through more than twenty degrees because my curtains are opening and closing by themselves. There is no hope of sleeping. Now there is a snapping crack from the cargo, then a long screech, now a resounding boom. There may be a pattern to the sounds, as there may be a pattern to the rolls, but it hovers just beyond the rhythm of prediction. Some subconscious part of you has feelings for which way the deck will tilt: your balance compensates for the churn, tug and shove of changing forces. But outside, in the rushing dark, every crash from the container stacks is sudden and angry, an unpredictable violence. I cower my way round the deck, heart beating like a bird's.

CHAPTER 11

China

The new world appears first as shallowing water, green under clouds like towering sea horses. Then it is a string of sandy islets, each bigger than the last, forming a chain we must pass through. There are thirty degrees of heat on deck and the sun has a yellow-grey bruise around its throbbing eye. More islands rise in small pointed mountains as we come upon a line of junks. It is like seeing New York's skyscrapers and yellow cabs for the first time, the same dizzy exultation at watching the legends resolve to truths in front of you.

The junks have formed a line abreast and are carrying out a sweeping trawl, their stern castles arranged in a neat curve. On the nearest deck ten men are bringing in miles of net, hauling by hand, a rhythmic tug-of-war with a tolerant sea. They wear blue boiler suits and conical straw hats. It is something about the overlap between what you have heard, what you have seen, the assumption you make that things are not quite like that and the discovery that the world really is like that which makes the sight of fishermen in conical hats so pleasing. Chinese junks and Chinese hats – what cliché next? A pilot whose exquisite manners will make us all feel like gauche yobs, perhaps. As we pass Zha Zhou Island the containers flicker with passengers stirring. Birds flap and flit-hop between crates; others take flight. The swallows have made it, and a pied wagtail, and a dove. The squat enduring heron has survived, too.

We are running through Guangzhou Large Vessels Typhoon Shelter, according to the chart, and it is well stocked. The great ships lie on the water, a clutch of blunt knives on a rucking green cloth, bows to the sea.

'You see he is rolling more than we are,' says the Captain, pointing at a black bulk carrier. 'I was leaving Cape Town in a tanker going to the Caribbean and where those currents meet, the Benguela and the Agullas current, even in a flat sea with no wind at all you will roll so waves break over the ship. This is current.'

'Crikey!'

'Oh yes. You see how they are anchored? The angle of the anchor chain tells you the strength of the current. You must reckon with it, passing these islands. You need plenty of speed here. At least twelve knots. At least. We cannot slow down here, no no no we cannot do it. Not with all these anchored ships.'

We are heading for the Lantau Channel as the pilot comes aboard. He will be our first contact with the world's next superpower, the hungry heir presumptive to the global throne.

The pilot takes a long time to entrust himself to our ladder. He gestures up at Chris vigorously but the same tactic the Suez crew employed has no more effect now. Flanking the pilot are two men who grab and tug at the ladder, pointlessly, while the pilot prowls and gestures and gives up and comes back, becoming entangled with his men's harnesses. Finally he makes his leap. He appears on the bridge soon afterwards.

'How do you do, Mr Pilot? Hello hello . . .' booms the Captain, in standard greeting.

'Why you no answer me?' shouts the pilot. He is trembling. 'I call you on thirty-seven, on twenty-four, on twelve, on thirty-seven . . . why you no answer?'

'We have only one radio,' the Captain says, taken aback, indicating the VHF. (Actually we have two, but one of them listens to Channel 16.)

'Why you no answer? You should answer!'

'We couldn't hear you because of all the talking on the radio,' Chris says. Chris suddenly looks like a defiant fifteen-year-old. His defence seems to me to be more like an admission of guilt, though it is true the radio is rarely silent or intelligible at the moment.

'Why you not answer when I call you you should answer me!' yells the pilot.

'You should not talk to me like this!' the Captain bellows, roaring anger like an oven billowing heat, his finger pointing skywards, possibly calling on Thor, Odin and Wodin to agree with him – or perhaps to indicate the position of the nearest of the microphones linked to the voyage data recorder.

Captain and pilot are now staring each other out.

The telepathy for 'Ignorant arrogant aggressive uncultured foreign megalomaniac . . .' is identical in Danish and Chinese.

'Would you like a cup of tea? Or coffee?' I try, aiming at the pilot.

'NO,' boils the Captain, 'I will do this.'

Chris and I watch the duel in silence. The pilot's blade-faced attack cannot match the Captain's thundering-bear defence. At the end of a stretched pause we all feel the pilot blink.

'What course and speed would you like, Mr Pilot?' the Captain inquires, in an effortfully neutral tone.

'Three fifty!' snaps the pilot. 'And not more than fifteen knots.'

Chris makes him some coffee.

Lantau Island is green, wet and gorsey: the wind comes straight off it and you can smell the vegetation. A stagger of promontories falls back, revealing the flashing lights and runways of Hong Kong's new airport. The air is loud with jets, the sea sliced with ships, but there is no sign of where all this transport is going, no hint of whatever is drawing so much here. The sea slides from moss-green to silt-brown to a yellow in which vague islands appear like preparatory sketches in the haze.

Now the mainland's arms spread ahead of us and the water muddies to a swatch of sludges. This is the Zhujiang estuary, the delta of the Pearl River. To port are Macau and Xiangzhou, to starboard Shenzen and Bao'an. Ahead somewhere is the city of Guangzhou. Though we are in a waterway so wide you need binoculars to see its borders we are confined to a narrow channel pulsing with other vessels. Junks with buckets and grabs attest that dredging in the Pearl estuary never stops. The great width of these surrounding waters and the harnessed profusion of boats and ships – something between a conveyor belt and an invasion fleet – gives the feeling of entering a world of the superlative. Perhaps it struck every wide-eyed Western mariner thus since the first European sailors reached here, via Malacca, from Portugal. We pass the spot where it happened, Neilingding Dao, an island like a two-humped tortoise nosing into the deep-water channel. Jorge Alvares raised the flag of Portugal there in 1513. By 1821 it was the transhipment point for nine hundred annual tonnes of opium from Bangalore. When the Chinese cracked down on the trade the British launched the First Opium War, and began what the Chinese still refer to as their Century of Humiliation. Steaming up Zhujiang estuary, you feel humiliation has since changed sides.

Taking the cities on the horizon together – nothing separates them but lines on maps – we are steaming into the middle of a megacity of forty million people, a conurbation second only to Greater Tokyo. The Pearl River delta has been turned into one of the earth's most economically productive landscapes. Consequently, we are churning our way up the world's most polluted waterway. Tankers, coasters, bulk carriers and container ships are pouring up with us or beating down past us, three abreast every few minutes. The city nearest us, Bao'an, is a line of white tower blocks. Identical in height and design, they look as though they were unwrapped and arranged along the shore just this morning. A brand new bulk carrier surges by, empty: whatever she had, cereal, coal or red bauxite, Guangzhou has swallowed it. Lumbering up with us are barges so loaded they have no freeboard, and junks and dredgers and small boats carrying three or four containers, as well as parades of giants our size, though all this renders our leviathan strangely small. We make lame jokes as though we are nervous. It is a common saying, and one of Chris's favourites, that we are just bus drivers. For the first time it feels as though our enterprise is rather smaller than that, more like pizza delivery. We pass two small tankers, *New Glory* and *Morning Breeze*, both daubed with two of the sea's most common signposts: 'Safety First – No Smoking'.

'*Morning Breeze*!' Sorin exclaims. 'You mean Smell-like-Shit poison chemicals . . .'

Wistful Chinese music weeps from the radio. Bao'an is now clearly visible under the heavy, fume-grey sky. The city's towers are dense as a quiver of arrows. Who lives there? Is the city waiting for a populace? We pass a red-flagged junk at anchor, riding the wake waves. Through binoculars I can see its master is smiling and his wife is heavily pregnant. I decide their baby will be a girl, and she will become the first female mayor of Bao'an.

Our destination is a scaffold of cranes on the west bank: Nansha, recently reopened after typhoon closure. We are nearly there when, three days to the hour after we left Vung Tau, our heron leaves us. He is last seen holding a steady course for an area marked 'Shellfish Farm' on the chart. I applaud the bird, and soon recognise the extent of his perspicacity. It is not just that the shellfish farm looks like the first heron-friendly spot we have seen, it is Nansha. Nansha to us is a hardened mudflat, tarmac glistening under rain slick, and stacks of containers, all marked COSCO, and tugs churning up water the colour of dirty elastoplast. Through a tiny portion of exhausted sky an orange sunset gleams like a cracked scab. Bats scatter over the containers, and men rig the gangway, and the stevedores board and cranes beep and boxes boom all through another night of loading and unloading and there are no shore passes. The small birds that failed to leave us earlier are befuddled by soaring containers and blazing lights.

'My kid could manoeuvre a ship better than that' is Sorin's verdict on the pilot who oversees our departure.

'What's he done?'

'He doesn't use the wind, he doesn't control the tugs . . .'

This is related with an air of absolute disgust. It is not as simple as a man being no good at his job. It is as though the pilot's incompetence is a moral failing, and the indictment of a port, of a whole district, almost of a culture. Perhaps our bitterness is a function of our evident insignificance. Perhaps this morning's pilot could not be bothered with us because he had heard about our clash with his colleague. Or perhaps the touchiness comes from our changed role. For these four days we are not in the business of intercontinental shipping, which is the *Gerd*'s cause and calling. Instead we are shuffling containers between Nansha, Yantian and Hong Kong. We are coasting, which is a different kind of work altogether.

'Goodbye, Nansha!'

'Good riddance,' says Sorin. 'Yantian is better – Yantian is nice.'

We steam into an angled bay below a steep green mountain. A spit of land supporting the container port forms two Yantians: we moor opposite the Yantian of pleasure, denoted by a scatter of coloured lights. On the other side of the headland is Yantian the town. A Chinese agent grants a lift to the port gates, most of a mile from our berth. He does not smile, perhaps because his car has no springs in seats or suspension, or perhaps he takes against me, or perhaps he is shy. How lost to supposition and imaginings is a dumb-tongued foreigner. Beyond the gates is a long road linking the two Yantians. It is Sunday morning, early, but every passing bus is full to the doors. Where is everyone going? There are Lycra packs of serious cyclists. The buildings are charmless utilitarian blocks but the town has a pleasant feeling: the embracing damp of the bambooed hill above it fills the atmosphere. Twenty students are queuing at the cashpoint. No shopkeeper is having a day off. Shops have a uniform signage, red and yellow on brown. They sell all the goods with which China floods the world, cheap suit-cases, blow-up toys, temporary umbrellas, every daily contortion of plastic. I had assumed that being clever enough to wash the rest of the planet in this stuff would imply the Chinese were clever enough to avoid it, but by the volume of shops offering dross they are, like a failing drug dealer, getting high on their own supply. Stalls sell yams and oranges. The town smells of plastic and imitation leather, cigarettes, mouldering cement and rotting fruit. Most of the people on the streets are young. Occasionally someone says 'Hallo!' and laughs – one radically coiffeured young hairdresser in particular.

Down at the waterfront an old Soviet aircraft carrier is rusting. The *Minsk* is a major attraction; scores of families stream on and off. In front of it an extremely beautiful young bride is being photographed with her handsome man. He wears a full dress naval uniform, complete with more medals than he could possibly have earned. There is an unreality about them, as though they are models, rather than a happy couple. Wedding photos are serious business in China. If you can afford it the thing to do is rent a series of costumes and be photographed in several scenarios, a creation of memories reminiscent of Philip K. Dick. Perhaps the happy couple are pretending to be a happy couple for a website or brochure for prospective happy couples. The undertaking has a certain satire about it, visible in the smiles of the bride-to-be and groom, if they are. The day-off atmosphere at the front contrasts with the solemnity of the administrative district, where red-starred party offices are closed.

The end of town is marked by the beginning of Chung Ying Street, once a dry riverbed lined on one bank with Hong Kongese shops, Chinese on the other. In 1979 the Chinese government allowed a cautious degree of free enterprise in Yantian, designating it a Special Economic Zone. Chung Ying Street became a place of encounter between Western capitalism and Chinese communism, and something of an attraction. There is now a museum commemorating this and you can walk down the memory of Chung Ying Street – but only if you have a special pass. I do not have a special pass, so walk three miles to the other end of town, arriving just in time for holiday luncheon.

The road runs to the sea and subsides in vehicles, the fat 4x4s favoured by the rich and tasteless everywhere. In a series of two-hundred-seat restaurants families are eating seafood – more kinds of spiky, squirming shelled and gilled creatures than I knew existed. I point and hope. Charred and spiny corpses are served, along with a pile of some sort of armoured crustacean. The latter avenge their deaths by lacerating my fingers. If only I knew the Mandarin for 'hammer'.

I am the sole Westerner in Yantian today. A construction worker in a hard hat is delighted by the appearance of this alien. He points and cries 'Ha-lo!' and shouts with laughter at the reply. Several children have the same reaction. Grumpy rain begins to fall but no spirits seem dampened. When a portable karaoke opportunity appears a hundred diners pause to see if I will make use of it. The proffered song is 'Country Roads' – which the song implores to take you home to the place you belong – and I am convinced this is satire, and find it very funny, until the karaoke master sings it for me with no evident understanding of the lyrics. Leaving a tip causes some confusion, at first, and then grave bows and smiles. It is a long walk back to the ship and there is no time for anything else. The way leads past bedraggled shack-like housing under the legs of a flyover. It's a poor, workhouse world again: coming ashore from seafaring brings you up to the surface of a country as if through its base-ment. You begin to see nations as theatre sets. Backstage, in their curtained-off ports, the cranes and crates and

stagehands supply the ever-multiplying audience, the limit-
less performance, the carnival without end or intermission
we call the day-to-day.

We have loaded volumes of Chinese cargo for the United
States almost beyond imagining. Two thousand tonnes of
knives, forks and other steel household goods will be laid
and deployed in homestead America, while three thousand
tonnes of tables and chairs are set and drawn up for the
meal. In the kitchens ninety tonnes of Chinese albacore and
cod will have been defrosted, with twenty tonnes of yellowfin
tuna caught in the Philippines. On the patio will be twenty
tonnes of new furniture, supporting twenty tonnes of dried
fruit and nuts offered in two hundred tonnes of ceramics.
The cook, using five hundred tonnes of kitchenware, will
call the family away from three and a half thousand tonnes
of phones, DVD players, televisions and stereos. The children
will have to be separated from three thousand tonnes of toys.
They will take their place looking smart in five hundred
tonnes of Chinese clothes. Four hundred tonnes of lamps
will light the meal, where discussion will cover today's
purchase of three thousand tonnes of manufactured goods
and nine hundred tonnes of new shoes. (Seafarers say these
are divided into containers of right feet and left feet, to stop
us helping ourselves, but this may be apocryphal, based on
the one time someone saw a container break.) After supper
someone will undertake a little DIY with a hundred tonnes
of hand tools and six tonnes of copper, mined in Zambia,
converted to pipes and wires. Walking the dog, which is
replete with its fourteen tonnes of pet food, forty-two tonnes
of Chinese umbrellas will fend off American rain.

Approaching Hong Kong even Chris and Sorin admit a measure of excitement. Beyond Beaufort Island, suddenly, mountains come toppling down to the pale sea. On every fringe and finger of the hills, poking between peaks and over passes are skyscrapers, towers and blocks. A yellow tangle like scrambled barbed wire is a rollercoaster. We pass Stanley Peninsula and Ocean Park; there are people on the beach in Repulse Bay. Through binoculars we can see a stadium full of pinhead faces at Ocean Park, and camera flashes: the great *Gerd* will make a tiny backdrop to the dolphin dance. As we enter the harbour Hong Kong opens and rises before us, a fanfare of technology being realised as you stare, the steel towers springing from slopes like armoured soldiers sprouting from sown dragon's teeth. Bushels of skyscrapers loom, the giants throwing the smaller ones into disproportion. The water is slashed and clotted with boats, many moored in rafts, chaotically, while those in motion follow three hundred different courses. There is a vertiginous sensation of certain collision with another giant, at least our size, as we head straight for the loop of Stonecutter Bridge, its cables hatched against a sky of mists. Hedges of harbour cranes are packed around the docks, crowded over by towers. There are motorways on stilts, traffic torrents and helicopters and our route turns right into the guts of it all. The Hong Kong harbour pilot says a European study surveyed the waterway but stopped short of the inner areas, the Rambler Channel and Victoria Harbour: 'They left it blank and wrote a note saying it was a miracle there had been no major accidents in twenty-five years.'

We tie up almost below Stonecutter Bridge, right in the middle of the action, it feels, though I am shortly and almost fatally to discover that this is not quite true. I charge down the gangway as soon as it is lowered. We have six hours of freedom and several of the crew intend to enjoy it. I am to meet an old friend: we have settled on the bar of a hotel I can see from the ship. It really should be easy from here.

On the dockside is Antonio, a Hong Kongese who used to live in Argentina where he was in the restaurant trade. He was happy there, but he has a wife, an ex-wife and children in Hong Kong, so here he is, working security on the dock. His cheekbones are high and sharp, his eyes narrow even by local standards. His smile reveals very long teeth.

'Are you happy in Hong Kong?'

'Hong Kong people, Chinese people only love money,' he says. The more he spoke of his home the lower his opinions sank. 'Love money not heart,' he says. He is a complete gentleman, escorting me on to the shuttle and helping solicitously with the port exit. Minutes after thanking Antonio and assuring him I will be fine I am not.

The hotel is not supposed to be approached without a combustion engine. I find myself in a storm drain below a motorway looking out for snakes and wondering why I sometimes end up in such places. Reversing the course I walk along a hard shoulder, then a no–hard–shoulder motorway sliproad. I imagine my (more cautious) brother's face shouting at me, telling me this is mad and insisting we go back. Death is postponed by a surprised taxi. The hotel has no bar; men clutch plastic bags of booze bought from the mall in the basement. Signs in the lobby warn of incoming typhoons and weighty rain falls outside.

My friend appears, Caroline, a photographer, ceramicist and teacher. She says the Chinese do their drinking in restaurants or at home. She has bought some cans in a plastic bag too, but though he agrees they are hers, the concierge cannot hand them over without authority from the reception manager. Everything in China takes ages, Caroline says, and deference to authority is automatic. We set off to town and I am beguiled by narrow trams curving through British street furniture: the bollards, lights and road marking could be in Luton. Central district has three canopy layers of human forest. At the base is a street-level strip of light and bustle, then up in the air are the mid-levels, which are high walkways, connecting to escalators which climb hills. Above all are the towers, so high they give the impression of having no tops, reaching like so many Babels to a dark and mastered heaven where the luxury, power and penthoused wealth can only be fantasised. Soho is steep streets and contours packed with bars, which are packed with Westerners.

The air seems full of sex and money, though I am head-spun and this is all relative to life in my cabin. It is Monday night but the drinkers are watching rugby on TV and getting smashed. We find a palace of kitsch which serves Chinese food. We smoke shisha pipes provided by an Egyptian who speaks no English. Above us lights burn in a sweatshop, its windows stuffed with new dresses. Hong Kongese girls drink cocktails and expats befriend one another in shouts. I rather long for an opium den. Caroline talks about the

ease with which her Western male friends have found
Chinese partners. It is more difficult for Western women,
she says. Chinese boys, raised as 'Little Emperors', in the
common phrase, regard Western women as too challenging.
We catch up on gossip from the other side of the world and
too soon it is ship time again. I walk back to the *Gerd*
between the containers. Her size is always a shock; you can
only see fractions of her at a time, giant fractions.

A few of the crew go ashore in the small hours, to buy
DVDs and compare the prices of electrical goods. Joel finds
some ice cream. Chris buys a tablet computer he is pleased
with but the internet has been unplugged: 'We maxed out
the download limit in two hours,' he says. The cranes work
in a frenzy. We are close to full at 4 a.m. and leave fully
laden in the morning, weighing 115,000 tonnes. Much of
the cargo was meant for other ships but they ran rather
than face the typhoon. MSC, CMA and Maersk have a
cargo-sharing agreement by which they pick up each other's
missed loads, the only way they can compete with the
Chinese giant, COSCO. We have four cylindrical forty-foot
tanks in the bow, labelled Super Heavy – Danger – Benzyl
Alcohol, made in India, destination Los Angeles. Sorin says
we have a lot of frozen shrimp in the reefers: close to a
thousand tonnes. 'Quite a prawn cocktail, eh?'

The manifest, which the company releases months later,
says America has ordered six hundred tonnes of televisions
and phones from Hong Kong, along with three hundred
tonnes of computers, twenty tonnes of clocks and watches,
ninety-five tonnes of books and magazines, fourteen tonnes
of batteries and sixteen tonnes of parts for cars and bikes.

American families will inspect our four hundred tonnes of handbags, wallets and school bags and wash with ten tonnes of soap. American children will play with our five hundred tonnes of toys. American aesthetes may make a distinction between 'art, antiques, collectors' pieces and bric-a-brac', but we do not, lumping three tonnes of them together in one forty-foot container. For Mexico we add seventeen tonnes of computers and a hundred tonnes of electronics, to be transhipped in Los Angeles. The load of the night is four tonnes of 'aircraft, spacecraft and parts thereof', made in India – most likely for an aircraft manufacturer, but just possibly for NASA.

CHAPTER 12

Pacific Diary

A s she curves out of Hong Kong, fully loaded, the *Gerd* heels over and stays tilted to starboard for twenty minutes before rolling back. Andreas says we used 175 tonnes of heavy fuel steaming fast through the big seas on the way to China. The relative value of oil versus freight rates forms the fulcrum on which shipping tilts between profit and loss. Currently oil prices are rising and freight is falling, so shipping lines are trapped in overcapacity and sliding profits. Everywhere we have been half-empty giants pass each other in the seaways. Maersk is also in the oil business: gains there are more or less balancing their losses in the ships, but it is tight. There is talk of a return to wind power, to a new generation of cargo ships which will have sails as well as engines. The sails will be rigid and retractable, echoing the great junks of China's age of exploration, which were ten times longer than the greatest European galleon.

Andreas says there is a problem with the shaft generator. It ought to use excess revolutions to make electrical power

but it is playing up. In Denmark they will be studying
printouts and tables of our kilowatts, speed and fuel
consumption and shaking their heads.

'A greener solution would be smaller engines which run
faster and make better use of less fuel,' Andreas said. 'But
the key to the whole thing is freight charges. If everyone
put them up there would be more jobs in Europe. We rear
chickens in Denmark but because the rates are so low we
carry them to China to be butchered and then carry them
back to Europe to the shops!'

Sorin talks about 'the windscreen wiper' – travelling
backwards and forwards across the Pacific on Great Circle
routes. 'Five-week trips over five months,' he says. He did
it for Hyundai Lines, carrying cars.

The night is wild in the Taiwan Strait, so dark you cannot
even see the water and a gale blowing, the wind roaring and
whistling round the bridge. The sea seems haunted sometimes.

'If we're going to sink,' says Chris, nodding at the radar
screen, 'this is a very good place to do it.'

The radar is spotted with small ships travelling between
Chinese ports, and smattered with heavy elephants like us,
bearing east for America. The difference here, compared to
everywhere else we have been, is that those ocean-going
ships are all huge, and they are all fully laden: the great
imbalance of trade in action.

4 October

A glumly grey sea and a heavy-feeling day which we
try to dispel with activity. Shubd and I hit a punchbag,

inconclusively. Sorin discovers me without shoes and says it is bad luck to go barefoot on steel, especially on a ship. Fishing fleets fill the night sea with their green and white fires.

5 October

Giant blue skies over a heaving royal sea, sparkling and braided with white. We are in the Japan Current, Kuro Shio, which gives us an extra two knots of speed, and passing between Kingushan, which we cannot see, and the islands of Mi Saki and Yakushima, which we can. The former is a battleship-shaped volcano. Our course takes us out of the East China Sea and into Nansei Shoto.

Now we are passing a volcano, Satsuma. It rises from the sea, bubbling white cloud. This is no Etna, but Satsuma's surge straight out of the water makes it monumental and alive.

'It glows at night,' says the Captain.

It must have been a beacon for mariners in these seas always. Satsuma's sides are scarred and dribbled stone. They are creatures, volcanoes, more than mountains. Just short of it is a green island of slopes, cliffs and bays, deserted but for a lighthouse. It looks as strange as a dream in the sun.

6 October

The calendar says we are nine days from America but we will repeat Tuesday when we cross the date line. New DVDs are available, purchased by Prashant in Hong Kong. These are not good, on the whole. I caught them watching

Thor last night, which was incomprehensibly poor, but there
is *Black Swan* among the new haul. Among the films posted
missing on the mess door are *Dirty Dancing* and *Sex Drive*.
Perhaps someone threw them overboard when they did not
live up to their titles. Sex is a distant thing now, a concept,
a memory, a somehow unbelievable hope. While the urge
for a drink fades with the wake, desire comes back in waves.
Our situation seems to amuse my female friends on email.
'Hello, sailor!' several of them say. A French ex-girlfriend
sends me a photograph of herself in her knickers, with
wishes for my satisfaction. It is impossible not to flirt
with certain correspondents: it is like being a teenager again,
returned to the stage when I saw pornography for the first
time. But sailors are not great consumers of porn because
the data download ration does not permit it. Some men load
films on to their computers before boarding: one of the
things the UK Customs 'Black Gang' were looking for when
they searched the ship in Felixstowe.

When I said I was going to sea there was a near-universal
catcall from my friends, with much bawdy advice about
watching out for sodomy and the lash. 'It's all boredom,
buggery and wanking, isn't it?' said one, a photographer,
and among the best-travelled men I know. There were
certainly broad strains, if not traditions, of sexual activity
among the male crews of sailing ships, both consensual and
abusive. Attacks on women are now more common on cruise
ships (where levels of assault are significantly higher than
they are on land) than on trading vessels, no doubt because
cargo shipping is an overwhelmingly male environment.
There are atrocities too. The International Transport

Workers' Federation reports that mistreatment, beatings, the enslavement of seafarers forced to work without pay, and rape are all common in the worst 10 per cent of the world's cargo fleet. Little escapes from that darkness and almost nothing of what happens there is reported. Peter Morris, formerly a transport minister in the Australian government, who became Chair of the International Commission on Shipping, described an infamous incident from this netherworld to a congress of the Apostleship of the Sea. The ship involved was the Panamanian-registered MV *Glory*:

'The Indonesian radio operator, Budi Santoso, died in the sea near the ship several hours after being beaten with an iron bar by officers before he and his five shipmates jumped into the sea about 1.30 a.m. on 1 November 1995 some ten miles off Port Dampier, north-west Australia. To the best of my knowledge Budi Santoso's death has not been investigated, no one has been charged, the ship was sold, changed its name, changed its flag and sails on merrily, no care, no responsibility.'

Morris's target was the grotesque irresponsibility of registeries like Panama which routinely fail to investigate incidents, and the cynicism of shipowners who flag their ships in countries they know will take no action. But horror also visits ships owned by companies as responsible as Maersk, flagged in states as ostensibly committed to human rights as the United Kingdom.

In 2010 the body of Akhona Geveza was found in the sea off Rieka in Croatia. An hour before the nineteen-year-old cadet disappeared, her co-cadet, Nokulunga Cele, told the captain that Akhona had been repeatedly raped by a senior officer. Their ship, the *Safmarine Kariba*, was owned by Maersk, operated by a Belgian subsidiary, Safmarine, and flagged in the UK. In a vicious irony, Akhona and Nokulunga were aboard as part of a South African-run training programme designed to encourage more women to go to sea.

After talking to the captain, Safmarine's then CEO, Thomas Dyrbye, reported that Akhona had told the captain she had not been subject to any abuse and had mentioned she had 'suicidal considerations'. Although Akhona had told Nokulunga that the chief officer had first tried to kiss her during a swimming lesson, then summoned her to his cabin in order to apologise to her, and there raped her, and subsequently forced himself on her 'many times', Safmarine and the Croatian police chose to believe she had simply jumped over the side.

Calls for action in the United Kingdom, including one in the House of Lords, brought no meaningful change. An investigation by the South African *Sunday Times* found several cadets on the training programme had been abused. Officers threatened their careers if they did not consent to sex. Two male and two female cadets said they were raped; a third man claimed to have been sent home for refusing sex. 'It was like we were dumped in the middle of a game park,' one female cadet told the newspaper: an analogy that gives an impression of the ravening reception the young people received, but which does not convey the particular hell of being stalked aboard a ship.

There is nowhere to go, only narrow corridors, workspaces and cramped messes where eyes are constantly on you. The ship house, the accommodation block, is all angles and nooks and tight corners where you are easily trapped. In the narrow passages bodies must squeeze by each other, and a cabin is a dreadful place for someone in despair. As small as a cell, shifting and never silent, never allowing the illusion that you are not where you are, and not safe, either: there is always a copy of your key somewhere. If you were being stalked by a senior officer there really would be no escape.

Croatia's Adriatic coast in mid-June is a sparkling littoral of wooded islands and clear waters. It must have seemed an alien and fearful place to Akhona. Her captain said she had agreed to leave the ship in Trieste, which was only two days away. The captain and the employer, Safmarine, are satisfied that rather than wait two days she chose to climb over the rail and jump, knowing that she was no strong swimmer. The chief officer involved was briefly suspended from duty. He has never been named, much less charged.

We sail in a benign environment, comparatively. In the workshop is a traditional calendar, familiar from the car repair garages of the 1980s, from which a young blonde woman, unencumbered by clothing, beams enthusiasm and felicity. At meals and on the bridge we do not talk of women; perhaps, like alcohol, they are better out of mind because out of sight. What takes place in the privacy of our cabins only we can know, but certainly Facebook and emails play their part. Flirting is wonderful, of course, but a conversation with N, a friend in the crew, reveals where it can lead.

N is in a terrible mess. He has a girl in Hong Kong who wants to marry him, and two girls in the Philippines, as well as a wife. He is torn four ways. It is obvious what they see in him: N is amused and amusing, open-souled and energetic, with a shout of a laugh. Our conversation about his love life descends into complete confusion. N is beset by wistfulness and longing on every side; it is difficult to keep up with which woman he is talking about.

'So what is the first thing you are going to do when you get home?'

'My car!'

'Your car?'

'Ahhh, my car, and my gun.'

'Your gun?'

'I have gun. I am police some time.'

'And what will you do with your money?'

'Money soon go! Go go go. Everybody comes, family, friends, one-day millionaire!'

'And this business with your wife, and the other women . . .'

'Ahhh don't know. You know is because internet. Meet on internet. And because I am seafarer you know.'

'You're popular.'

'Too popular!'

All afternoon we sail up the Japanese coast, which is high, high mountains along the skyline. The last sights of land are the peaks and ridges in the dimming air and a red sun sinking behind them.

7 October

It is another beautiful, confusing day on the fringe of the western North Pacific, a hundred nautical miles off Japan,

bright blue again, after a peachy dawn. We eat a good breakfast because at 10 a.m. all the clocks go forward to 1 p.m.,
the same time zone as Vladivostok.

'We will have pancakes today!' says the Captain.

'Why's that, Captain?'

'Why not?'

So we eat pancakes mid-morning, which is now early
afternoon. The wind is freshening; a strong north-westerly,
thirty-four knots, blows over a sea hard blue, ridden by
foaming horses. In the engine room they are cleaning a
piston and changing some oil but we still make twenty-one
knots. The Captain is dealing with the long arm of Homeland
Security, which wants to know my visa number. There are
mutterings about the kind of reception we can expect.

In the afternoon I walk up to the fo'c'sle to see the bulbous
bow buried deep in the water and listen to the blade of the
forefoot cutting fast through the waves. The only sounds here
are the sliced slush of the ocean splitting open and the curled
rush of the bow wave. The sea is scattered with the broken
remains of pine trees, logs, twigs, branches, what might have
been a barn door, a smashed container – and plastic. There
are plastic bottles, a bucket, broken yellow shards, plastic
boxes, crates, bags and crisp packets. The North Pacific gyre
is a purgatory of waste. We are carrying a thousand tonnes
of 'plastic articles, new and used' and a further four thousand
tonnes of 'miscellaneous manufactured articles' from China.
A percentage of them will end up in the Pacific, in a rubbish
patch said to be the size of Texas. We are only skimming its
fringe: the main body is to the south of us, circling in the
centre of the gyre, the convergence zone.

Two white birds, egret-like, approach but do not land. Bronze-backed cormorants hunt flying fish off the bow.

We surge on, accompanied by one ship, *Ever Charming*, which has the same destination and date as us but is on a different course, peeling away to the south. Our ship's heart-beat never stops. I have never known a machine do so much mighty work so unceasingly; machines have always been something you switch on and off.

At midnight Shubd says, 'You are starting your first Great Circle navigation!'

He shows me the course, sixty degrees: we are going up one side of the globe's greatest ocean and down the other. We have entered the North Pacific proper, having crossed the Japan Trench.

'It's 6,431.75 nautical miles to our berth in Long Beach,' Chris says.

It is a warm night, twenty-two degrees, and the sea is calm with occasional breakers. There are few clouds and a waxing moon. Earlier we had strong wind on the port quarter so Chris trimmed the ship, shifting water ballast to that side to correct the heel. In the evening a light roll becomes a gentle surging motion. At 3 a.m. the rolls become sharper and the two-thirds moon turns heavy gold and sinks, leaving a ruddy aura. The wind seems to come from the stars.

8 October

Reflections on *Titanic* at breakfast; I watched the film last night. Sorin says I was wrong to mock the helmsman for turning the wheel to port when the command was clearly starboard: when rudders were controlled by ropes you did indeed spin the wheel the opposite way from your intended direction, he says. The Captain says SOLAS, the society for saving lives at sea, originates from the disaster. This thought is interrupted by Sorin's discovery that our orange juice is good until 2212. We will be 150 years in our graves but the juice will still be fine.

'We carry tonnes of the syrup in stainless-steel tanks,' says the Captain. He does not drink the juice.

We watch two of our smoke-jumpers being 'killed' during the fire drill as they simulate opening the engine room hatch, behind which is the 'fire'.

'They stood on the wrong side,' Chris says, 'the hinge side, so when they touch the pins the pressure differential blows it open – bang!' He smacks his fist into his palm.

The officers say there is a problem with the fire hoses. They are too heavy, wide and hard to handle under pressure. Even getting them around corners is tricky. There is a narrower gauge with a better – adjustable – spray available, which is used by the Danish fire brigade, but they cost more. The lifeboat still gives me the creeps.

Another high-skied day, with the wind now cooler than the sun is hot. In the afternoon we all assemble to watch a corporate safety video. It is a classic of the genre. You can almost hear every eyeball in the room swivelling to the only woman in it. Sadly the actress is playing a bozo sitting at a table of bozos in a ghastly office while an irritating Scottish bozo asks rhetorical questions. We all struggle to stay tuned until we come to horrifying footage of a cargo ship on fire. The irritating Scot identifies something he calls OAD syndrome – only a drill – but insists we should drill until procedures become second nature. Then he admits that, were we faced with the real thing, everything would change constantly. Great emphasis is placed on the Captain going to the bridge and staying there, and ensuring that the fire plan is followed. The chief would be his eyes, the crew would fight the flames and do barrier cooling. The Scot says fires at sea are very rare. The Captain grunts and says he has had many small fires in his career. They must have been small, considering he was on supertankers.

'Horace! Come to bridge.'

There's a bird, one of the red-footed boobies, doing a stiff-winged albatross impression over the bow.

'It will stay with us all the way and catch another ship back,' Sorin says. I am doubtful but he says he has seen this many times.

The visibility was thirty miles at least this evening and tonight it is not much less; the sea heaving, alive everywhere and moonlit.

'I saw a fishing boat earlier,' Shubd says, 'on AIS. Going back to Japan.' He studies charts which are only white depths, but for a shred of Kamchatka and the tail of the Aleutian Islands, at the very top.

9 October

Pancakes and time-jump again. America says I have the wrong visa, though I went to Naples to get the one specified by the company.

'Welcome to our life!' says Andreas.

'Problems,' says the Captain. We send a volley of documents to the Americans. When they come aboard they will take over the library and process us. Smart dress and best behaviour is the plan. The dining table becomes a trumping match of horror stories. The Captain recalls a Danish master who started his ship without permission after an inspection.

'The coastguard come back and arrest him and put him in jail. Six months!'

Sorin and his entire crew were lined up on deck in Seattle, hands on the rail.

'Meatheads,' he says. 'With guns, on steroids.'

'In special tight trousers,' adds the Captain.

Sorin's ship was raided by a team armed with machine guns. One of them, his finger on the trigger, slipped – and emptied half a magazine into the walls and floor of the bridge.

'Just because we are seafarers why do they treat us like criminals?' asks Andreas, plaintively. 'They asked one Filipino if he was married. Yes. And kids? Yes. So how many girlfriends do you have here in the US? This is an outrageous question!'

The discussion closes with a seafarer's maxim: 'Better a sister in the whorehouse than a brother in the US Coastguard,' says someone, to sniggers.

Outside there are vast horizons, thirty-mile views in all directions, low squadrons of white cloud, no ship on any screen and invigoratingly clean air. Later our bird reappears, riding the updraught at the bow. It has companions with black backs, white fronts and a black band on their tails.

They look like albatrosses. They slice away and plunge on the weather side, chasing flying fish. Sorin saw a dolphin family in a sea the colour of rain. The sunlight is cold; an eerie calm. Our Great Circle takes us across the North Pacific Basin, five to six kilometres deep, to the Emperor Seamount chain, which are south-running mountains, some with peaks rising to nine hundred metres below the surface. We will cross them and steam over the Emperor Trough, seven kilometres deep in places, then out towards the Chinook Trough. Sunset is cold and we are still bearing northerly.

10 October

I draw the curtains and there is a whale outside, a humpback. It seems extraordinary to come across him – how much life there must be below us, from krill to submarines. Later there are two more whales, one surfacing in the only streak of sun, a splash of gold in hundreds of square miles of hard grey sea.

Breakfast news is a bleak and typical selection of the doings of the sea. Eleven Chinese sailors have been killed in the Mekong delta, near Burma, over heroin, it is thought. A Costamare vessel has run aground on a reef in the Bay of Plenty, New Zealand, and spilled much oil. The crew are safe. She was doing seventeen knots in clear weather and the reef is well charted. In Gioia Tauro, Calabria, one of Europe's larger container ports, a hundred and thirty-five million euros' worth of cocaine has been confiscated from the 'Ndrangheta, the Calabrian Mafia, who plunder the docks at will.

We are travelling in the middle of a high pressure and the sea is very strange today, grey dark and slippy-sloppy, like a great frying pan full of water, unstable in its own mass. There are no waves. We are still seeing scraps and fragments of plastic.

'Ten years ago we throw everything over the side,' Sorin says. 'Paper, card and metal still.' But he is proud that Maersk is a signatory to the ISO convention against pollution.

'The Indian Ocean can be calm like this in the north-east monsoon season,' Shubd says. 'Like a lake.'

There are some small birds on the containers behind the bridge. In defiance of regulations I throw them some cake, but I fear they did not eat it. The US Coastguard would be very angry: food anywhere on the ship earns you serious trouble. Sorin found some small birds dead. He says the big ocean-goers are perching around the bow: 'They like to hide up there.'

11 October (the first)

'We are on the far side of the world,' says Chris. I spend the morning in the engine room and the bilges, the lowest accessible part of the ship, joining the day shift at 0530. We drink coffee and say nothing. The expressions of the crew are like those of farmers, that same shyness and a phlegmatic blend of resolve and resignation at the start of work. Who am I to understand their world? I have posted a blog address in the lift and some have read it. Joel and Noel are particularly enthusiastic about someone telling their story; the others are not sure. I do not speak Tagalog and most of them have seafaring English at best. One, G, is extremely cautious around me because he had his computer seized at Felixstowe by the Black Gang – UK Customs inspectors. Whatever they found on his hard drive rated as 'explicit material' and was confiscated. I would like to know if this was just pornography, or appalling evil, but can find no way to ask. At six o'clock we go down, boilersuited, to the engine room. G clearly does not want to talk about it. Hermanath, Rohan's replacement, is wide awake, assigning men to the day's tasks. Hermanath is an energetic young man from New Delhi, bright and alert as a light. 'We have an oil leak in the motor for the port stabiliser,' he announces with enthusiasm. 'Let's go!'

From the engine room you duck through a half-sized hatch into the engineers' passage, a grey and dim-lit corridor running the length of the ship. This is the refuge in the event of a pirate attack and the only means of going forward in bad weather. It would be a desperate place in which to hide from pirates: nothing to sit on, no daylight, no communications and no sense of the world at all, just an elongated cell stretched as long as the ship. You imagine the fear, the waiting and listening. A third of the way along it Hermanath opens a hatch in the floor.

'Careful here. Go down only when the man below is out of the way.'

We descend five ladders, each room-high, to the bilges. Here is a riddled honeycomb of steel compartments and high sills, narrow spaces and pressing bulkheads which conspire to trip and bump you. We work our way backward

to a point where the hull starts to curve in towards us, and
here is Roy, on all fours, rags on his hands and knees,
mopping up the oil spill by crawling in it. There is nothing
else to see and Roy is in no position to be interviewed.
Hermanath leads the climb back to the engine room. Here
the deck shakes crazily under your feet, your teeth pretty
well chatter and the noise is horrendous, even through
earplugs. The heat washes over you off the engine in waves
which seem to push you back. A shift lasts all day with
breaks for breakfast at 7.30, coffee at ten, and lunch.

Hermanath continues on his rounds. He is twenty-nine
and has been ten years at sea; he has the same bounce as
Joel, the lightness of men who were born to it. He talks
about the satisfaction of his work.

'Yes, it's a real man's job!' he says. 'I can't sleep without
the noise of the engine. If it stops you get your shoes on.'

When he is on watch (three nights on, three nights off)
he has an alarm in his cabin which sounds when any of the
ship's thousand alarm points trips. Everyone says there are
too many alarms.

'It's because they can't have a monitoring point without
an alarm,' says the chief, scornfully.

In the repair shop Prashant is wielding a sledgehammer,
banging a bolt out of a scorched and pitted injection unit,
which is a thing like a milled steel traffic cone. He jumps
up on to the workbench to get a better swing. By lunch I
am woozy with the noise and the scrambling up and down.
I have been using the gym but I can see why most of the
crew do not need it. We put the clocks forward again
yesterday: the Captain says everyone is tired on the day after

time change. But we agree it has been a good Tuesday, so we might as well have another one tomorrow. We cross the date line tonight.

11 October (the second)

Wakeful at 3 a.m. I go up to the bridge. There is a single puddle of full moonlight dead astern.

'You never see the Pacific this calm,' says Chris, in the darkness. 'I had one captain who was out here in a storm, a real bad one,' he says, quietly. 'All you can do is turn the ship into it and ride it until you break out. That one lasted three days and at one point they had an engine shutdown. Within five minutes they were beam-on to the waves. They were rolling forty-five degrees but since the indicator only went to forty-five degrees it was probably further.'

'What do you do then?'

'Strap yourself in and pray.'

'Sheesh.'

'We don't want that,' Chris said, with feeling. Our GM – our centre of gravity – is currently so low that the graphs say we could roll fifty-eight degrees before the ship becomes 'unstable'.

'What does that mean?'

'We capsize.'

Joel is in the mess at dawn. He is up early because he slept through his alarm yesterday. Sorin says he could not get out of his bunk either. Joel says that whenever they hear of a ship in trouble all their stomachs lurch. 'First we want to know if the crew are OK, then we want to learn something from it.'

12 October

The sea is cold shades of blue. Rings of sun spotlight puddles of gold behind us. We are at latitude 45 degrees 31 minutes North and making southwards, so we have passed the zenith of our Great Circle. Our longitude is 167 degrees 25 minutes West, which puts us at the eastern end of the Chinook Trough, which is five and a half kilometres deep below our keel. We are rolling gently, placidly, about halfway between the Bay of Alaska and Hawaii.

The Aleutian Trench is off to the north of us and our next conquest will be the Surveyor Fracture Zone. We are a week from land in any direction and Conrad's peace of God is here with us. The wars of men will not be forgotten, however. We have received a warning about missile testing in Naval Air Warfare Center's sea range, just off the coast of California, in an area we will steam straight through. In the evening I subject Prashant and Hermanath to *The Ghost Writer*, in revenge for them putting me through *Thor*. They think it pretty terrible.

It is a strange night. I wake at quarter to two, convinced by body clock and lighted darkness outside that it must be nearly morning. The night is overcast and there has been rain; the air has the fresh cold smell of it. Chris is on the bridge. He says he likes the midnight to 4 a.m. watch.

'Lots of chief officers say they miss it. You can do whatever you want!'

(As long as you do it in darkness, maintain your night vision, do not fall asleep, answer all your alarms, which bleat every ten minutes, keep a good watch and do not leave the bridge.)

The night becomes very beautiful, the moon full and bright, lighting silver splashes on the sea. Huge clouds glow low over waters of dark imperial blue. On the return trip they will circle north of the Aleutian Islands and sail down the east coast of Japan. It will be much colder and the ship will be covered with ice.

Chris will have five hours ashore in LA before the voyage to Shanghai, because he will have to unplug reefers and keep an eye on the stevedores. The engineers have more time off in port: Hermanath referred to the deck officers' job as 'staring out of the window'. There does not seem to be much of that going on: Chris is plotting the next Great Circle and the course back to China.

I fall asleep listening to the engine beating its rhythm. She has a fine, gentle sway-roll on her: it is like being rocked in the arms of someone walking. With crews always male, or overwhelmingly so, the ship becomes a strange plait of feminine archetypes – wife, mother and mistress. They tend to her constantly and she holds them while they sleep.

13 October

The wind is cold and strong enough to blow you over on deck, and the sea is all colour: purple, green, black-brown and turquoise. There are bodies on the steel, a dead cockroach and a dead fledgling. How did the fledgling get here?

A nest on a container? We have seen no birds for two days, only water, clouds, stars, moon and sun. There is no more rubbish on the surface, just the keen feeling of our speed, twenty-two knots. The roll is bigger and the waves seem to race past, jumping. Our starboard side is all salt-crystallised, though the wind comes from port: the ship's high sides make it eddy back strongly on the sheltered side, blowing the tops off the leeward waves so that their spray streams back towards us, white as a sea wizard's hair. The roll is particular. She has this one version whereby you lean to starboard, pause, and when you think she is going to roll back she rolls further.

We are over the Surveyor Fracture; next is the Medocino Fracture. The westward movement of the Pacific plate over the last seventy million years has created this stretched riddle of fissures and ridges, the mightiest of which is the seven-thousand-kilometre-long Emperor Seamount range. The tail of these mountains reaches all the way down to Hawaii.

Take a mental image of the younger volcanoes of Hawaii, of their striated and scarred sides rising thousands of feet, towering ridges and peaks, and submerge them in kilometres of water. No light from the surface penetrates down here; this a world of utmost black, an upthrust of mountains of monstrous height and depth. The creatures living on their sides and gliding like slow birds over their deeps are only vaguely known to science. Now and then nets are lowered down from the bluey-silver regions miles above, as remote from these depths as the upper atmosphere is from the surface of the earth. The nets are held open by steel plates, 'canyonbusters', which weigh up to five tonnes. The cable at the net's mouth is threaded through chafing gear, steel balls or rollers which measure up to a metre in diameter. The whole assemblage is dragged through the canyons and over the ridges of the seamount.

Life grows slowly in the depths of the ocean, lives long and does not replace itself swiftly. The deep trawl scoops up whatever it happens upon and leaves rubble. Tons of corals are uprooted and destroyed – there are many more coral species in the deep seas than in shallow tropical waters. These corals support entire communities of specific, endemic species which are wiped out with them. The haul often contains new and 'relic' species, previously known only from fossils. From the 1960s to the early 1990s the Emperor Seamounts were particularly targeted by Japanese and Russian trawlers in search of such deepwater fish as armorhead and alfonsino. Annual catches fell from 35,000 to 5,000 tonnes before the practice was abandoned. The fisheries are not expected to recover. Fish caught and discarded as bycatch included two previously unknown species of dragonets (which look like they have stepped out of fossils – long, fan-finned, big-eyed beasts like miniature Chinese dragons) and the highfin dogfish, only twenty-one specimens of which have ever been recorded. The Jurassic period has not finished down here. Conservationists fear the effect of seamount trawling on small populations with a limited range and slow reproductive cycle is catastrophic. One study followed the course of a trawl in the Gulf of Alaska. Seven years after the dragnets were hauled up there was no sign of any young coral in place of what had been destroyed.

Seen from the perspective of the deep we are alien, a quasi-Martian species inhabiting a universe of almost entirely different physical and temporal conditions. As the *Gerd* pounds on far above it is as if she is a spacecraft, one of many in her vastly high orbit. Now and then one gropes down, blindly, with a net. Plunder and pollution are our only contributions to the worlds under the sea.

14 October

Early bed under glittering stars, then woke at 4.45, so got up. Others were up too. Joel said: 'Thank God for the stabilisers! If they weren't out, in this weather, no sleep!'

Another dawn, another breakfast: conversation is fitful these days. The sea is growing off the port bow, where it has been all this time. Bands of clear follow bands of mist over water an astonishing colour, blue and purple–black and bustling with waves: it is strange and exciting to look out from the deck all the way to the horizon and see nothing still anywhere. Busy wraiths in squalls of rain hurry over us, coming and going, commuting to infinity.

Chris is in an excellent mood. Everyone is excited about LA – we're still more than two days out but it feels just over the horizon. You can feel the forces acting to bend the ship, and you feel her flexing against them.

'You should see the atmosphere on a ship after three days of storms and no sleep,' Chris says, with grim relish.

'Pretty bad?'

'Poison.'

The forces are peculiar and intermittent, like hands pressing down on your shoulders and your neck. Sorin says you need to drink a lot of water in storms, 'Because all the guys are sick.'

He is in a meditative mood during his watch. He is also flying home from LA.

'What does it take to be a good officer, Sorin?'

He thinks for a moment. 'You need to be able to feel the ship – like a body. Like a creature.'

'Is this a good ship?'

He looks down her, all the way to the foremast and the Pacific.

'Oh yeah, she is good ship.'

'What else?'

'To be good seafarer? I think you need to feel salt on your skin. Once a seaman always a seaman.'

'And suppose your son says he wants to go to sea. What will you say?'

'I would respect him, but I would warn him. About loneliness . . . isolation. About needing to be strong with yourself.'

It is dark and rainy now and very lively. Outside the cargo is singing and thumping in whines and bangs; loose things in the crates are booming. We have been boarded by pirate poltergeists. Showers flood, wardrobe doors fling themselves open, batteries and lighters fly off desks, a pencil crosses the chart table of its own accord, my lamp revolves on its base and the bed refuses sleep.

15 October

As I go up to the fo'c'sle at daybreak it is still dark under the containers. The prow is silent and the ocean streams towards us; weather here comes right down to the water as we drive into it and through it, through patches of light and towers of dim, through trunks of rain like a forest. We steam under low arches of cloud, through columns of vapour, the sea black beneath silver pillars. Now it is day, now it is night, the sea's surface unbroken and heaving like the flanks of a beast breathing. There are spirits of blue rain. You would not be astonished to see phantom ships, sea monsters or the edge of the world. How those old sailors needed their courage, even in morning warmth. The day then breaks into a vaulting blue with scars of white cloud high in the clearest air I have ever seen, and a patina of vapour like an eggshell glaze, translucent in one quadrant, and everywhere else screaming clear, sun scintillant on the waters, which are stilled.

The Captain disengages the autopilot and takes the helm. In order to approach America we must confirm that we have tested the steering gear. He turns his ship to port and to starboard. He slows her, stops her, goes astern and spins her on her axis. These feats accomplished, we resume our course towards Long Beach.

To take a vessel to the Land of the Free you must clean the entire ship. You must search end to end for moths, particularly the Asian Gypsy Moth, and destroy them, plunging any colonies of eggs you find in boiling alcohol. You must switch from burning heavy fuel to low-sulphur diesel. You must submit crew details and an effects list, to ensure that no one tries to sell a load of Hong Kong iPads on the sly. You must destroy or remove any spills, garbage or organic matter. You must lock all meat, fruit and veg in stores and seal them. You must convert the library into an interview room – we will stand a metre away from the table, with nothing in our pockets and our hands where they can see them. I have been repeatedly told that a Filipino on his first voyage to the US is not allowed to land. Presumably by not blowing up his ship in port, and by returning, he proves he is neither a terrorist nor immigration-inclined. Finally, when you have done all this you sail in across a firing range. The Captain is particularly concerned about the state of the bins in our cabins. 'Not one apple core. Not one piece of orange peel or we will have all kinds of bullshit. We will be fined!'

'Someone always forgets this,' Andreas confides.

I go on the rounds with Joel and Prashant, completing a checklist. We climb up inside the funnel casing, a huge, hot and oily vertical chimney veined with a single ladder. The steel of the rungs and guard rails is hot. I have no idea of the temperature in here but it feels like forty degrees. Joel and Prashant test fire hatches and hydraulic systems with blasts of compressed air. Everything works, all the boxes are ticked. The men are bubbly at the prospect of land.

Over lunch Andreas talks about bunkering, which we are due for in LA. 'When you take on 3,450 tonnes of fuel the thing to worry about is the force of the air pressure. As it is expelled from the tanks you get static, so you can get static discharge and fire.'

Somehow we get on to the Old Days again.

'You used to get two beers, thirty-three centilitres, every day, one bottle of whisky a month, and some wine. Then you could get together and have a party. The old ships had bars and smoking saloons adjoining the mess, with a sliding partition between the officers and the men. But now no alcohol. No conversation either!'

He laments that no concessions are made at Christmas.

'Before 2008 we used to get buckets of no-alcohol beer on Sundays,' Shubd says. 'And much better contracts.'

An entertaining conversation develops with Hermanath about the next generation of ships, the Triple Es. They have two engines.

'How would you feel about two engines, Hermanath?'

He looks rather shocked.

'It would be like having two wives!'

There is a lovely moment on the bridge towards sunset. The Captain is in his chair, arms crossed, leaning back, relaxed. Chris is looking at something on the computer and Andreas has joined us. The Captain and the chief talk quietly in Danish and then they fall silent. The sun makes bright bars as it sinks and the sea is an endless dream, as though it has forgotten it can be anything but kind. I look at the faces of the men as they look at the sea, with equanimity, with satisfaction and an unexpressed awareness of the temporary and the timeless, with acceptance and certainty that this was all and nothing at all, and that everything is always changeable, and that they are a crew whose completeness would only be proved tomorrow when it will be broken, and that they had brought their great ship to land again, almost, and that foul weather and hardship lay in her futures and in all their separate courses, and that there would be ports, hopefully, at the end of them. And I thought for a moment I understood a little of seafaring men.

It was after this, in the lift, that the Captain said:

'No one understands, when you are at home. They ask you about what it is like and maybe they have a few pictures. But all they think is sunsets and sunrises, clouds. They have no idea, actually, how *vast* the oceans are.'

A dark calm night and the voices of America reach us across the water. The radio crackles for the first time for over a week. We hear two women, San Francisco and Los Angeles Coastguards. I cannot resist teasing Shubd.

'I like the sound of this San Francisco girl, Shubd. She sounds like a natural woman.'

'Oh yes, I think this is true.'

'But this LA woman, she is a babe.'

'Ha ha! You think she is beautiful?'

'Don't you? Listen to her!'

'Yes. Perhaps she is.'

'She's incredibly beautiful. Blonde or brunette?'

'Blonde maybe.'

'Blonde for sure. I think she may have had breast enlargements and liposuction. If it's a choice I'm going with San Francisco.'

'You have a very good imagination.'

He calls Plead control, the missile people, and pleads with them not to rocket us. The LA woman tells us to carry on.

16 October

A changed beat from the engine jolts me awake – what has happened? Then it comes back: this is the last morning of the voyage, we are slowing down. Day opens in dark low cloud and a brownish sea, with a line of fanned light streaming below the lid, and there off the port bow are promontories, the tumbled arms of America. They are mountainous, dark crumpled gold; a monumental wild land seems to hove over the horizon, as though it is resolving out of low cloud and spreading towards us over the sea. It seems amazing that the ocean has a limit, a shore, and we have reached it. We are somewhere north of Los Angeles; the coast is too distant to make out detail but it looks uninhabited and – peerless. What a landfall! No one knows who first crossed this ocean the way we have, from the Orient to America. When the old sailors spoke of the New World they referred to its east coast, but the shock of this grandeur, of these dark mountains which answer the ocean's might and scale – this is a new world, now, here, for ever. The Cantonese word for this coast is 'gumshan', gold mountain. Originally it referred to the gold rush, which inspired tens of thousands of Chinese to voyage this way in the late 1840s, but it is an accurate term this morning. The mountains are still giants of darkly glittering ore.

The Captain is unusually loquacious. 'We will berth near the *Queen Mary*. This is a beautiful ship – you will see her. She made over one thousand Atlantic crossings, during the war also. I have keyring made out of bronze from her propeller.'

He also has a 'magic priority pass' for airports.

'I have three hours in Amsterdam so I can get some breakfast. Some beer. Some more beer. Some cognac!'

The islands of Santa Rosa and Santa Cruz roll by off our port side and we drive east towards Santa Catalina. Joel finds a minute to come up to the fo'c'sle.

'Ah, I love it here! This is beautiful.'

'Do you ever come here, normally?'

'Ahhh no! Not really, no.'

'Because you're always in the engine room.'

'I like the engine room.'

'But how can you? It's terrible!'

'Nooo! I like it. It's a puzzle. You have to think about it and – try things. And you are always learning, and I like that.'

'You seem such a happy man, Joel – are you really?'

'Yes. Yes I am. You have to be. This is very important. You have to do your job and not worry too much. You must be positive. Or – you cannot do your job.'

'OK, but the thing is, I find it – extraordinary, that you can have two men, let's say two engineers, doing exactly the same job, the same rank, but they are not paid the same because they have different passports. You told me the Filipinos are 25 per cent of the world's seafarers, and yet you are paid far less because you are Filipino. How can that possibly be right?'

'Mmm – but this is the market.'

'But it's not fair, is it?'

'If you don't like your contract you don't sign it. If you don't like the terms that are offered don't take the job! But if you sign the contract and take the job you can't complain.'

'But – oh! Look!'

As I am asking the question there is a splashing in the sea and a school of dolphin cut across our bow.

'In Argentina we had to slow right down because there were so many whales. They were spouting! There are many whales there in September.'

'Where do you like, in the world?'

'I like Gioia Tauro. You can see the volcano – Etna. And the sunsets and the sunrises. The sky . . .'

Now Santa Catalina comes out of the haze, huge, pitted and mountainous with high cliffs. We see something tossing and splashing in the sea – killer whale? – and a head – a manatee? Probably a sea lion. The waters are full of life and mystery, including a sinister ship, CS *Global Sentinel*, which is laying fifty-two kilometres of cable from Monterey with an earthquake sensor on the end and low-light cameras. Why? What is there to see down there? The island of Santa Barbara passes, looking like a pirate HQ. I was sad when I woke but the approach to this other empire is full of beauty. And such colour! Californian sunshine beats Chinese tone and gloom. There is far more wildlife here; there are brown pelicans, dolphins, glossy gulls and a hummingbird, a moment ago, buzzing from Santa Catalina to the mainland. The Captain compares the port of LA by area to the goings-on in China. They have six kilometres of the biggest cranes in Shanghai, which is the world's busiest port; apparently Los Angeles is the biggest by area. The train schedules in Los Angeles are the key to the whole thing, the Captain says.

We approach the mainland from the north across the Gulf of Catalina. The Palos Verdes Hills are green, some ridges are built over but many not, because the hills are sand and cannot support structures. Through binoculars we study bluffs, and then a lighthouse like an old pepperpot. It is the Angels Gate Light, position 33 degrees 42 minutes 31 seconds North, 118 degrees 15 minutes 03 seconds West.

Chinese coastal waters are thick with fishermen: here there are one or two trawlers and long-liners going out of San Pedro Bay but the sea is scattered with yachts and two-masted schooners and water skiers and fast ferries; the champion spends while the contender earns. It is evidently cheaper to catch all the fish in the East and bring them to the West Coast than it is to catch them in the West, or even to catch half of the fish in each place and leave the rest to swim.

A low speed limit makes us sedate and there is very little container traffic compared to China: six or seven ships. There are bars of grey pollution above the land now and mountains in the far distance; Los Angeles lies below and between. Down the coast is Orange County, Laguna and La Jolla. The names and their associations contain America's trick of preparing everything for you in a thousand ways, prophesying itself, upstaging your discoveries.

After all, leaving was so quick.

'What's the plan tonight?' I asked Joel.

'We're going to Walmart!'

'Really? Why?'

'Really cheap, yeah, cheap.'

So at the end of their voyage the sailors go to the shop which sells the goods their ship has carried, and they buy some of them.

'What are we doing tonight, Chris?'

'Going to Hooters.'

'Hooters! What – isn't that where the waitresses . . . ?'

'They have really good chicken.'

'O-K. Look, I might see you but I think I'm going to go out on the town actually . . .'

US Customs could not have been more pleasant. Backed up by a couple of big officers, a young woman with a gun at her hip studies all our passports and takes details and issues shore passes. The Captain was entirely charming – the officer was charmed, as you would be – and our agent, Divna, stood by, seeing all well. Divna is an Amazonian blonde and very famous in our world, like certain captains. She was waiting on the quay using her phone as Captain Larsen brought the *Gerd* alongside for the final time.

'Ah, there is Divna!' he cried, spotting her as a tiny blonde blob. 'Good, we will use her to position the ship.'

He did, too.

'Do you see the time, Clare? Two thirty.'

After two months, ten ports, half the globe, a cracked cylinder casing, pirate dangers, a fuel leak, one confiscated computer, visa problems (mine), a typhoon, four dodgy pilots, several storms, multiple corruption demands, multiple, multiple collision opportunities and God knows how many carrots eaten resoundingly by his chief officer, the Captain has brought his ship, crew and a record cargo into Los Angeles to the hour, to the minute, and, the log will show, to the second. Stand up, stand up for Captain Larsen, and for all of his kind!

There are no emotional farewells. Sorin gives me a Maersk T-shirt of which I am inordinately proud; Chris presents a laminated copy of the ship's vital statistics. I had not realised we had lamination facilities and the gesture is typical of Chris: sweet, and highly practical. We joke in the queue for the library where the immigration officers are and for once we are all together, all in the same boat, our hierarchy that of boys in a line, or on a team bus – irrelevant. Whoever is funniest holds the floor. Andreas looks truly playful for the first time, and – he is very tall – is subconsciously appointed head boy in the playground. We make jokes to make him laugh particularly. Every time a name is called we all shake our heads and groan. No way will they let Joel in! But of course they do. I had not understood at first that seafarers' goodbyes are a peculiarly final kind. When will we ship together again? Apart from the back-to-back officers, probably never. Will we meet in our own lands, or someone else's? Probably not. Handshakes with everyone, thank everyone, and Divna says OK, are you ready? And I am.

PART TWO

North

CHAPTER 13

The Zeemanshuis

I wanted cold, I wanted storms and I wanted a ship nothing like the great *Gerd*. In size and sophistication she was near the crow's nest of container shipping: now I wanted to experience life in the bilges. Maersk runs a regular service between the Low Countries and Montreal, using old ships. In the middle of a hard winter I asked for a place on the *Maersk Pembroke*, which plies between the ports of northern Europe and eastern Canada. Photographs of the ship showed a ragged old battler, pummelled and butted by the Atlantic.

It seemed I might be able to join her in Rotterdam, the shipping capital of Europe. The Zeemanshuis, the Seaman's House, a cheap hotel on the banks of the Nieuw Mass river, is not necessarily the place you would choose to stay if you had just spent nine months on a ship and wanted a change, but it offers discounts for seafarers.

There are mooring posts in the dining room and pictures of ships on every wall. There are tugs in the stairwells and tankers in the bar. There are liners and caravels in glass cases and many, many photographs of brave, clean, modern ships, all sailing under blue skies, all impressive and all ugly; most of them very ugly. Seafaring gave the world its most exalting technology, the tall ship, then replaced it with boxy utility. We build few beautiful vessels now. Writing in 1822, Chateaubriand describes what we have all but lost.

> The lone vessel is a fine sight: responding to the lightest touch of the tiller, a hippogriff or winged courser, obedient to the pilot's hand, like a horse under the hand of a rider. The elegance of the masts and rigging, the agility of the sailors as they scramble along the yards, the different aspects in which the ship presents itself, leaning into a hostile southerly, or fleeing swiftly before a favourable northerly, make this sentient structure one of the wonders of human ingenuity. Now the foaming wave strikes and spurts against the hull; now the peaceful waters divide, without resistance, before the prow. Flags, flames, sails complete the beauty of this palace of Neptune: the lowest sails, deployed to their full width, swell like vast cylinders; the topsails, reefed in the middle, resemble the breasts of a Siren. Animated by an impetuous breeze, the ship with its keel, as with the blade of a plough, cuts with a loud noise through the fields of the sea . . .

Only two aspects of this wonderful roll endure: ships are still sentient structures, and they still cut the fields of the sea. I am desperate to join mine, now, but she is eluding me. She may not be coming into Rotterdam after all. I await news, and study the workers of Europe's busiest container port.

Breakfast in the Zeemanshuis finishes at 0930. At 0928 a Filipino comes in, followed by another, followed by thirty more. People at the tables start to smile at the scale of the invasion. Placid and inexorable, a quiet wave of men breaks around the buffet, sweeping up eggs, bread, juice, tinned fruit and coffee: a breakfast such as they eat on their ships, if they are lucky, and much of it carried here by their ships, of course. Bags crowd the reception area, tagged Cathay Pacific. Their owners are far from feeble men but it takes two to lift some of the suitcases. They bulge with the hoards of those signing off, their goods gathered who knows where, and the provisions of those signing on.

Some of the men have just landed, others are checking out, and there is a whiff of diesel in the dining room now; some have just come ashore. All have timed their run on breakfast to perfection. The first finishers collect on the pavement in front of the hotel, smoking, wincing at the sun on the river and watching the passing barges. You can feel their jetlag. They are dressed alike in puffy bomber jackets and woolly hats.

Four doors down the quay from the Zeemanshuis are the offices of Marlow Navigation, a company based in what it calls 'the favourable business climate of Cyprus'. Marlow is a manning agency, specialising in supplying crews to shipowners. You can almost smell the laundered shirts of the men inside, as they tap keyboards and make calls. They employ 13,000 seafarers, half Filipino, a third Ukrainian. Marlow recruits all levels, from master to able seamen, but the domination of Filipinos – and their traditional relegation to the lower decks – means that it is the supply of poor men desperate for work to rich men hungry for profit that makes the company money.

Marlow cannot be blamed for the way the globalised world works, but its operation is a feudal and racial pyramid, with the white and powerful at the top. This is clear in Marlow's first newsletter, published in 2007 on the occasion of the company's twenty-fifth birthday. The letter names men who have been with the company for more than seventeen years: each is to be given a watch. Of 111 Filipinos receiving watches, only three are captains. Of seventeen Germans, eleven are captains, the rest chief officers.

A third engineer leans against the railing outside the hotel, feet braced.

'Reeper ship,' he says.

He's signing on to the *Nagato Reefer*, Japanese-owned, Panama-flagged. She's currently a few miles downriver, coming in. She will be leaving this evening. She began life travelling between New Zealand and Wilmington on the US East Coast, carrying apples, pears, kiwi fruit and meat.

'Now Rotterdam Las Palmas Rotterdam . . . maybe Russia in May.'

He was on tankers for the last nine months; for the next nine he will live on *Nagato Reefer*. He is employed not by the shipowner, of course, but by a crewing agency like Marlow. (I do not ask which.) Sometimes it will be good, he says, sometimes hard. He is not complaining.

'Life is sometimes, sometimes. Don't want waves, just plain seas – plain! These are good cigarettes from the Philippines – Blueseal. You take one?'

A Dutch girl jogs past.

'All ports are good ports,' says the third engineer, watching her, 'ex-ceb Nigeria.'

The third engineer may have a fair idea of the conditions which await him on the *Nagato Reefer*, which is only a month out of detention in Southampton, where she was inspected by Britain's Maritime and Coastguard Agency. The inspector's report may go some way to explaining the man's phlegmatism, as he draws on his cigarette. Although some of the deficiencies must have been remedied before she was released, in the event of an emergency the third engineer's next ship would have been little short of lethal to her crew.

'The vessel was detained in Southampton because none of the lifeboats had drain plugs and the No. 1 battery was discharged in each lifeboat; the magnetic compass bowl contained a large bubble; the officer responsible for the radio operation was not familiar with the power supply arrangement; the chief engineer could not explain the operation of the CO_2 fire-fighting system; none of the engineers knew which steering gear was fed from the emergency power supply and the port life-raft painter was tied to the ship and not to the weak link. In addition the records of rest for the chief engineer were false on a number of days during November and there were no records of rest kept for December; two out of three deck-head lights were inoperative in the CO_2 room; and there was no record of the last annual survey on the International Oil Pollution Prevention (IOPP) certificate.'

Now the men group on the quayside. They have changed into hooded tops; some of the younger ones are in T-shirts, though it was snowing yesterday and there are slicks of ice in the river. The men photograph each other and set out for the sights.

'The Filipinos are amazing,' said Chris, my Danish friend. 'Put them in any port and in no time at all they find the cheapest shops, the best bars and the worst women . . .'

No man walks alone; two are briefly arm in arm. Whatever else you may think of their lives their comradeship seems enviable.

The Reverend Steve Axtell ministers to the Seaman's Mission in Rotterdam: he sees the solidarity and vulnerability of these men in a way others do not.

'The last thing was a tanker, she was carrying edible oil. A man had died on the voyage, a Filipino, and the crew wanted a mass for him,' his voice softens. 'And they wanted me to bless their ship. Worried about the bad vibes.'

The vibes in the Zeemanshuis vary. Two Filipinos are caught out: they have no room, no money for sightseeing, they are shattered and their pick-up is not until later. They sleep on a bench in the lobby. Not long after nightfall a Marlow minibus turns up.

No one would accuse Marlow of being a gangmaster of the sea. The company could point to its training facilities, its international certification and reputation, its pedigree and blue-chip clients. Is it Marlow's fault that the industry allows it to profit from absolving shipowners of responsibility for the men who do their dirtiest work? (The local Maersk office is an extravagant double skyscraper a mile up the quay. They can certainly see the port from up there, and the ships, but not the Zeemanshuis, which falls below their sightline.) Two miles from here, across the river, Glenn Cuevas, a thirty-six-year-old father of two from the Philippines, was crushed to death by an eight-tonne container. In the pre-dawn darkness of 21 January 2007, Mr Cuevas was placing twistlocks on top of a container when another was lowered down on top of him. An able seaman, he was employed by Marlow Navigation as a crewman on the coaster *Eucon Leader*. Marlow also managed the vessel. Cuevas should never have touched the steel boxes that killed him. International agreements forbid crews from handling containers: this is partly because the men are often drained, exhausted and overworked when they arrive in port, and partly because cargo handling is the union-protected province of dockers and stevedores, who are expert at it. It is possible for a master to ask a local union to waive their right to handle his cargo but no such agreement was reached. Mr Cuevas's captain was in the habit of ordering his crew to lash and unlash the containers despite having been warned about it – severally, according to the International Transport Workers' Federation. The *Eucon Leader* was covered by an ITF agreement which specifically forbade cargo handling by the crew.

Who put Glenn Cuevas in harm's way? Seven years after the incident a legal case to determine liability is still ongoing. The Captain had questions to answer: what happens on his ship is his responsibility. But captains act at the shipowner's behest, certainly where savings and expenditure are concerned. A family firm, Bernd Becker GmbH have been in the business for over a century. They either ordered or approved the practice, or had no knowledge of the regime on the vessel – in which case they must have wondered how the Captain was saving them so much on dockers' fees. Thanks to the efforts of the ITF and the Dutch FNV Bondgenoten union, Marlow and its insurers paid $200,000 compensation to the family of Mr Cuevas.

The lovely islands of Antigua and Barbuda are also implicated, since the Beckers flag their ships there. This means it is the Antiguan authorities' prerogative to investigate the incident. No such action was taken. Indeed, such an investigation would have made news throughout the shipping world. The reason so many owners flag their vessels in countries like Liberia, Panama and Antigua is precisely because shipowners know that in the event of incident or disaster the authorities of these places will not hold them to any significant account.

Are there outstanding questions for Marlow Navigation? The company employed Mr Cuevas: one can only speculate whose side it would have taken if Mr Cuevas had complained that the Captain was asking him to risk his life. Would Marlow have allied itself with a lowly seafarer? Would any manning agency make common cause with an aggrieved individual among the hundreds of thousands of men they supply to the market, and with him confront a shipowner, one of their prized clients? Perhaps it would indeed – which would make his death Mr Cuevas's own fault, for not complaining or refusing.

(Fortunately, blacklisting in the industry is universally denied, at least by shipowners and crewing agencies, so it cannot have been fear of losing his livelihood that made Mr Cuevas attempt a deadly job he was not qualified to do.)

It surely was not the ship's fault, anyway: the *Eucon Leader* is a smart blue and orange coastal feeder, engaged in shifting containers between Germany and the Low Countries. She was shiny new, barely two months out of her Romanian shipyard, when Mr Cuevas was killed. Strangely, she is the only element of this story which was verifiably changed by the death of Glenn Cuevas. The *Eucon Leader* has been renamed *Jork Ruler* and is now flagged in Cyprus. The Beckers welcome inquiries from paying passengers who might like to travel on her.

History may conclude that Glenn Cuevas died by his own decisions. Like many crewmen, he may well have been eager to do the unlashing work, despite the dangers, because it is paid cash in hand. If he made more than three hundred dollars on the day he died it would be surprising. But then the sea is a surprising place: perhaps his captain and the Beckers paid him far above the going rate.

It is not surprising that nothing of this makes that inaugural Marlow newsletter, which came out at the end of 2007. (Mr Cuevas had died that January.) You would not hurry to take the matter up with the butch Dutch skinhead who comes to collect the next batch of Filipinos from the Zeemanshuis. He rides shotgun next to the driver in the Marlow minibus. He sees his tired charges safely inside, slams the door on the small, pale brown men, and they are off to sea again.

You wonder, watching them go, if Marlow Navigation was named after Joseph Conrad's Marlow, seaman, navigator and the narrator of *Heart of Darkness*, that feverish indictment of colonialism.

CHAPTER 14

The Hard-driven Ship

The pick-up in Rotterdam is changed to Antwerp. Antwerp in February is funereal. The city's population of Orthodox Jews wear plastic bags over their black hats in defence against the scudding rain. There is a mile of diamond dealerships wrapped around the station, most of them closed. It is as if there was once a population here who ate diamonds, drank diamonds, read diamonds, smoked diamonds and died out, leaving the little white stones to gather dust behind steel grilles. A hotel near the port seems a good idea until you reach it. The Etap in Luithagen Haven is a frontier post surrounded by miles of spray and trucks, and containers, containers everywhere and not a ship to carry them. The pilots of Antwerp are on strike. Among the charging lorries the only life forms are two magpies speaking Flemish, and one fellow guest, a professional diver.

'It's the third most dangerous job in the world,' he says.

'After what?'

'Astronaut, baby, diver – we all have lifelines.'

'Good money?'

'No, not really,' he laughs. 'Not so much. Everyone thinks so . . .'

'Why then?'

'I was on dredgers. Building windmills in the North Sea. We lost an anchor and we had to send a diver down to get it. I wanted to get it!'

Chemical mist from the nearest refinery blows out of a sodium sky. There are five oil refineries around Antwerp's docks, attended by a cluster of petrochemical works whose density is only surpassed by Houston, Texas. Their products taint the daybreak, fouling the wind and the February rain, which stings like blown grit.

The diver flicks his cigarette butt away. 'I will be in the water in an hour,' he says, contentedly. 'I love the water. Must have water. I live in Ostend, right by the sea.'

'Are you diving in the port?'

'In the industrial area. Measuring depth for concrete.'

'No point telling you to keep warm, is there?'

'I have four layers! Underwear, jumpsuit, woolly bear, diving suit. Like the Michelin Man.'

The strike has been called off. Igor's taxi turns up in the mid-afternoon. Igor is from Ukraine. He loves Putin and he hates the BBC.

'Liars, liars, liars!' he jeers.

'Do you think I am a liar?'

'I don't know.'

'I'm not. And nor are the men and women in the BBC, my friends and colleagues, who risk their lives to tell you the truth. Just because you don't like what they say . . .'

'Agh!' Igor sneers. 'This is all shit.'

'It is NOT shit! How can you sit here in your taxi in a Western democracy where we don't kill journalists, where we don't defraud our elections, where a vote actually means something, and support a monster like Putin who put that scurvy, lying, homicidal, disgusting, torturing, murderous, megalomaniac wanker Ramzan Kadyrov in charge of Chechnya?'

Igor permits himself a near-smile. 'You are right about Kadyrov.'

By the time the lorryways open into a single broad square in a wasteland, where the superstructures of ships appear like space stations on a barren planet, we have become something like friends.

'Nuclear power station,' he nods. The heads of the cooling towers are capped in low cloud, as if they are pumping out the sky.

'That's nice.'

'Not Chernobyl,' he says. 'We were very lucky wind was blowing away from town.'

Igor thinks Belgium the best country in Europe. On this, too, we are implacably opposed.

His destination is a building like a broken brick, set in a moonscape. It seems empty but for a desk and a security door and a rough-skinned young man behind the desk.

'*Nastravia*,' says Igor, with a charming smile, his first, and goes.

'*Maersk Pembroke*?' says the young man. 'Are you crew?'

'Sort of.'

'Ah yes,' he smiles, 'straight through.'

A minibus waits in the rain. The other passenger is an extraordinary figure in seaman's gear. He wears a yachting

cap and donkey jacket, sports a white beard and carries an
attaché case. He must be a diamond smuggler. The bus tears
past the *Maersk Essex*, one of the world's biggest and ugliest
container ships. Then we pass a really rotten-looking ship,
so low in the water her deck is level with the quay. She
weeps rust. She is a mess.

'Oh God, not her,' I mutter.

Frankly, she looks dangerous. Now we approach a fine
big ship, registered in Monrovia. The diamond smuggler
disembarks the bus, turns up his collar against the rain and
begins to climb the ladder. Apart from the power station,
the chemical clouds and the desolation of containers there
is nothing for the eye anywhere. The bus turns and heads
for the rotten ship. It stops and the driver invites me to
alight. We have found the *Maersk Pembroke*.

They seem to be having some trouble bringing her
alongside. Is she aground? Ropes trail uselessly in the
muddy water. Stevedores stand around smoking. Up
above, in the rain, heads peer over the sides of the bridge
wing. The bridge wings are open to the elements! I start
to smile.

Her keel was laid down in 1997 and she was named P&O
Nedlloyd Sydney, a proud member of the then recently
combined fleets of Britain's P&O Containers and the
Netherlands' Royal Nedlloyd Lines. She is beautiful in
the pictures of her pomp, with her white superstructure,
her black hull painted red below the Plimsoll line, and an
elegant poop and stern, which now look perilously close to
the water. Her parent company was the third largest cargo
shipping line in the world: much of the *Sydney*'s business

was in the southern oceans. Her senior officers were Dutch, naturally. In 2005 Maersk bought P&O Nedlloyd for over two billion euros. The *Sydney* was rechristened *Maersk Pembroke*. Only two of her Dutch officers now remain: the Captain and the chief engineer. The ship's repaint job, an all-over coat of Maersk Lines' light blue, never very convincing, one feels, is a disgrace now. Thumped, rust-pored and tug-bashed, her undercoats and previous livery show through in Rothko patches.

She does not berth so much as decide she is near enough. Apropos of nothing she vomits hot spray in a lateral jet from a concealed pipe somewhere in the superstructure, catching me with a steamy, greasy blast. You cannot help laughing. Faces smile from the deck and the crew wave and call out. They have been anchored in the Steenbank Roads for the last two days, while the Captain emailed me counselling patience and we all waited for the pilots to call off their strike.

It was difficult to know whom to curse. The pilots are well paid. They retire at sixty-two. The whole world is taking a cut of some sort at the moment, except for the rich. The strike was never going to win anything; it was gesture politics and they must have known it. My time trickled away and my funds diminished with every night in the vile Etap hotel, and why oh why could the pilots not just accept the increase in retirement age to sixty-four?

On the other hand, the pilots do a dangerous, difficult and crucial job, and who would want their grandfather scaling the sides of ships in the freezing storms of the North Sea winter at the age of sixty-four? Why oh why could the wretched Belgian government, or whatever passes for it, not back down? And so I seethed, and forgave everyone everything the day the strike ended and I received the message from the agent, a young Belgian named Arthur, that the ship would be alongside from 4 p.m., and that I was welcome to join her. I could have hugged the young man in reception at the Etap. I could even have hugged Igor.

Agent Arthur looks ill but a lot of Antwerpers look ill. It must be the weather and the season. The stevedores do not look healthy but they seem indestructible, in the way of stevedores. The only man among us who appears thoroughly well, in the very pink, is the pilot. He is leaning over the rail of the ship gossiping with a camera crew, who are filming him for this evening's local news. He looks amused, very smart in expensive foul-weather gear, and tough. He gives brief, wry answers to the camera.

According to the authorities of the Port of Antwerp, the strike, which lasted three days, cost a million euros an hour. Fleets of ships backed up in the Channel anchorages and global schedules went to pieces, leaving shipowners liable for compensation. The Swiss shipping company MSC announced it was switching its entire operation to Rotterdam, thereby jeopardising two thousand Antwerp jobs. The pilots returned to work. They had successfully extracted a promise that a committee would be formed to study the problem of their retirement age. So it goes.

The young Filipino chief officer, Erwin, invites us aboard. After Sorin's height and authority Erwin seems too young for his role, but though shy he is firm and self-contained. Agent Arthur and I follow him through a hatch into a sheltered area with duckboards on the deck. There is that smell of institutionalised cooking again, and diesel. All the air inside reeks softly of diesel but the *Pembroke* is not bunkering, she just smells. We descend a stairway to where a pirate-proof gate stands open. In a small room beyond this is the Captain. He seems to take up half the space.

'Pete Koop!' he cries.

With a big smile a bigger hand shoots out. We shake. His eyes, an indeterminate grey, are very keen. His smile has teeth under a grey moustache. He has a round strong frame which fills the white uniform shirt, on which a faded yellow stain looks as though it has defied a few washes. A fifty-euro note shows through the top pocket. There is proper old gold braid on his shoulders, four stripes and the loop. He is in his early sixties and quick; he makes it seem the age to be. He is humorous and chatty.

'So we will meet in the bar,' he says, 'at six thirty, before we go down.'

There is a moment of wild hope. Have the Dutch won an exemption from the abstemious Danes?

'For a *drink*, Captain?'

'No! No. First they took away the beer. Then, in 2008, things not so good, they took away the soft drinks!'

Instead of a lift there is an unenclosed and airy iron stairway. You need a bit of strength just to open the door on deck one. Constant draughts patrol this stairway in whistles and moans.

My cabin comprises a lumpy double bed, a non-functioning strip light with exposed bulb over the pillow, desk, chair and a brass-rimmed porthole. The Captain appears, apparently delivering a letter to the electrician's cabin next door. He looks queryingly at me as I look queryingly at my cabin.

'Captain! Can I get to the bridge?'

'Yes but only at sea, it's locked when we're in port.'

'Can I go out?'

'Only where you came in.'

'Is there internet?'

'Not really! Well, yes, sometimes, a bit.'

'Can I smoke?'

'In your cabin, on the bridge if the officer of the watch doesn't mind, and in the bar.'

We warm to each other: he sees I like her and he likes her very much. Captain Petrus Paulus Maria Koop comes from a Catholic family. His father was a bishop in Brazil. Petrus was selected for the seminary, did a bit, got out and went looking for a ship.

'I always wanted to go to sea,' he says.

His ship was launched in eastern Germany in 1998, but her architects and designers must have acquired their principles in an earlier era. When I succeed in gaining entry to the navigation bridge I find a room like a seventies space mission; form is placed at the complete service of function, but function is rendered in pleasingly human terms. There are two soft seats either side of the central control console, with seat belts. After the *Gerd*'s austere standing spaces and multiple computer screens this seems both superannuated and decadent. Apparently we are slightly longer than the average wave length: riding them will be entertaining, but the thought of seat belts rather alarms.

'So we go up, up, and down down!' says the Captain, grinning like a shark. She is 210 metres long so he must be talking about mighty waves. Force eight to nine is forecast.

'What are we carrying, Captain?'

'Well, we don't know, but definitely expensive cars – they don't want someone driving them on and off a car carrier. And milk and cheese. We take our milk and cheese to Montreal and bring their milk and cheese back.'

Similarly, he says, countries swap hi-fis and electrical goods.

'We take Philips and Grundig and Bang & Olufsen to the East and bring Sony and Hitachi back.'

If global trade is a question of swapping brands across the oceans it is no surprise it is faltering.

'On the way back from Halifax we bring live shellfish. Lobsters. Two tanks in forty-foot refrigerated containers. The crew must check them every four hours.'

Nestor Loste, the electrician, my neighbour in the next cabin, will risk his life climbing a ladder while freezing gales threaten to throw him tumbledown to the heaving deck to make sure the poor buggers are still alive *every four hours*? The Captain smiles at my incredulity.

At quarter past six we meet in the bar, preparatory to 'going down'. Two Europeans sit with the Captain under strip lighting in the mess which adjoins the bar. The room is bare but for three pot plants and a few chairs. The bar makes a recessed and inviting cove of warm lights and colours, opposite. Its walls are decorated with the ship's battle honours, plaques and photographs presented to her on the occasion of her first visits to various ports. None of them refer to the ship by her present identity. The effect is a small and surreal display commemorating the first arrivals of a ship named P&O *Nedlloyd Sydney* in Portland, Hong Kong, Seattle, Barcelona, Southampton and Auckland.

A small case contains three coins and an inscription: 'A Guilder, a Pound and a Mark were placed under the keel at the Keel Laying Ceremony 3rd November 1997 to wish the ship a prosperous life'. The following year, according to another notice, the MV P&O *Nedlloyd Sydney* was christened by her 'Godmother', a Mrs Gail Fletcher. All this ceremony, recalling the Peninsular & Orient Line's traditions, which go back to the company's founding in 1822, comes to an end with a laminated notice run up by someone on a computer.

'Welcome to the Beer Museum', it begins. 'Historic Facts: 1st April 2007, A sad day in the history of shipping. It was the day that Maersk Line forced ex PONL ships to implement "Zero Alcohol" policy. On display are two rare items of alcoholic beverage, as was enjoyed by staff, officers and crew after a hard days work. Please, do not touch the items on display. Look at them and let your mind wander to days of ships with happy crews. Free admission.'

'It was a very social place,' the Captain says, 'before.'

Our assembly in the adjoining room is a strange mixture of awkwardness and charm. Because the bar serves no drinks no one has anything in his hands. There are no snacks or anything that can be asked for, passed or partaken. There is no moment at which the ritual naturally ends. In a lull in the conversation Captain Koop jerks his hands, drums them once on his seat and says 'OK! Let's see what we have tonight!'

At this we rise and descend six floors to the dining room. The high spirits which accompany this descent are partly a function of relief at escaping from the mess, a room which seemed to solicit awkward silences, and partly due to the anticipation of food. In the bar, often, we sit in each other's company and wonder what to say.

This first night, though, is a joy. Pieter Mulder is the chief engineer. Unlike his peers on the *Gerd* he also wears full uniform. Johannes, a tough-looking Dutchman, our mechanic, never does. Pieter is a sweet, gentle man with the kind of face you want to see smile and laugh, which it does eagerly, sympathetically, at the least excuse.

'I wanted to join the Dutch navy,' he says at dinner, 'but they said I was "not assertive enough".'

'You're too nice, clearly,' I say, angry on his behalf.

Johannes – Jannie – is another kind man, eyes bagged like a smoking dog, gentle and possessed of a great store of stories, one of the best on the ship. His English is an embarrassment to him so many of these come out in Dutch, engrossing the chief and the Captain.

'I speak Indonesian,' he explains, 'but I never sailed with Filipinos before and I can't get their language at all. What is it, a mixture of Spanish and Chinese?'

Dinner begins with an atrocious soup, salt solution with coloured lumps. Things pick up with the main: perfect broccoli, roast potatoes with rosemary and lamb chops.

'Annabelle has done well,' the Captain pronounces. Our chief cook is not a man – the first woman the Captain has ever sailed with. Our chief steward, Mark, evidently works out. He is constantly smiling, friendly and so generous with his sing-song deference you almost feel uneasy. It takes me two days to stop him calling me 'Sir' and get him on to Horace instead.

The Captain has a rather old-fashioned approach to the division of rank. He expects to be waited on well. Mark obliges. The formality is of a piece with the uniforms and the ritual honouring of the past. In the age of the liners, crossing the Atlantic was a serious culinary experience and a great social occasion, part trial, part triumph. In the 1890s Cunard was pleased to offer its first-class passengers ten meals every day. A typical menu ran:

Before breakfast: grapes, melons, etc.
Breakfast: 'Almost anything on earth'
11 a.m.: Pint cup of bouillon
Noon: Sandwiches carried about the decks
1 p.m.: Lunch
3 p.m.: Trays of ices
4 p.m.: Tea
5 p.m.: Toffee or sweets carried round on trays
7 p.m.: Dinner
9 p.m.: Supper

That 'Almost anything on earth' was not a whimsical proposition. Before the age of luxury sea travel ended in the 1960s, an American oil magnate, travelling on the *Queen Mary*, took seriously the menu's urging not to limit his choice to the listings, and asked for rattlesnake steaks for four.

'His order was gravely taken, and his party was served eels in a silver salver borne by two stewards shaking rattles.

There were sixteen kinds of breakfast cereal every morning, and each liner, on each crossing, carried fifty pounds of mint leaves to make mint juleps.'[2]

From the end of the nineteenth century to the middle of the twentieth, war years excepted, the ocean liners ruled the Atlantic. They were the biggest, regularly the fastest and certainly the most luxurious passenger ships ever seen. On the maiden voyage of the *Normandie* in 1935 the suite of the wife of the French President, Madame Lebrun, was guarded by a sailor with a pike. Crown Prince Akihito of Japan won the table-tennis tournament on the *Queen Elizabeth*. The Duchess of Windsor ordered the colour of her suites in advance. She liked electric greens and blues. On the *Pembroke* we have no mint, no juleps and no pikes, but we do dress for dinner, or at least shower for it, and there is royalty at the Captain's table.

A portrait of Queen Beatrix of the Netherlands overlooks us from the bulkhead. She is smiling kindly.

'She's much better-looking than those miserable royals who watch over you on Danish ships.'

Roars of laughter greet this sally, encouraging further forays.

'Since our Danish friends – invited us to join them . . .' Pieter says, shaking his head. All three mourn the Maersk purchase of Nedlloyd. The Old Days were clearly more fun here too: how much more fun will become horribly clear. I congratulate them on their potted plants, which line the

[2] Terry Coleman, *The Liners: A History of the North Atlantic Crossing*, Allen Lane, London 1976.

windows. The Captain pretends he has never noticed them before.

'Aren't they all dead?'

'No,' Pieter says, 'but look, they are all trying to get out! They are trying to get to the kitchen!'

And they are, they all strain towards the door. We find this very funny. There is also laughter from the kitchen, and from the crew mess beyond. You can hear men singing, and strange, eerie piano music playing. She seems a happy and haunted ship. The cranes have only worked for an hour or two but already we are higher in the water. The Captain says she is never fully loaded on this run because of minimum draughts on the St Lawrence River. She was built for the South Pacific, he says, Australia particularly, hence the open bridge wings – the part of the bridge which extends as far as the side of the ship. When you manoeuvre a ship close to shore, or if a boat comes alongside, you have to stand on the wings to see what is going on. Doing that on this run will be bitter. The Captain has seen a hundred shores from up here. He was first mate on her before he got his master's ticket and command.

'Have you met John? He's a character,' says Pieter.

'Oh he's quite a character,' the Captain chuckles. Jannie grins and shakes his head.

John Holmshaw, the second mate, is a Geordie. We snap together in the corridor like old friends. A fellow Brit! What a treat. John is tall and broad, a fine fighting outline overlaid with softness. The expression is warm and friendly, humour in the eyes given an exclamation mark by a wayward tooth. He can look unbelievably shabby, a sea tramp, or surpris-

ingly smart in uniform. His legs seem permanently bent at
the knee. This gives him a miraculous, shuffling stability.
He immediately informs me that he is the best-paid second
officer in the fleet.

'Ah've got a master's certificate, like, and they want me
to sit for chief officer, but naa, ah don't want to. Too much
work. Ah'm happy with second.'

A lot of John's conversation is conveyed with gestures
and expressions. His face is compelling, with appealing eyes
below black, once-thick hair and above a chin of two pendu-
lous bulbs. He shows me a picture of Theresa, his girl, who
spends part of her time on the Tyne, waiting for him at his
place in South Shields, and part of it on the Gold Coast of
Australia, where she has a house. John's favourite picture
of Theresa has her sitting on a bed in a cell, behind bars.

'Locked her in,' he burbles happily, 'so she'll be waiting
for me when I come home.' Theresa is blonde and beautiful
and she gazes at John's camera with utter love.

John's cabin, next to mine, is worse than any teenager's
room. It looks as though it has been shelled. Everything is
broken. The drawers under the bed are held shut, or perhaps
together, by gaffer tape. An extraordinary thing like an art
installation dangles from the air vent in the ceiling, apparently an unsuccessful attempt to block it, giving the impression of a giant dressing hanging off a wound.

John says we may do a Great Circle to avoid the storms.
In any case we will pass far north of where the *Titanic*
foundered, in April 1912.

He has been thirty-two years at sea and he collects
disaster stories. John's stories should be heard in a Geordie

accent. They are accompanied by an intense, assessing gaze on the part of the teller. His eyes search your expression for gratifying signs of horror, distress and amazement. Within about five minutes of meeting John I am engrossed in the fate of a ferry making a run from Savannah, Georgia, up to New York.

'The Captain dies, so everyone moves up. But they didn't know their jobs. A fire breaks out in the bow, right, and the chief officer, who's the Captain now, increases speed. Increases! So of course the flames blow back over the ship. People tried to get out of their cabin windows but they didn't quite fit, and that's how they found them . . .'

I feel a bit sick. John continues.

'There was a British ship on the River Plate passing a tanker in fog. And they touch, you know, and fire breaks out. The air rushing to the fire causes a vacuum. Seventy-two people died. Asphyxiated. The tanker crew survived by jumping into the water on the opposite side.'

'Christ.'

'It's my job to show you the lifeboats and things but there's no rush,' he says.

'John, if anything happens I'm sticking to you.'

He shows me the controls on the bridge as if at some point I will be taking over. My favourite detail is a piece of A4 paper mounted on the chart table, a hand-drawn map labelled NEWARK. Red crayoned arrows coming up from the south turn left short of the Statue of Liberty, encounter a felt-tipped green TUG, pass a tank farm and a football field, turn right, avoiding New York container berth, which is marked with a cross, before turning left and coming to rest at the foot of a sketched aeroplane on the runway at Newark airport. Whatever else happens, the *Pembroke* will always be able to find her way there.

I go up and down the ship after this, doing my washing and feeling her spirits. She may be at the furthest end of the aesthetic spectrum from the tall ships Chateaubriand describes, but she is still a sentient structure, invitingly higgledy-piggledy. There is a library of near-smashed paperbacks. Hammond Innes, Ken Follett, James Hadley Chase, Clancy . . . You feel she has been lived in and loved in and loved.

'She has been all over the world,' the Captain said, and the bow shows it. Driving through westerlies and pushing through ice up the St Lawrence, she is down to her bare iron.

'If we can do without an icebreaker we will but sometimes you hit it and it does not move,' said the Captain.

CHAPTER 15

Down-Channel

The pillowcases smell of old sweat, the sheets of unwashed men and tobacco. You wake to reeks of diesel. The ship gently lists as containers are loaded, rising from the deck and approaching the level of my window. If only one could disable the ventilator the diesel fumes might be stemmed. I resolve to sleep with the door open. On the way to breakfast I meet a man called Book. He is a fitter, a junior mechanic who leads the oilers and wipers in maintenance work in the engine room.

'Why are you called Book?'

'Because I am handsome!'

'OK!'

He talks about being chased by pirates. 'We should be pirates,' he laughs. Book wears a pirate headscarf.

All day, under rain and container booms, the ship lists and twitches as if she is being slowly beaten. The draughts in the stairwell complain. The crane operators break for lunch and tea. You would not see that in the East.

At 1630 we leave the berth. The Schelde out of Antwerp must present the least promising, most grey and rainswept, most blurred and smoking, towered and glowering, twisted, flat-banked and ship-stormed road to the ocean in all the world. The Deurganck nuclear power station pours steam unbroken into cloud and the river seethes at its outfall. The turns are tight as we join a press of ships, all leaving on the tide. The southern shore is a low marsh of dreary non-colours. The opposite bank is fired with refinery towers and warning lights. The river looks closer to dirt than water, thrashed by the passage of the ships.

The *King Daniel*, home port Palermo, is a villainous tanker. There are Hapag-Lloyd container carriers and the *Philadelphia Express*, a fat car carrier, and even they look smarter than poor *Pembroke*. The cargo planners have broken our lines into lumps of containers, apparently scattered at random. Naked grey hatch covers shine with rain. Asymmetric blocks of reefers catch the wind, which is strong from the south-west and growling around the bridge.

After the *Gerd* we seem quixotic, a battering barge to her cargo liner. How much difference can our containers possibly make to the vast hinterlands of Montreal? With freight rates currently below the cost of shipping the containers, and the oil price high, our only certain achievement is a speck of red on the chart of the company's losses. But the ship rushes on, fixed on the doing of the thing; the why of it as little concern as the low green farmland and the black trees darkening behind the dykes. We alter course every few minutes, three hundred degrees now, as the river turns north-west. The bo'sun, Edgar 'Sumy' Sumudlayon, is at

the wheel. Sumy is the tallest of the Filipinos, a tough young
man whose attention switches between the course, the river
and the rate-of-turn indicator. In the left seat is the pilot;
Captain Koop on the right. Flemish and Dutch come over
the radio and the river switches again.

'Starboard twenty!'

That is a rate of turn. Now the pilot asks for ten more
degrees and we round another red buoy. We pass grain
elevators, cement works and jumbles of boats as a flight of
greylag geese come over, thirty birds in five skeins.

'Full ahead!'

A container carrier comes up, *A La Marne*, blue and red,
carrying K-Line and Hamburg Sud boxes, her bows like
ours a snarl of rusted steel. The sky is towering and gigantic
now, grey-white cumulus to the horizon. We overhaul a
Dutch barge. They look so mighty on the Maas, as you walk
in Rotterdam, but they are bike couriers on this coast. The
north shore is closer as we come back to 325, blocky buildings behind sprays of bare woods with pylons behind them.
Ships travelling at speed heel over as they make their turns.
There are lilac clouds now and the river is rot-gut green.
It is thrilling, this weather, this twisting exit, this speed, as
we turn into the Overloop Van Hansweert, which leads to
the bend of Gat Van Ossenisse. We will soon be down there,
where the Das Van Terneuzen leads to the Rede Van
Vlissingen, Flushing Roads. The Captain shows the bend
on the chart, just after our dog-leg out of Deurganck, where
container ships go aground. We are deep in the water, ten
and a half metres: going into Flushing there are only five
or six metres of water under the keel.

Flushing Roads in a February dusk is no place for an amateur; I am surely the only one out here, circling the deck as the light dies. The walkway is narrow, pitted and sheened with spray and grease. The wind bursts between the cargo stacks and ships bigger than ours pass, dark and huge in the dim. Our foremost cargo is some sort of tractor, wrapped in a flapping tarpaulin. The bow is too slippery, too low-gunnelled to be safe. I skid from hand hold to hand hold and retreat, wuthered, chilled and trepid as a kitten. After a bolted supper I am back on the bridge.

'Force six-o-seven, Captain?'

'Ah, she always sounds loud! Five-o-six. Maybe seven further out. I hope we can get the pilots on and off . . .'

In Flushing Roads the river pilot puts the ship hard to port, making a lee in which the pilot boat approaches. The Captain hauls on his jacket and cracks open the iron dogs, the clips which secure the bridge doors. He peers out into the rain while the river pilot descends and the sea pilot comes up, blowing into his extravagant beard. The forecast is gales from the south-west.

The *Pembroke* is a living thing tonight. She helps you open some doors and puts an invisible shoulder against others. When the draughts around her bridge are not moaning they cheep and whistle to themselves like birds. The windscreen wipers take irregular rests between wheezing cycles. As the slacking tide meets the sea you can feel the ship wobble, like someone stepping into sudden darkness. Beyond the screens there is blackness, rain, the channel markers and now the low orange glow of Zeebrugge to the south.

It is impossible to pass the harbour lights and not think of another bitter night, 6 March 1987, when the ferry *Herald of Free Enterprise* capsized there. Within two minutes of leaving Zeebrugge harbour with her bow doors open the ship was on her side, resting on a sandbar. Many of the passengers had saved up coupons from the *Sun* newspaper which promised a day return to Belgium for a pound. One of those, Simon Osborne, was then nineteen years old.

'The noise was horrendous from start to finish,' he told the BBC, 'a terrible, unbelievable mechanic grinding noise, breaking glass and the screams of people who were injured, falling or terrified. I was trapped in the lounge area of the ship. There were a lot of people around me, but as time wore on it became clear that many were dying, presumably from the cold . . .'

A hundred and ninety-three people perished in the worst disaster involving a British ship in peacetime since the *Titanic*. For weeks the media carried images of the bright orange corpse of the ferry lying in the water under the lights of rescue vessels, and of the haunted faces of survivors and the bereaved.

The immediate cause of the ferry's capsize was the negligence of two seafarers – the assistant bo'sun, who had overslept, and the first officer, who was hurrying to return to his station on the bridge. Each thought the other would close the doors. But if the *Herald of Free Enterprise* was a symptom of her era, then, according to the findings of the inquiry into the sinking, 1987 was a time of a corporate hunger for profit which alienated workers from management. Seamen's requests for a monitoring system to inform captains that the bow was secured for sea had been dismissed as unnecessary expense. The ship left her berth in a rush, as was her custom, and slightly overweight. The cross-Channel ferries were still immensely lucrative in the years before the Channel Tunnel opened; the *Herald* was designed to load and unload quickly, and to accelerate fast. She reached eighteen knots only ninety seconds after leaving the harbour, piling up a bow wave which swept inboard and sank her 'as quickly as a glass of water falling over', Simon Osborne said.

Though the Court of Inquiry condemned 'a disease of sloppiness' 'infecting every level of the company', a charge of corporate manslaughter against the operators collapsed, the judge directing the jury to acquit the company and its management. No evidence existed to show that a single senior figure had behaved recklessly, he said. Perhaps the most telling aspect of the tragedy is this failure of the law to hold the parent company, P&O European Ferries, to account. At the time corporate manslaughter was much more likely to be pursued successfully against small companies in which one person could be held to be a 'controlling mind'. Suits against large corporations were (and still are) rarely successful because the bigger the company, and the higher the degree of delegation within it, the less chance there is that one person could be said to be 'a controlling mind'. A revision of the law in 2007 exempts individuals from prosecution, allowing instead for companies to be fined. In the months after the disaster Labour Members of Parliament expressed outrage that a management shuffle was the only apparent price paid by the ferry company.

Hansard records a typical reaction from the left-wing benches to a statement on the disaster by the then Secretary of State for Transport, Paul Channon.

> Mr Max Madden (Bradford, West): Is the epitaph of the tragedy that profit prevailed over safety? [. . .] Will the Secretary of State understand that many people believe that the captain and crew have been made scapegoats and that the company has been protected, as a major contributor to the Conservative party?

> Mr Channon: I hope that, on reflection, the hon. Gentleman will regret that remark. [. . .] I have been extremely scathing about the company, and in doing so I have echoed what the judge said.

The controlling mind on the *Pembroke* seems at ease this evening. As the lights of Walcheren in the Netherlands diminish behind us the Captain whistles 'The Magic Flute', unconcerned by any superstition. The names of the sandbars around us could have been announced by the rolls of the tide on the dark thrusts of the banks themselves: Raan, Droogte Van Schoonveldt, Wandelaar.

At 2130 the pilot leaves us, taken off by a scarlet catamaran. Two searchlights blaze the water as men in red and yellow safety suits catch the pilot and haul him down to safety.

'They use the catarmaran in force seven or above,' shouts the Captain, watching from the bridge wing. 'But it damages very easily. It's always off for repairs.'

Twenty-seven ships light the sea ahead, anchored off the Wandelaar Bank. We bear west into the oil-black Channel. The clouds part ahead and we sail into a cold and moonless clear; Venus is so bright we mistake it for a helicopter. Orion shows to the south and the lights of the coast are French now, not Belgian. The chart is shoaled with banks to landward, the memories of a continent that once reached further west. They set the autopilot, turn out all the deck lights and the gangway crew stand down. No one else will leave or join us and we will touch no land until Canada. Even the little blue leading light on the foremast is dimmed. The Captain shows me the Aldis lamp, familiar from war films in which they were used to flash Morse code from ship to ship. He talks of rumours that GPS is going to become less reliable: 'The satellites are getting old. They'll have to shoot stars again!'

Studying the automatic identification system, the radar, and the lights outside, the Channel seems busy to me, even by its standards of five hundred ship passages every twenty-four hours. It is glutted with vessels, many, like us, plunging to repair deadlines broken by the strike. We are cutting north-west across the traffic to the south-bound lane on the English side. We will turn south once we reach it and follow the lanes and traffic control schemes all the way to the Scillies.

'It's all different now,' the Captain says. 'When I first went to South America we carried the equivalent of three hundred and fifty containers but there were no containers then. Ships had two derricks, you linked one to a line from a crane on shore and controlled them both. You had to be pretty handy! Mostly it was done by stevedores.'

Their route went Amsterdam, Bremerhaven, Hamburg, Recife, Buenos Aires. They took cars and electrical goods to Latin America, bringing back coffee, tobacco, hardwoods and beef, the latter in freezing holds.

'You would be a week unloading and a week loading! Wonderful! You did not want to come back. I did not save any money . . .'

The shorescapes of Captain Koop's memories were gradually then entirely erased by what became known as the intermodal shipping container. Our steel boxes were invented in 1955 by Malcolm Maclean, the owner of a trucking company in North Carolina. By the end of the following decade, centuries-old cultures of rackety docks and sailors with the time to spend wages were gone or going, along with the waterfront worlds the Captain remembers. Container ships needed deep quays which could support huge cranes; the containers needed miles of space where they could be stacked and shunted; the trucks that carried them to and from the ports needed fast connections to motorways. The piers and warehouses of some of the world's greatest cities, the capitals of the ages of sail and steam, were now obsolete: London, Manhattan and San Francisco still have their docklands and wharves but the only cargo ships that work them are becalmed in photographs on the walls of bars and restaurants. Big ships still ply the lower Thames, and the Mersey, but they are straggled remnants of the great fleets of the past. Even here in the Channel, the world's busiest freight lane, the Captain says there are fewer ships these days. Trade has shrunk since 2008, and ships have grown bigger, he says.

He brings up an electronic chart of the Atlantic and clicks though the weather map. The ocean is swirled around with fletched arrows in spirals, indicating wind directions. Each feather on an arrow's tail indicates ten knots of wind speed. The western ocean is dark blue with projections of low pressure and high waves. Our course leads into an area of forty-knot winds and four- to five-metre swells.

'We can survive that, but no bigger,' he says. 'If you go too fast in six metres you kill your ship. The bow cannot take it.'

The Captain is desperate for speed but whichever way he plots the course the map's predicted waves demand a day of slow steaming, survival speed, at no more than ten knots. This means we need speed now, as we turn into the southbound lane at South Falls buoy, a critical point for ships transiting the Channel. Heavy traffic converges here and the sand waves on the seabed are in constant migration, monitored annually by the United Kingdom Hydrographic Office, which frets about vessels of ever-deeper draught on ever-tightening schedules making this crucial turn over sands that are never still. Our instruments say we are making eighteen knots' speed over ground, minus one knot of counter-current: the flow of the ebbing tide we came out on. We can see the lights of the French coast to port; to starboard is the orange twinkling of Ramsgate. We head straight for Orion and it is a freezing night.

I miss Shubd and Chris and Sorin! It's true, I miss my shipmates, Joel especially, and their mighty machine. I do like *Pembroke–Sydney* – she is a beguiling character – but the *Gerd* will always be the ship to measure others by. And Captain Larsen, so inimitably himself, so fearsome and gruffly kind, is my template. Captain Koop, with his moustache, looks a little like a rugby-playing John Cleese. He is entirely obliging and tirelessly helpful – 'Look, I'll show you' is his catchphrase. The third mate, Chicoy, has the size and shyness of a boy. He wears it severely, humourlessly, as if in compensation. I wait up for John, though time is confusing here. We are going back an hour at some point. He should be up soon.

The *Gerd* was such a luxurious machine, with miles of glass bridge wings and the wonderful after deck: there was always somewhere sheltered from the wind. *Pembroke* has iron emplacements on either side of the bridge which you can imagine shooting from, and nowhere to hide from the weather. She is much more feminine, with her homely and scattered accumulation of books, charts, coffee cups, magazines; her curtained-off radio and computer area, her wind-chatter and history. She seems to demand an equal return of masculinity: Captain Koop, with his bulk, is her perfect counterpoint. But there is an apprehension sailing with us. We are behind schedule, heading into bad weather, with boy-men instead of the easy professionals of the *Gerd*'s crew and only old and battered bow plates between us and the ocean which is always angry, so sailors say. This is what I hoped and bargained for but I feel a little like I did on my first night away from home.

Chicoy is excited about the Dover Strait because he will get a signal on his phone. Even with the lights of shores on either side of us he says, plaintively, 'Just like the Atlantic

– no ships!' (It must be a relative judgement as I can see several.) He says we will not see any when we get out beyond the Scillies. From Bishop Rock, to the west of the Scillies, we will make a Great Circle into the cold, in the hope of outmanoeuvring the weather.

The sea can take for ever and swallow it but land goes quickly. After Ramsgate come the lights of Dover; a ferry to Calais crosses the black water ahead, lit like a festival. The duty-free shops, the bars and cabins, the food . . . Does some smoker on deck see our lights? Certainly they do on her bridge, as we pass behind her.

Dover Coastguard, the voice of England, sounds tired, but his questions are all alert. By his tone you picture a man no longer young, in a white shirt – clean on today but past its best – with insignia on the shoulders, sleeves rolled up. Perhaps there is grey in his hair, which is retreating fast, and a coffee cup not far away, though not near enough to the instruments to cause any damage in case of upset. He is wearing a headset, the microphone suspended in front of his chin. The windows above his screen are dark and the light in the room comes from the computers. He looks at us, a triangle denoted by our name and call sign, Papa Delta Hotel Yankee, with our course, speed and destination all a button-press away. He recognises us, perhaps. He has a host of ships to contact; he may be weary but his questions are very courteous and he listens carefully to what we tell him. He knows dozens of ships can hear him, tuned in to his frequency, and dozens of judgements may be made each time he speaks. I cannot help wondering if he has a wife and children waiting for him somewhere in the dark mass of England, not far away. He sounds as though he has. You can imagine him serving toast to a teenager. He is not quite paternal with us, but he is not quite fraternal either. We are all working, this freezing black night. His voice has the assuredness of dry land about it but all his attention is out in the Channel with us. It is not surprising he sounds tired; it must be a stressful time for him. The coastguards are under assault from government cuts: eight of nineteen stations are being closed. Those remaining are tasked to cover wider areas and more ships with fewer officers. Our guardian, overseeing the world's busiest shipping lane, is now manning a downsized twenty-four-hour 'substation'.

'*Maersk Pembroke, Maersk Pembroke*, Dover Coastguard, Dover Coastguard, over.'

Once contact has been established the questions come.

'*Maersk Pembroke*, what is your last port of call, over?'

Chicoy tells him.

'And your next destination, over?'

'Montreal,' Chicoy says.

'How many persons on board, please?'

'Twenty-four, figures two four, over.'

'Thank you – and are you carrying any dangerous cargo, over?'

Chicoy replies in the affirmative and reads a list of number and letter codes, corresponding to the contents of our dangerous, lethal and pollutant-carrying tanks and containers.

'And do you have any dangers or deficiencies to report, over?'

'Negative, Dover,' Chicoy says.

'*Maersk Pembroke*, Dover Coastguard, thank you. Have a good watch and a safe passage to your next destination.'

He wishes everyone the same thing. Each time the benediction sounds sincere.

'Thank you, sir, same to you,' says a Russian officer. He is going to Vigo with a long list of dangerous cargo. A Swede is going to Shoreham with a cargo of timber; a Brit is planning to 'steam up and down and kill time' until the tide is right at Rochester. An Indian is going to Santa Marta, Colombia, arriving on 1 March. What an exotic and curious place is the Channel! Add the stories of the hundreds on the ferries, and the ghosts of night-fighters and bombers in the air above us, not to mention the late long-haul flights and the last of the day's low-cost flocks, and the plans and tales of the seafarers, and the gripes and scores of the fishermen, and the missions, hopes and love-longings of those in the last trains in the tunnel below the seabed, and the English Channel is a universe, a dizzying nebula of life and history, all around us in the night.

When William of Orange dispatched four hundred ships through here in November 1688, on the way to Torbay, the landing site for his invasion of England, his fleet was so large it was able to salute Dover and Calais simultaneously. On our right lie the Goodwin Sands, 'a very dangerous flat and fatal, where the carcasses of many a tall ship lie buried, as they say', Salarino describes them in *The Merchant of Venice*. The chronicles of the crossings of this narrow sea begin with human history almost as far back as we can measure it. The first identifiable individual who made the journey did so around 2300 BC, in the very early Bronze

Age. Known as 'the Archer' because of the sixteen arrow-heads interred with him, he was buried with great wealth and ceremony at Amesbury, near Stonehenge, but oxygen isotopes in his teeth reveal he grew up in Switzerland or the Tyrol. He is likely to have made the voyage on a very calm day in a sewn-plank boat. The oldest example of a seagoing craft of this kind, dating to 1550 BC, was discovered beneath the streets of Dover in 1992. Before the invention of nails their planks were stitched together with roots and flexible wooden fibres. The enterprise and courage of the Archer notwithstanding, more than two millennia after his crossing, in 55 BC, Julius Caesar's legionaries protested that his expedition to Britain would require them to fight on the other side of what Romans called 'the green sea of darkness'. The Emperor Claudius had the same problem in AD 43. On being ordered to board their transports some of his soldiers sat on their spears and objected to fighting 'beyond the inhabited earth'.

John's alarm clock rings for a full minute before he is awake enough to silence it. He comes up to the bridge, acknowledging Chicoy's handover in gentle grunts, sleepy but interested. John produces his BlackBerry and mourns the absence of signal. He shows me some more pictures of smiling Theresa. He scrolls down to find some 'which show her figure'.

They are going to marry this year.

'She misses me terribly when I go to sea.'

When they have been together for two years the company will let him bring her aboard for a trip. As we pass over power lines and the Channel Tunnel, John recounts his education at a 'terrible school'. 'No English O-level, but I did get Chemistry, Physics and Maths. Went to sea with BP – four years on VLCCs – you know? Very Large Crude Carriers. You get a purge pipe spouting thirty foot of petrol, straight up. You're soaked in it. And you're in the Gulf, it's hot there and you're breathing petrol the whole time – you're high.'

Next he was on bulk carriers, which was much better, and then a multi-purpose carrier, which was the best.

'Party every night! The Captain was great, yeah. He let us do cargo-watch from the bar. Went to Rio a lot, girls and dancing, you know . . .'

All our lives are in John's hands until 4 a.m.; within moments this sleepy-looking man spots a crucial mistake. Chicoy has missed a waypoint, a course change, and plotted our progress straight into the south cardinal buoy at the tip of Varne Bank. John fiddles with the computer, lower lip stuck out, until we are safe. The threatened gale is beginning as a fresh wind from the English side. We have passed Boulogne and Dungeness now, Orion has ridden westwards and the sea ahead is so dark you cannot believe that there is anything there at all. John wants to talk on, about photography, but I must, must sleep.

CHAPTER 16

The Western Approaches

We sail through an exhilaration of white horses and rainbowed spray, into a clear morning with gannets diving. The temperature is six degrees but the wind is teary cold. Portland is just visible to the north and the Cherbourg peninsula of France is a low line to the south: it is a surprise to be able to see both at once, this far west. From a beach in Dorset you feel France might be out there somewhere, but to paddle for it you would have to be either mad or expert. By 750 BC there was a busy trade between the two; Britons exchanged metals for wine and pottery from Amorica. This morning all the trade is passing through the Channel rather than across it. There are ships in lanes around us, mostly small coasters, and two large carriers out ahead, one off each side of the bow.

Erwin is on the bridge, a young man with a real thrust to his jaw, such as you would need if you were to be a chief officer at the age of twenty-eight. His last run was the Gulf to Somalia and back, over and over again, carrying containers. He puts his success down to luck and learning. He and

Chicoy are the same height, barely five and a half feet, but Erwin is a lesson in accrued authority, lightly worn.

The chart says we are heading into the Western Approaches. To preceding generations, and to anyone reared on the novels of Nicholas Monsarrat, Alistair MacLean or Geoffrey Jenkins, the phrase means more than the sea area it describes. The Western Approaches were the first of the killing grounds of the struggle at sea in the Great War, and, even more terribly, during the Battle of the Atlantic, 1939–45. That conflict took the lives of more than 100,000 seamen and sent more than fourteen and a half million tonnes of merchant ships to the bottom, along with 175 of the Allied warships that tried to protect them and 783 German submarines sent out to destroy. As we surge three abreast with two coasters, on this gannets' morning, with the sun bright behind us and England falling back into Lyme Bay, we are setting out across a monstrous graveyard.

On the seabed directly ahead of us, upside down in sixty metres of water, is the wreck of HMS *Formidable*, a British battleship torpedoed in the small hours of New Year's Day 1915. As dusk fell on the first year of the Great War, *Formidable* was returning from gunnery exercises with her full complement of 780 men. She had been launched in 1898; for all her Krupp armour and fifty-tonne guns she was obsolete when war broke out. A submarine had been reported in the area but the weather was so rough it was thought that no U-boat could attack. The *U-24*, under the command of Rudolf Schneider, struck at twenty past two in the morning, torpedoing the ship's starboard side. *Formidable*'s Captain, Noel Loxley, thought at first that he might make land, but the battleship listed rapidly. In gale-force winds, rain and hail, with swells running to nine metres high, Loxley gave the order to abandon ship. To lower a boat in such conditions would be a desperate business even from a modern vessel in perfect working order. As *Formidable* leaned twenty degrees to starboard the crew struggled to get their boats away. Some hit the water upside down, some were smashed as they fell, others were swamped. Schneider's second torpedo struck the ship's port side. It was reported by survivors that in her final moments, when the ship gave a tremendous lurch, Captain Loxley cried, 'Lads, this is the last, all hands for themselves, and may God bless you and guide you to safety.' He is then said to have lit a cigarette and walked to the forebridge. The battleship capsized, rolling over men in the water as she sank. Five hundred and forty-seven died, including the Captain.

Most of the dead have no headstone. 'Auf einem Seemannsgrab, da blühen keine Rosen' ran a German folk-song of the era: 'On a sailor's grave no roses bloom'. Among those whose bodies were washed or carried ashore were twins, John and Henri Villiers-Russell, aged twenty-nine, who are buried in the churchyard of St Michael's Coppenhall in Cheshire. Employed at the Crewe Railway Works, they were also members of the St John Ambulance Brigade and the Royal Navy Sick Berth Reserve. During their summer holiday of 1914 they joined *Formidable* for a week's training. War broke out when they were aboard and they volunteered to stay on. Like those of many of their shipmates, the twins' names are recorded on a memorial to the dead in the parish where they grew up; many more of the names of the ship's dead are inscribed on panels around the bases of the Naval Memorial obelisks at Chatham, Portsmouth and Plymouth. The body of Captain Loxley's fox terrier, Bruce, was washed ashore. As a war dog, his grave is kept at Abbotsbury Gardens in Dorset.

The volunteering twins, the scattered memorials to the crew, Loxley's perfect fulfilment of naval archetype and the grave of his dog seem to cut a cross section across the grain of the Great War, and of the spirit of the dying Empire: class, rank, heroic tradition and reverence for animals, all undone by the assumption that new weapons would not work in foul weather. HMS *Formidable* was the first British battleship to be sunk by enemy attack in the First World War, her fate a sign of the terrible efficacy of the U-boat campaigns. By mid-1916 Britain's food stocks were perilously low; at the end of the year the Admiralty was reporting to David Lloyd George, the new Prime Minister, that the war at sea was all but lost, and advising him to negotiate a peace with Germany. Lloyd George refused, and ordered the inauguration of the convoy system. The idea of grouping merchant ships together under naval escort faced great resistance, not least from shipowners and speculators, war profiteers, who were making huge sums out of insurance on ships that were sunk, as well as government subsidies and dividends paid to investors in shipping. The contrast between the situation of these figures and that of the men who crewed their ships could scarcely be more savage. A merchant seaman's pay was stopped from the moment he took to his lifeboat. If he survived he could not expect to be paid again until he joined another ship in one of the convoys which saw the country through the end of the first war and sustained it throughout the second. Some men were torpedoed and rescued three times: 100,000 of them were less lucky. It is the heaving grave-waters of the convoys' crews and the sailors who fought to protect them that we will travel through. Most of the iron carcasses we will pass over will not be warships, but merchant vessels, the ancestors of our own.

Breakfast is mango yoghurt, hard fried eggs and something like catfood with potatoes. Annabelle is making beautiful cinnamon and apple tarts. She gives me to understand that 8.15 is rather late. Mark, the steward, says his admirable figure is thanks to his use of dumb-bells. 'I quit smoking!' he cries triumphantly, then confides, 'I saw all these actors with good bodies and I wanted to have one too.'

Now there are heather-coloured cloud shadows on the green water.

'Warship *Dragon*, Warship *Dragon*, Warship *Dragon*,' announces the radio. 'Live firing, Lyme Bay. Go to channel eight, out.'

Tune in or get shot, runs the apparent subtext.

Someone ignores him magnificently. Warship *Dragon* – one of Britain's new Type 45 destroyers, carrying one of the world's most sophisticated radar systems and enough weaponry, it is reported, to down all the warplanes in South America pretty well simultaneously – calls repeatedly, imploring the renegade to respond. Warship *Dragon* gives his antagonist's course (220 degrees), position (seven miles south-west of Portland) and speed, thirteen knots, and receives no reply. The mystery vessel lets him sweat for a while (there is no way they cannot hear *Dragon*), until at last a laid-back Indian-sounding voice acknowledges.

'We are about to commence gunnery firing,' says *Dragon*, sounding more conciliatory now. 'Could you alter your course southwards, so that we can proceed with our serial, over?'

The Indian lets him sweat again. By the time he agrees to go to Channel 8 to discuss the matter Warship *Dragon* is calling him 'sir'.

Now a French fishing vessel, *Flaneur*, crosses our wake coming up from the south and heading into Lyme Bay. He immediately attracts *Dragon*'s attention. The fisherman calls *Dragon* 'sir' in the most delightful French accent but fails to change his course by a single degree. I wish I could see *Dragon*; she must be lying to the north-east where there is a warship-coloured haze against the land. The rest of the horizon is a sharp cut line, slightly bowed.

Coffee is taken at 10.30 in the harbour control room, a happy occasion, blessed with Annabelle's cinnamon apple tart. Pieter makes us all laugh, Jannie makes the Dutch laugh in Dutch and the Captain tells a story about the Filipinos' love of music. Apparently their union, which struggles to protect or significantly enrich them, has won them the right to have a karaoke machine on any ship with a given number of Filipino crew.

'One captain of the *Palermo* [our sister ship, on the same run] bought them a drum kit, keyboards and two guitars. The next captain hates the noise they make, so he has it all shifted to another ship. Two weeks after he's done it he gets transferred to the same ship!'

On the bridge, studying the day and the instruments, I note that she claims to have done 608,738 nautical miles. This indicates that *Pembroke* is just embarking on the equivalent of her second return leg from the moon. She is burning seventy tonnes of fuel a day at our present speed – eighteen knots – and thereby costing the company over fifty-six thousand US dollars every twenty-four hours. At twenty-three dollars a day the services of Richard, our assistant steward, are cheap indeed.

'It's always warm down here,' says Pieter, as a lovely pre-spring day passes by outside. There are five black-backed gulls in the water; I wonder which pirates' souls they are. Judging by our position, south-east of Plymouth, probably Drake and his men. Their voyage around the world, only the second circumnavigation of the globe, started badly hereabouts, according to Francis Pretty, a gentleman at arms who sailed with him.

The 15th day of November, in the year of our Lord 1577, Master Francis Drake, with a fleet of five ships and barks, and to the number of 164 men, gentlemen and sailors, departed from Plymouth, giving out his pretended voyage for Alexandria. But the wind falling contrary, he was forced the next morning to put into Falmouth Haven, in Cornwall, where such and so terrible a tempest took us, as few men have seen the like, and was indeed so vehement that all our ships were like to have gone to wrack. But it pleased God to preserve us from that extremity, and to afflict us only for that present with these two particulars: the mast of our

Admiral, which was the *Pelican*, was cut overboard for the safeguard of the ship, and the *Marigold* was driven ashore, and somewhat bruised. For the repairing of which damages we returned again to Plymouth; and having recovered those harms, and brought the ships again to good state, we set forth the second time from Plymouth, and set sail the 13th day of December following . . .

British understatement has been somewhat diluted by time. A contemporary writer would struggle not to make more of the dire battle to cut the mainmast off the *Pelican* (later renamed *Golden Hind*) in order to save the ship from the tempest. Being driven ashore in the *Marigold* at the height of the gale would surely leave her and her crew, now, more than 'somewhat bruised'.

There are a few trawlers about, and the gannets still, but it is the land which draws the eye. Francis Pretty must have glanced back at it four hundred years ago. What that low green line has meant to so many, over so many ages! Ever since we went to sea it has been our home, for home is a thing sailors and travellers have to leave to know. You can still hear the leavened joy of reaquaintance on the deck of a ferry approaching Dover. You detect something of what the Welsh call *hiraeth*, a kind of longing, when your aeroplane drops below the cloud base on approach to Heathrow. People peer down at sodden fields and motorways of rain and say, 'Oh God, look at it!' with mock-horrified affection.

As the coast curves away towards Fowey and St Austell, and the voice of Brixham Coastguard comes over Channel 16, I match the names on the chart to the little clusters of habitation, staring through binoculars and sounding their syllables with a funny feeling in my stomach. Salcombe, Plymouth, Falmouth . . . is it sentimental, is it silly, to feel this – whatever it is – at their parade of echo and associ- ation? People from these shores and their hinterlands have set so much by them, done so much from them and for them. The towns on the edge of the sea have so rung with news of blood and valour. It means what, that I feel I can almost hear it? That I am British? That I am one of the tiny multitudes who recognise these places, though I do not know them, though I have no personal connection with any, beyond this feeling, a throb like lost familiarity? To the majority of passing seafarers – even to the minority who actually see them, those on the bridges of ships who unfold this scroll of places with their charts – the names and the notches of coves, the white crumbs of structures and the lights that signify them at night tow no freight of meaning, tell no story, teach nothing.

I know a man who met a pirate off Brixham. Pete was sailing with his brother when a vicious-looking man in a speedboat pulled up alongside and gave Pete an evil look. Pete called his brother up to the deck, and the man powered off. A few minutes later there was a shout over the radio and a puff of flame and smoke from a yacht ahead of them. The pirate had thrown a petrol bomb at it. Pete and his brother went to give assistance, the fire was extinguished, the yacht saved and a search launched for the pirate. He was found, later, having lost his boat, clinging to a buoy.

*   *   *

Chicoy is talkative this morning. Neither of us could believe the other's age: he is thirty-six, and looks much younger. He thought I was younger too. He has three children.

'When you need money you have to go to sea,' he says. He sadly regrets not buying property years ago – now land in the Philippines is very expensive. Manila is jammed with traffic, and he needs money, money, money. How far from home he is in this foreign sea. He would do three months on, three months off if it were not for the money. He sees no way around this exile.

'No chop-chop for voyage contractor,' he smiles, bitterly, rubbing thumb and finger together. 'No chop-chop . . .'

He says he could not sleep after his watch last night, because he was worrying about money. His sparse beard makes him look so young.

Eight fishing boats surround us now, including one with a red mizzen sail from Guernsey. When the nets are down rafts of gulls sit on the water, waiting for the hauling to begin, whereupon they fill the air, a white and screaming sky-wake. Fulmars are the most active of all the birds, in their ceaseless soaring.

By noon the thermometer shows thirteen degrees and it is hot on the bridge with all the radiators on. Cornwall is blue as hardened sky. We seem to have sailed into the first day of spring. The sea is soft and we ride soporifically.

John comes up at ten to twelve, splendid in white uniform shirt and polished boots. He shows me where the life jackets are, five floors below us, in a red box on the deck on the port side. I am assigned to the port lifeboat. Even if we are fleeing over the starboard side I must still go to port to get my jacket. If any alarm goes off my station is on the bridge. An emergency seemed thoroughly unlikely on the *Gerd* but quite possible here.

The gannets have found a shoal, five of them are missiling into it, throwing up gouts of white spray, as the Cornish coast curves back towards us. The land slopes, low rumpled hills flatten down to the Lizard. Two tankers – I am learning to call them Very Large Crude Carriers – are moored at the pilot station off Falmouth. John thinks they are waiting for a space at Milford Haven or taking on North Sea pilots. The tankers are forbidding-looking hulks, but at least Falmouth Roads, once the most vibrant anchorage in all the world, is not entirely empty.

From before Drake's time until 1850, when steam replaced the sail-driven packet ships, Falmouth was the principal landfall for the information Britain gathered from the globe. Rather than have ships sail on up the Channel, risking Ushant and the Goodwins before negotiating the Thames estuary, their tidings were transferred to mail coach at Falmouth. News of fortune, disaster, triumph and reversal came ashore here, systematised with the Falmouth Packets in 1688. These light, fast ships carried mail to and from the garrisons, embassies, courts and governments of Europe and the New World, at first via Spain and the Caribbean, later via New York, Charleston and Halifax. Sending a letter from London to New York in 1788 cost four pennyweight of silver, currently worth about three pounds; the fastest Post Office service today costs £7.78! (Though your missive should arrive within six working days; in 1788 the typical run of a packet ship beating 'uphill', west across the Atlantic against the prevailing winds, was the best part of two months.)

The dish aerials at Goonhilly Down point towards America. We can see wind turbines and cliffs, and a shore more bittern-brown than green. Could it be any northern isle? Something about the slanted light, this Sunday afternoon, and the indeterminate season speaks of England, though John, in his torn chair, as he gazes without expression at the waves, looks like a man who could be anywhere.

We pass the Helford river, St Mawes, Porthscatho, the Whelps and the Bellows. Five gannets use our bow wave of air for a lift, sometimes resting on the fo'c'sle. South of St Michael's Mount the mobile signal comes and goes. John curses. One gannet cruises by the bridge wing, giving us the eye.

Porthcurno passes, then Land's End. Nine miles out is Wolf Rock, its tower a vertical scratch on the horizon, an apple stalk standing on the sea. It took three years to lay the first thirty-seven stones of its granite lighthouse, so difficult were the conditions on *an melv*, 'the lip', Wolf's Cornish name. An alternative explanation suggests the builders' challenge: wind scouring through the rock's fissures sounds like a lupine howl. The charts and pilot books of this sea are stippled with peril. Carn Base is marked by an east cardinal buoy, and the chart notes 'Heavy seas during gales'. 'Many of the dangers in this area are steep-to and the soundings do not provide a warning of approach,' say the sailing directions. 'It is essential to use every opportunity to ascertain the vessel's position. Careful consideration should be given to the effects of wind, currents, and tidal current in order to ensure keeping S of the Scilly Isles. Recent prevailing S and SW winds, combined with the influence of surface drift and tidal current, almost always result in a N set.'

In 1967 this confluence of forces and that 'North set' were partly to blame for catastrophe.

'There's plenty of room between Carn and the Seven Stones,' John says. 'Seven Stones reef, you know, where the *Torrey Canyon* struck?'

John tells the story. A series of miscommunications, an inexperienced navigating officer, contradictory course alterations, the set of the drift and tide, confusion, then panic combined to run the supertanker *Torrey Canyon* aground on Pollard's Rock, one of the Seven Stones. At ten to nine on the morning of 18 March 1967 she hit as squarely as if she had come thousands of miles from Kuwait, via the Cape of Good Hope (she was too big to pass through Suez) like a slow arrow, perfectly flighted to the target.

There are two extraordinary pictures of the *Torrey Canyon*'s master. Captain Pastrengo Rugiati was photographed on the bridge of his ship, then one of the largest in the world, when she was hard aground. Half the face almost lifts towards the lens, the way faces do, in an instinctive desire to put on some kind of show. Rugiati had served in an Italian submarine in the Atlantic during the Second World War, later transferring to a destroyer. When this ship was seized by Germany, Rugiati was sent to a concentration camp in Poland. Under his beret is half of a captain's face, rugged and set, the face of a man who has seen and endured indescribable scenes, and surpassed them, and risen to the height of professional seafaring. He is still a captain, and still on the bridge of his ship, though he looks like a bystander with the slackness of shock about him. The other half of his features, furthest from the camera and out of shadow, appear to have been washed out by light or surprise. All expression falls from this face; it looks like the sketch of a spectre. The second photograph shows him cowering on his side, cramped into a space like a locker. This picture was taken two months later in an Italian hospital. In dressing gown and pyjamas, his knees drawn up towards his chest, Rugiati is under his bed in a foetal curl, as if in fear of some nightmarish beast. In fact he is trying to hide from journalists. He gapes at someone behind and to the left of whoever took the picture: more than one paparazzo has found his way into the ward. In Rugiati's face is something which horror films aspire towards and will never attain. Terrorpale, the eyes bulging black, the brows high on the forehead in disbelief, the picture shows a man in the instant that the monster discovers him. He does not scream; he stares. The expression is that of someone – something – hunted, trapped and still looking for a way out.

The *Torrey Canyon* was carrying over 119,000 tonnes of heavy Kuwaiti crude. The grounding caused the world's worst oil spill. Rugiati's last, frantic spinning of the ship's wheel brought her round through ten degrees, audible on the bridge as the gyro compass clicked through each one, slowly. He knew the impossibility of changing a supertanker's destiny in a hurry; he saw the inevitable moments after it became so and had to watch as he bore down upon it. In his face you seem to see it all.

After the Scilly Isles the echo sounder loses signal as the depths drop away. We ride the swells, taking longer steps now. The ship is now burning high-sulphur fuel – Pieter made the switch as we crossed the Marine Pollution Line south of Mount's Bay. The afternoon colours change, clouds come down, the sea seems to be pondering. At sunset the Scillies are over our starboard shoulder, lying low off the coast. A lash of cloud supports the Bishop Rock light.

'When you see that you know you're home,' John says.

We steer west-north-westerly, course 278 degrees, starting our Great Circle. The Scillies are tiny, tinier and gone, and now there are bigger waves. There is only one ship on the radar, inbound to the south of us under mares' tails of cloud. We are nodding through a still evening with no whitecaps and only one bird, a gannet that has taken the albatross station over the foremast.

It seems amazing that this time yesterday we were snaking out through the rain and surrealism of the Schelde. The sea treats time, distance and men's lives as mutable things, unfixed. For example, John has two weeks to add to his thirty-two years before we get back to Bremerhaven, then he will be off for a month and a half. After that he has no idea what ship he will be sent to, sailing where, with whom, for what, in what condition. Custom and tradition are his only certainties: John knows his watches will start at noon and midnight and end at four and four.

He told me horrifying stories this afternoon as we swept slowly out past the end of Cornwall. It was very funny in an awful way, trying to extend one's feeling to the place's moment, with the mariner tipping appalling tales into your ear. They are better set down at night.

As the sun sinks Captain Koop does his exercises. He marches the length of the bridge with great vigour, arms not quite swinging, then turns and marches back, accelerating towards the centre of the bridge like a man with a plane to catch, before slowing rapidly at the end, turning on his heel and setting off again. Captain Koop is pacing the Atlantic out with a mighty pathos, a formidable determination to have more life, more days on land. With every stride he is reclaiming time, paying into a pension of existence beyond his coffin-shaped ship. Captain Koop is defying the sea. It seems an eminently sensible policy, pursued with manic commitment. He would run you over, you think. I do not know how many widths he sets himself but he surely hits his target.

Dinner is at the bar because it is Sunday. Pieter the chief engineer gives out lemonade and alcohol-free beer and relaxes on a stool behind the counter, happy. There are no uniforms tonight; the Captain is dressed as if for football. We eat chicken again, with green beans and noodles, straw-berries for pudding. The strawberries have done their share of seafaring, from Kenya to the Netherlands to the Atlantic. The mood is jolly.

'We had to bribe Lagos Customs with cigarettes,' Pieter grins. 'And we had these cigarettes, they have – they're from Canada? – they have these photos of cancers, lungs, horrible stuff – and the Nigerians didn't want them! No, no, not these! Marlboro Red – didn't want them! We had to – [Pieter relishes English and often seeks the *mot juste*] – compensate them with extra Coca-Cola.'

There is much laughter from all three of them at the legendary chief mate who 'couldn't see' the Cambodian and Vietnamese boat people, who fled the aftermath of the Vietnam War in the late 1970s, taking small boats into the international shipping lanes in the hope of rescue and resettlement.

'Couldn't see them!' they chortle.

In his cadet year Pieter was with a ship that picked up sixty boat people and took them to Singapore. The Dutch government accepted them. Pieter recently had a letter from one of the refugees, a young boy at the time, who is organising a reunion. Untold numbers of boat people died at sea: the UN estimates up to a quarter of a million. It is not the numbers that make an impression on the Dutchmen, but the means. They have all done sea-survival courses.

'The tricky bit is getting into the life raft from the water,' Pieter says, not laughing. The talk turns to drowning, to water in the lungs and how long the brain survives without oxygen, and hydrostatic pressure, when the squeeze of the water around the legs keeps blood near the vital organs. When you lift the body out of the water the pressure is removed and blood drains back to the legs. This is why some victims of the storm which struck the Fastnet race in 1979 waved to rescue helicopters from the water but were dead by the time they had been winched up. Casualties are now lifted in slings or baskets, horizontally.

The ship enters the Celtic Sea. Below us is the Jones Bank: 70 metres, 180 metres, 90 metres, the depths shift like waves and the chart shows a dozen wrecks near to us.

None is named or dated on the chart. The sailing directions describe the world in which they lie. 'The bottom of the Western approaches to the English Channel appears to consist mainly of fine or coarse sand, a great deal of broken shell, and occasional patches of pebbles, gravel and small stones. Mud may be found in places now and then. The sand is mostly white; although, in many places it is yellow, with black specks. The black specks are often found mixed both with the white and yellow sand; they are very fine, resembling fine cinder dust.'

As we rumble over this submarine desolation there is a sudden lift: 'Swells.' 'Swells already,' say the Captain and Pieter at once, exchanging a glance. Pieter tilts his head as though listening for something. The Captain nods, frowning so that his jaw juts.

Now they chat about Egypt and Hong Kong and Nigeria, and as they laugh, surrounded by *Pembroke*'s old honours from ports across the oceans, there is something quietly magnificent about these three Dutch seafarers, something in and out of time, at once nostalgic and actual. I cannot characterise the feeling at first. Each has a personal isolation about him, a sense of a world of worries confined to his cabin, which is familiar, but their cares are padded with a sardonic humour and a sea-companionship I have not noticed among other nationalities I have sailed with. Hendrik Willem Van Loon, writing in 1916, would have had no difficulty ascribing it. His collection *The Golden Book of the Dutch Navigators* begins with a vision of the Low Countries towards the end of the 1500s, on the eve of the Netherlands' great age.

'Wherever a man went in the country there was the high sky of the coastal region, and the canals which would carry his small vessel to the main roads of trade and ultimate prosperity. The sea reached up to his very front door. It supported him in his struggle for a living, and it was his best ally in his fight for independence. Half of his family and friends lived on and by the sea. The nautical terms of the forecastle became the language of his land. His house reminded the foreign visitor of a ship's cabin. And finally his state became a large naval Commonwealth, with a number of shipowners as a board of directors and a foreign policy dictated by the needs of commerce. The history of Holland is the story of the conquest of the sea . . .' Van Loon dedicates his book to his sons with a homily: 'I want you to know about these men because they are your ancestors. If you have inherited any of their good qualities, make the best of them; they will prove to be worthwhile. If you have got your share of their bad ones, fight these as hard as you can; for they will lead you a merry chase before you get through.'

The three descendants of Van Loon's Dutch navigators are now discussing pilots: the man who saw us through Flushing Roads last night was of the old school, in his tattered jumper and sea monster's beard, and he knew what he was doing. 'You know they train the new ones on simulators now?' says the Captain, sceptically.

'So I guess we'll find out about that, one way or another,' Pieter laughs. 'You know we are retarding the clocks another hour tonight?'

'Oh? Thank you. It's confusing . . .'

'You should have been here when the ships went slower – we used to go back by half-hours.'

Jannie claps his hand to his forehead. 'Each twelve hours divided in three watches, so ten minutes different for you, ten minutes for him, my ten minutes – the calculations!'

Nymphe Bank is to the north, Cockburn ahead and below the horizons small unnamed banks, each worked by a solitary fishing boat. The Porcupine Sea Bight, the edge of the European Continental Shelf, is out beyond Cockburn Bank. We are coming up on the line dividing United Kingdom from Irish waters. There are over 350 known wrecks in the chart of our current position, in the south-western approaches to St George's Channel. The oldest marked is the *Thomasina*, a full-rigged sailing ship launched in 1873 and sunk by gunfire from the *U-35* in 1915, an extraordinary confrontation between the Victorian era and the modern age. Appropriately, perhaps, there was no loss of life: the crew were allowed to take to their boats, from which they were later rescued, before the U-boat fired. Conduct of this kind attended many sinkings of cargo ships in the first war, and persisted sporadically into the beginning of the Battle of the Atlantic. The list of the lost encompasses the end of the age of sail, recording forty more tall ships sent to the bottom in the Great War, several of them by torpedo.

The records are full of echoes – *Thistlebank*, another sailing ship, was carrying wheat to Ireland from Argentina when she was torpedoed in June 1916 by the same Rudolf Schneider who six months before had sunk HMS *Formidable*. A third sailer, *Sunlight*, carrying molasses from Hispaniola to Glasgow for Lever Brothers, was sunk in the same area

by another U-boat five days later. In late 1940 there is a
spate of six vessels in sequence, three cargo ships and three
trawlers, all sunk by air attack. France had fallen: Channel
shipping was within easy reach of German aircraft. There
is another cluster, this time of U-boats, all destroyed during
and after 1943 when the Battle of the Atlantic turned decisively against them. In the latter part of the century fishing
boats are undone by explosions, freighters go down when
their cargoes shift in storms, yachts suffer flooding and
heavy seas and one boat dives down a wave at thirty-eight
knots and ruptures her hull – the end of *Virgin Atlantic
Challenger* and her attempt on the Atlantic speed record in
1985.

I end the day writing down two of John's stories. We
returned to the tragedy of the *Royston Castle*, and the
vacuum created by burning oil, which left no one aboard
alive. He has survived 'loads of fires, aye!' without encoun-
tering disaster: 'Engine room fires mostly. The suppressors
dealt with them.'

Then he tells the tale of the worst thing he ever saw.

'He was an electrician, a Geordie, only young. Twenty-
four. He goes to get a torch off the roof of a lift. Someone
had dropped it down there, you know, and he thought he'd
climb down and get it? It was the case that changed safety
regulations about lifts – and I was the one that found it,'
he says, proudly, twice.

'I get in the lift and it's all red. So I think, uh? And I
look into the gap, and there's a hand.'

The sun was out and the daffodils were in bloom above
St Michael's Mount, as John described discovering the

young Geordie's corpse, the flattened head 'three times
the size of a head'.

The most sinister story comes from John's time on the
Foreland, a bulker, an ore carrier renamed seven times, a
sister ship to the *Derbyshire*, which went down with all hands
when the seas broke off her hatch covers. The *Foreland* was
moored at Hunterstone on the coast of Scotland. This is a
chillingly bleak harbour, little more then a terminal at the
end of a pier that feeds a power station.

'I knew it was a strange ship when I first went on but I
didn't know it was an evil ship. My mother came up to see
me but when she got there, as soon as she saw it, she said:
"I'm not going on that ship." I said: "Why not? You've come
all the way up to Scotland to see us – what do you mean
you're not coming on?"

'She says: "I'm not going on that ship." Wouldn't say why.
In the end I took her hand and dragged her up the gangway.
She goes straight to my cabin and she wouldn't come
out. She'd been on loads of ships but she wouldn't leave the
cabin. Offered her a tour of the ship – didn't want it. The
captain said she could stay the night – she wouldn't have it.
She stayed in the cabin until she left and I said: "What was
all that about?"

'"Something terrible happened on that ship," she says. I
knew what it was, but she didn't. I hadn't said anything
about it. This was in the days before the internet and whatever so she couldn't have looked it up or anything – she
couldn't have known.'

'What happened, John?' I blurt.

'One of the crew had gone mad and stabbed some of the others. He killed a few of them. I said, "What was all that about?" She said: "Something terrible happened on that ship. Men died on that ship." I said, "Yes, but how did you know?" She said: "I could see them."'

CHAPTER 17

When Something Snaps

There are swells in the night as we cross the banks and the wind backs westerly. We wake to misted sky and sea the colour of a submarine. At ten there is a full meeting in the harbour control room. The Captain and Pieter, the chief, are there first.

'Have you heard about the *Maersk Luz*?' asks the Captain.

'No?'

'A fight in the crew. Filipino guys. Two dead and there's one in custody in Buenos Aires.'

'Jesus, what happened?'

'We don't know, they don't tell us. Maybe the Filipinos know. This is bad stuff. If men are at sea too long . . . they are such happy-go-lucky guys, eh? But if something snaps . . .'

Erwin arrives, downcast. The Captain prompts him:

'The *Maersk Luz*?'

'I know one who was killed,' Erwin says, quietly.

'You know him?' the Captain repeats.

'Marlon. I sailed with him, a long time. Months. He was a good guy, really a good guy.'

He shakes his head and more of the junior officers appear, all wearing the same expression. The second and third engineers, Reyje and Filemon, Sumy the bo'sun, Erwin and Annabelle are from the same town as Marlon. It is as though all the Filipinos on all the world's seas are one crew, and all their ships one fleet. By the atmosphere in the room the two dead men are next door.

The Captain goes briskly around the table. The chief engineer is responsible for ordering materials and stores: Annabelle tells Pieter she needs soap powder and soap.

'It's not going to be there when we get back to Rotterdam,' he says, 'so it's going to take two months.'

Annabelle says we also need fresh vegetables.

'Montreal?'

Next come questions about a flight to Cebu for Reyje, the second engineer, a young man with an extraordinary haircut, like a guardsman's busby, and questions from Filemon, his deputy, about signing off in March.

'What does your contract say?'

'April, Captain.'

The Captain makes an eloquent shrug. Erwin asks, on behalf of the crew, if there might be fifty dollars available for new DVDs?

'Yes, but after we spend three hundred of the remaining twelve hundred to update the anti-virus software in Montreal.'

There is a brief discussion about the lashing bonus. Like Glenn Cuevas, killed by a crate in Rotterdam, this crew will also be doing stevedores' work, because of safety regulations in Montreal, ironically. At least they will not be doing it while the cranes are working overhead, as Mr Cuevas was.

'In Montreal they don't work the cranes until the cargo is unlashed, and the stevedores don't lash until the cranes have finished loading. That's five hours – we can't wait. So the crew do it,' the Captain explains. A bonus is paid in cash and everyone wants in – only the Captain and the chief engineer exempt themselves.

The meeting breaks up and Pieter offers a tour of his engine room. He shows me around with the same thoroughness with which John showed me the bridge. The engine is an eight-cylinder B&W two-stroke diesel, capable of 28,000 kilowatts of power. The heat and fury, the noise and the gigantic scale are all reminiscent of the *Gerd* but here brass thermometers protrude everywhere like periscopes. I find the engine control strangely touching. There is a control rod which descends from the bridge. There is a red knob and a brass wheel marked 'More' with an anti-clockwise arrow. All this enormous complexity comes down to such a simple, humble control. Constellations of pipes and wires and washers and valves add up, in the end, to a shaft which you can spin 'more', 'less' and either way. We descend three decks to the level of the shaft, a grease-black whirl of constant motion (we must hope and hope) spinning eighty-five times a minute. The ship's tail narrows elegantly, like a ribbed fish, cold to the touch.

'Colder in Montreal,' says Pieter. 'You can hear the ice scraping along the sides. It's fine if it stays out there.'

We tour pumps, coolers, heaters and condensers. He stops by each of his charges and screams its function into my ear. There is a lot of fuel filtering down here because cargo ships use the cheapest, dirtiest diesel. 'And fuel pumps are very sensitive things!' Pieter touches pipes, warm and hot; the very hot he pats. Moving parts are daubed lovingly with grease.

Reyje, the second engineer, and Jannie, the electrician, are working on a cylinder head for one of the generators: it has done 12,000 hours of labour since it was last cleaned; when they have finished it will be ready for its next 12,000. They conduct a conversation about a level measurement with Pieter almost entirely in sign language, topped off with a bit of screaming. Eight hours down here with two breaks, with the deck shaking and the roar gouging at the little plugs in your ears! It takes shipping, the history of shipping, to make this seem reasonable. For all the ferocities of the age of sail, it was steam that reintroduced hell to a seafarer's existence, hell of a day-to-day quality not seen since the slave galleys.

The 'Black Gang' now refers to Customs officers; originally it was the appellation of the stokers and trimmers whose labour drove the turbines of the age of steam. R. M. Dunshea, apprentice on the cargo liner *Maimoa*, described the conditions in which her Black Gang fought the Battle of the Atlantic. The ship was twenty years old when the war began:

'Each man had to feed his three furnaces with two tonnes of coal every four-hour watch, as well as slicing and raking the fires to ensure good consumption. At the beginning of

each watch ash-pits had to be cleaned. Each watch was accommodated in a single, badly-ventilated room in the fo'c'sle. At
sea with a seven-day week they had no diversions, in port
they usually sought solace in dockland hostelries . . . many
fell foul of the ladies, the effects manifesting themselves a
few weeks later.'

Lady Nancy Astor suggested that merchant seamen be
compelled to wear yellow armbands on shore, as a sign of
their potential for carrying venereal disease. In 1938 she
told Parliament that a colleague who had seen the way
seamen lived 'said he would not expect ferrets to live in
such conditions'.

The young Eugene O'Neill came rather closer to the
actuality of the stokehold when he shipped as a deckhand
on runs between New York, Southampton and Buenos
Aires. When ashore he frequented a New York dive called
Jimmy the Priest's, where, O'Neill said, 'you could sleep
with your head on the table if you bought a schooner of
beer'.

'I shouldn't have known the stokers if I hadn't happened
to scrape an acquaintance with one of our own furnace-
room gang at Jimmy the Priest's. His name was Driscoll,
and he was a Liverpool Irishman. It seems that years ago
some Irish families settled in Liverpool. Most of them
followed the sea, and they were a hard lot. To sailors all
over the world, a "Liverpool Irishman" is the synonym
for a tough customer. It was through Driscoll that I got
to know the other stokers. Driscoll himself came to a
strange end. He committed suicide by jumping overboard
in mid-ocean.'

O'Neill addressed the conditions of the stokers in his play *The Hairy Ape*. His stage directions for its third scene are more telling than any photograph:

> The stokehole. In the rear, the dimly-outlined bulks of the furnaces and boilers. High overhead one hanging electric bulb sheds just enough light through the murky air laden with coal dust to pile up masses of shadows everywhere. A line of men, stripped to the waist, is before the furnace doors. They bend over, looking neither to right nor left, handling their shovels as if they were part of their bodies, with a strange, awkward, swinging rhythm. They use the shovels to throw open the furnace doors. Then from these fiery round holes in the black a flood of terrific light and heat pours full upon the men who are outlined in silhouette in the crouching, inhuman attitudes of chained gorillas. The men shovel with a rhythmic motion, swinging as on a pivot from the coal which lies in heaps on the floor behind to hurl it into the flaming mouths before them. There is a tumult of noise – the brazen clang of the furnace doors as they are flung open or slammed shut, the grating, teeth-gritting grind of steel against steel, of crunching coal. This clash of sounds stuns one's ears with its rending dissonance . . . And rising above all, making the air hum with the quiver of liberated energy, the roar of leaping flames in the furnaces, the monotonous throbbing beat of the engines.

The lowest of the gang in wages and status were the trimmers, who retrieved coal from the bunkers, spread it out evenly at the feet of the stokers, raked out the ashes and disposed of them. The worst work of the men of the *Indian Empire* – as they flung coal up an incline in the holds of a ship on her side in the Pacific – was the daily routine of the trimmers. They bunkered coal and balanced its bulk, moving it around as it was depleted, to keep the ship level. As stocks in the lower bunkers were burned the trimmers shifted tonnes out of higher bunkers, so the longer the voyage went on the more labour they had to accomplish. The only concession to their health and safety amid the choking dust was a wet rag tied across the mouth.

Nor was it enough that the stokers should simply shovel the coal, as in O'Neill's description. They must also ensure it burned 'like an incandescent cloud of vapour rushing from the top of coals towards the rear of the furnaces – it was not a "fire", but a bed of incandescent fuel on the grate'.[3] In wartime it was particularly important that this ferocious combustion was achieved: anything less and the ship would produce undue smoke and fall astern of its convoy, making it easy to spot and easy to sink. This meant a stoker had to be close enough to the blaze to use his tools effectively, the names of which speak eloquently of the work. He broke up clinkers of unburned coal with a slice bar, or dragged them out with a devil's claw. He raked the gratings clear of ash with a pricker bar and levelled the surface of the inferno with a firing hoe before adding more coal, and repeating the process. To complete the echo of the age of the galley slaves, the work in the stokehold on many ships

[3] David Simpson et al., 'Firemen, Trimmers and Stokers: The Real Heroes of World War Two', 2008. Available at www.barrymerchantseamen.org.uk.

was coordinated by the mechanical striking of Kilroy's Stoking Indicator, which beat a metallic time.

U-boat commanders knew where the guts of a ship were by the placing of her funnel. Directly below it, beneath the waterline, were the furnaces and the boilers. In the roar of Pieter's engine room, with the waterline above us, it is still difficult to picture the full horror of a torpedo strike: the explosion, the darkness, the burning oil and scalding steam, the screams of the injured and terrorised, the eruptions of flames, the in-gush of freezing water, and the press of men trying to get out through hatches buckled or jammed – and, for any who did get out, wearing the stoker's garb of vest and trousers, the bitter North Atlantic, slicked with oil and flame. If such a man made it to a lifeboat or raft he was extremely lucky. If he was not one of the first to die there from hypothermia, in cases where rescue was not quick, then he was luckier still.

There is a famous photograph of one such lucky man. He sits on the deck of the naval escort that has rescued him, one arm over the rail, one leg dangling below it. He wears a short-sleeved shirt. The wretched cork boards of a primitive life jacket are askew on his chest. He is covered in oil; the left side of his face shines as though moulded into a plastic mask. His eyes are narrowed almost shut and his mouth gasps blackly open, the human equivalent of an oiled seabird. He is not in the ship's sickroom, which suggests that he is a low priority case: much worse is taking place out of shot. Whoever holds the camera regards him as sufficiently ubiquitous that he can be photographed, rather than assisted.

The most comprehensive factual account of the merchant navy in the Battle of the Atlantic is Richard Woodman's book *The Real Cruel Sea*. In his acknowledgements Woodman pays one particular tribute: 'For a powerful evocation there can be none better than that of Nicholas Monsarrat in *The Cruel Sea*, the reading of which was, in its navigational sense, my own point of departure', Woodman writes, deferring to an eyewitness and participant whose novel could not be more 'real'.

Monsarrat served as a lieutenant in the Royal Navy Voluntary Reserve. *The Cruel Sea* is a fictional shaping of what he saw and did on the Atlantic convoys, and his book stands alongside the work of Conrad and Melville as the most perfect and terrible testament to the era of seafaring it describes. The oiled survivor of the photograph might have come straight from its pages. Monsarrat saw and wrote about many such men, and also those who were less lucky.

In one episode, 'The Time of the Burning Tanker', 'the time that seemed to synthesise the whole, corpse-ridden ocean', Monsarrat describes a tanker of which the crew of his protagonists' corvette, the *Compass Rose*, has become particularly fond, in the way that convoy escorts became fond of certain of their charges: ships are characters, after all, a sum of their parts and the personalities of their crews and captains. This tanker has almost reached safety, having been shepherded and defended all the way across the ocean from Halifax, and is almost within sight of the Scottish hills when she is torpedoed. As she blooms vast fires the surviving crew gather on deck. The *Compass Rose* cannot go closer to them because of the heat of the flames.

And then, in ones and twos, hesitating, changing their minds, they did begin to jump: successive splashes showed suddenly white against the dark grey hull, and soon all twenty of them were down, and on their way across. From the bridge of the *Compass Rose* and from the men thronging her rail came encouraging shouts as the gap of water between them narrowed.

Then they noticed that the oil, spreading over the surface of the water and catching fire as it spread, was moving faster than any of the men could swim. They noticed it before the swimmers, but soon the swimmers noticed it too. They began to scream as they swam, and to look back over their shoulders, and thrash and claw their way through the water as if suddenly insane.

But one by one they were caught. The older ones went first, and then the men who couldn't swim fast because of their life jackets, and then the strong swimmers, without life jackets, last of all. But perhaps it was better not to be a strong swimmer on that day, because none of them was strong enough: one by one they were over-taken, and licked by flame, and fried, and left behind.

Reading the book on a trading ship on the same ocean, in the same weather, with the same sea hissing along the sides of the hull, it is almost unbelievable that any man who survived one crossing – over two weeks of fear for the slower convoys, daubed with terror and horror – should have had the courage to face doing it ever again. In 1941 the Essential Work (Merchant Navy) Order forced seamen between the ages of eighteen and sixty to register for sea duty, and barred them from working ashore. Sixteen-year-olds belonging to

the Sea Scouts, Cadets and Boys' Brigade were encouraged
to volunteer for merchant ships, though they were still too
young to fight. What kind of men and boys they were is
described by Commander Frederick Watt of the Canadian
Boarding Service, who inspected ships gathered in Halifax
awaiting convoys.

> Certain nations, and within them certain shipping lines,
> maintained standards of performance that made them the
> front line of the maritime community. Their tradition of
> seamanship was as jealously guarded as that of any other
> long-established calling. These were the elite. There was
> also a type of independent-minded seaman who seemed to
> prefer a berth lacking spit and polish or an ordered future,
> who yet had his own brand of grainy pride, competence and
> dependability. But beyond that category were the embittered,
> the slovenly and the fearful – mariners to whom the sea
> was an economic fact of life, inescapable because there was
> nowhere else to turn. They were exploited by their masters
> on the basis of that hard truth.

Minus the slovenliness, and for the most part the bitterness and fear, every other element of this description is
present on the *Pembroke*, applying in different degrees
throughout the hierarchy, from the wipers and oilers to the
Captain. The men who fought the Battle of the Atlantic
were my shipmates, in fact. Richard Woodman's assessment
of the ships' crews has a particular resonance: 'All classes
of merchant ships employed large numbers of non-
Europeans. They were all paid less than their white

colleagues, lascars, for example, receiving around 30 rupees a month, about £2 5s., while their living conditions were abominable.'

John and I sit in the pilots' seats either side of the main controls, and watch the Atlantic well up, from blunt grey force five to choppy and whitened six, and back down to rumbling monotony, and we sail through rain into mist, through grey into sickly yellow cloud, with the visibility shortening and stretching, and the current eddying, sometimes a knot with us, sometimes a knot against.

'Oh I love storms me, love 'em, yeah. I've been through hurricanes and typhoons. Love 'em! Why? Why not? Exciting. I was on a small ship, smaller than this, and she stood up like that!'

He points a flat hand at the ceiling.

'We thought she was going to fall over backwards. The chief officer's wife was on board, poor woman . . . When you go to bed you have to lock your hands behind you, right? Like that? Lock them behind you under the mattress, or you fly off – she hits waves and stops dead. Everything's just smashed. In tankers the sea breaks over the ship. You can watch big ships bending because of the torsion, twisting like, so you steer one way and the bow goes the other.

'Once I was blind for five minutes. We were coming into the Malacca Strait and a lightning bolt hit one wing of the bridge, came right through the bridge and hit the other wing. It went between me and the captain, just this incredibly bright white light. We had both doors open, it came in there and went out there. There was this smell of burning – rubber from the deck. It left a scorch mark the width of the bridge.

'I've seen lightning hit a thirty-foot mast and leave nothing but a tiny stump. The Captain was right by it, he nearly had a heart attack. Same place, the Malacca Strait, I saw lightning cut a VLCC in half. Half a million tonnes, she was. We were going parallel to them, tank cleaning, and they were cleaning tanks too. We had an inert gas system for safety but they didn't. The lightning hits them, massive bang, and when I saw them again the whole ship was split down the middle, opened up like a sardine can. Her cranes were in the water. The people in the accommodation survived. But not the people on the deck.'

It is almost dark as we drive hard into the swells. The wind has been growing again, throwing spray high over the containers where it hangs in the air like rogue spells. We have had our heavy weather briefing and been told to lash everything down.

'We should be prepared for pitching, rolling, cork-screwing and slamming,' the Captain says. Slamming is the one which interests me. At supper Pieter recalls a typhoon: 'We still talk about it. It didn't last very long but you don't need a typhoon to last very long. We did our heavy weather preparation and there was a steel block in the engine room, it must have weighed two hundred kilogrammes. I checked and thought, yeah, it's not going anywhere. When I found it again it had jumped two five-inch sills, gone along the deck and fallen two decks down. It wasn't too good . . .'

Pieter has a sweetly patient grin, much used but not worn out.

By 2030 hours we are off the southern tip of the Isengaard Ridge with eight kilometres of water beneath the keel. The ship stumbles and rears. Our course is more northerly, 282 degrees; our speed a steady eighteen knots. There is utter, utter darkness outside and the radar is a green and yellow sunburst of wave-echoes. As we pitch and buck there is a feeling of madness, of dashing wildness on the bridge. The digital chart displays its customary caution: 'This chart is not up to date – DO NOT USE FOR NAVIGATION.' Oh well . . .

We may be one of six hundred in the Maersk fleet but we feel like a lone tramp tonight, running blind. There has been a shadow aboard since the awful news about the *Maersk Luz* this morning. People still sing and whoop but you can hear the defiance in it.

Chicoy is very solemn. I fear he is prone to sulks. The bridge during his night watch is Filipino territory, you feel. There is a sense of division on this ship which is marked compared to the *Gerd*: white Dutch officers, brown Filipino crew, and no Indians, Russians or Romanians to bridge the gap or bring the two groups together in English. The Captain is quicker with 'they' than 'the crew'.

'They sort out their problems themselves,' he said.

Procedure is different, too. There has been no tour of the ship, apart from my informal explorations. We have emergency drill once a month, John says, and I would not want to find out how the lifeboats perform if they are of a piece with the reeking, leaking diesel fumes, the broken lock on my cabin door and the chart we navigate by.

After midnight John takes the watch.

'Have you ever seen something you couldn't explain, John?'

'Oh aye, I saw a flying saucer in the Indian Ocean. The

mate says have you seen this? There was this blue light in
the sky. I thought it was a plane or something, but it came
right at us, too fast for a plane, and it was leaving this neon
blue trail, bright neon blue. As it came over we could see
it was a cigar shape, blue, and leaving this neon blue trail
which lasted for some time. I thought no plane can leave
that, no rocket can do that . . . I've seen some rare weather
conditions. Greece? No, Turkey, there was a spinning cloud
in the sky, and the water was spinning, like a tornado, but
there was nothing in between. Just the cloud spinning and
the water spinning. I thought it was going to hit us but it
went behind. Do you know about that lighthouse in
Scotland? All the keepers disappeared. The table was set
for a meal and they were all just – gone.'

It is terrifying on the bridge wing now, the sky angry
and torn, the clouds ripped open to a few shards of stars.
You feel your courage cowed out there, as you cling to the
steel and the wind rips tears from your eyes while the ship
dives into invisible troughs, thump-thunders and totters up,
the forces pulling you backwards, and waves of God knows
what size and intention, indistinguishable but palpable, are
in motion everywhere, the darkness racingly alive.

To even consider a convoy on a night like this is to realise
how ringed the seamen were with devil's alternatives. No
sailor wants storms – apart from John – but here you did
not want calms either, because storms kept the U-boats down.
Peter-Erich Cremer commanded the *U-333* in the winter of
1942. 'North Atlantic winter! In such weather waging war
stops of its own accord because everyone has enough on his
hands without it – even when we unexpectedly sighted a

tanker about 3000 metres away. I tried to keep contact . . .
it being impossible to attack straight away because of the
high seas and colossal swell. Wind force 10. At one moment
the tanker was on a mountainous wave, the next she had
disappeared into the valley. Then I lost sight of her
altogether.'[4]

Cremer would have found us hard to hit tonight: at
eighteen knots we are going at three times the speed of the
slow convoys, which crept along at six. You shudder at
the thought of trying to launch a lifeboat into the freezing,
unstable immensity. Being in the water or on a raft is un-
imaginable. You wanted moonless darkness because the
attacks generally came at night, and when the ships were
silhouetted the hunters were more likely to be successful.
But such a wild blackout as this made keeping station in
the zig-zagging convoy harder, and the possibility of collision greater, along with the danger of falling out of sequence,
and the light breaking to reveal that you had straggled
outside the formation and were suddenly easy meat.

Perhaps it is the echo of the men who crossed it or died
in the attempt that gives this ocean a loneliness and a chaos
absent from the North Pacific. That was incomprehensibly
vast, with horizons weeks beyond horizons, and the *Gerd* a
speck between the Aleutians and Hawaii. This is different.
The Atlantic tonight is like Hamlet's infinite space, bounded
in the nutshell of its coasts, beset with bad dreams. The
ancient Greeks believed it had no end in this life; what was
beyond it, the afterlife, existed only in intuition and myth.

[4] Peter Cremer, *U-333: Story of a U-boat Ace*, Bodley Head, London, 1984.

The water below us now is too deep for the chart to show wrecks. Anything that went down here might as well have been erased from the planet. Flapping and screeching noises come from the stacks.

'God bless,' says the watchman, as I go down around 3 a.m. I experiment with John's storm prescription, aiming to work my arms behind me under the mattress and link my hands together, but my arms are too short. We are due south of Iceland as I fall asleep thinking of the bow, battering the endless sea.

CHAPTER 18

The Eye

T he wastes have a watchful feeling about them. With wind and swells heavy off the port quarter I now know why John's drawers are taped shut. The sky is soft grey, beautiful in its freshness and clarity, the sea dark purple and iron-coloured. Swells flex their white-streaked shoulders and the horizon is a long emptiness, hypnotic in its totality. At 51 degrees 2 minutes 93 seconds North, and 26 degrees 14 minutes 41 seconds West on a map of the Atlantic war we are in great danger here: too far west for planes flying cover from Britain, too far south for those based in Iceland, and a long way east of Newfoundland. This is the beginning of what was known as the Black Hole, or the Air Gap. This was also at the point where early in the war convoys dispersed, and where, later, naval escort ships from Iceland handed over to those from Britain: a region in which submarines could be sure of finding targets. These waters have consumed men by the thousand and ships in hundreds, and their freights – potash, wheat, cotton, beef, sulphur, butter, fruit, tinned foods, mails, timber and general cargoes totalling millions of tonnes – and digested them all to nothingness. But millions more tonnes of zinc, manganese, iron ore, steel, copper and coal, enough to invigorate the descendant of the economy they were bound for, lie strewn in the deeps below us. Cargoes of metals, ores and coal were particularly frightening to transport. While munition ships blew apart and tankers blazed, those heavy bulk ships, once hit, broke and sank in moments.

Two fulmars accompany us as Chicoy clicks through the forecast on the computer. Twenty-five-knot winds at the moment (fifty kilometres an hour), forty knots tomorrow afternoon, and the waves will be six metres.

Over coffee at ten the Captain reveals the real treat.

'Bad weather tonight, then real bad weather, then the bad weather. The low is deepening.' He points to a spot on the world map where two systems are coming together ahead of us. 'There are ten-metre waves at the entrance to Cabot Strait,' he says.

As he says 'the low is deepening,' Jannie adds, 'widening . . .' and Pieter puts in 'lengthening!' and we all laugh.

I had thought we would go into the Gulf of St Lawrence through the north channel, Belle Isle Strait, around the top of Newfoundland Island, but it is iced up: we will make for the mouth of the Cabot Strait, further south. We are not far off the L in 'Mid-Atlantic Ridge' and aim to make our turn south not far short of the Hecate Seamount. That will bring us bow-on to the weather, which will be a relief. Blue nylon ropes have appeared around the chair backs, lashing them to the tables, and yellow cords loop around the bins. I walk the deck – the poop seems lower than the wave tops and the bow booms a warning as I approach. The plastic tarpaulins over the tractor near the fo'c'sle are being torn to bits. The ship reels and groans.

Fire in Bay 7, acetone. From the bridge we watch the stalwart little figures making their way up the starboard side to die. They drive a notional pin into the container and report things go well. Another team sprays the containers on either side, attacking a fantasy easy to imagine. Slamming into the storm some of the chemicals in the bow become unstable and ignite. With the weather the Captain must choose between turning to make a lee, a windbreak, in which case she rolls so wickedly the fire can barely be fought, or holding into the sea, allowing the wind to madden the flames.

Boat drill is more entertaining than frightening as we do not go near the boat. Mark has the best life jacket; I would give my journal to him. We stand under the boat and run through the list of who is responsible for bringing the blankets, who the provisions and who frees the life rafts. In this wind we would never see them again. Erwin says the whole lot was overhauled last year, so we know the lifeboat engines started then. No wonder some of the crew have faraway looks.

Around this meridian, to the north of us, lies the wreck of the *City of Benares*, a liner torpedoed in the early hours of 18 September 1940. She was carrying 231 children, evacuees from the Blitz and mostly working-class. They were to have been resettled in Canada at government expense in an initiative designed to redress the imbalance of children who had been sent to safety, the majority of whom were sons and daughters of the well-off. The Captain, the convoy's commodore and 120 of her sailors and officers went down with the ship. Over 150 of the children were saved, including six boys in the care of one Miss Mary Cornish, who were taken into a lifeboat commanded by the fourth officer, Ronald Cooper. In the North Atlantic in an open boat, through gale-force winds and heavy squalls, with their meagre water supply running out, heartbroken by the sight of a ship that might have rescued them turning away oblivious, with their food ration running out, and despite cases of delirium, depression, hallucinations and trench foot among adult survivors, the quietly extraordinary Cornish and Cooper contrived to keep the children occupied and the little vessel afloat and running eastwards through six nights, seven days and nineteen hours.

Miss Cornish led the singing of popular songs and devised games. She and a Father O'Sullivan told the children stories. 'When she detected whimpering, Miss Cornish would brusquely ask "Don't you realise that you're the heroes in a real adventure story? Did you ever hear of a hero who snivelled?"' She massaged the boys' limbs 'continuously', Cooper reported, while he made or lowered sail depending on the wind, streamed a sea anchor to thwart a gale which threatened to capsize them, and ensured that the spray broke over him, in the stern, rather than the children huddled under the cover of a hood in the fore end. When they were eventually rescued 'all the children were in good form', Cooper said. 'Everyone behaved very well, and a spirit of loyalty to orders and comparative cheerfulness prevailed.' You cannot help wondering how we would do in similar circumstances, our enclosed boat notwithstanding.

The word is that a painter on the *Maersk Luz* stabbed Marlon and the other man to death. The painter had 'trouble at home', apparently.

'If they are on for nine months it's too much,' the Captain says. 'People start to gather in places around the ship. Production goes down. And still people ask for extensions; seven months, eleven, thirteen . . .'

'Can you do that?'

'Now some ports want to see the contracts but if I have a fax for extension then it's fine.'

'Seven months is too much,' Erwin said quietly. 'Go crazy.'

'Six months is enough,' the Captain agrees. 'Maybe this will change things.'

Maybe. The International Transport Workers' Federation will have to be busy, because Maersk is unlikely to publicise the incident and needy seafarers will push for more time on board and captains and shipowners will look for ways around any new limit, and many countries will not check contracts. It might be different if Filipino seafarers were better or even fairly paid, but no one on any of the seven seas believes that is about to happen.

'At sea there is no hope that the road, or the host, or the lodging will improve; everything grows steadily worse; the ship labours more and more and the food gets scantier and nastier every day,' wrote Eugenio de Salazar of his Atlantic crossing in 1573, when he took his wife and children to Hispaniola on the *Nuestra Señora de Los*

Remedios, a ship which Salazar judged 'better by name than nature'.

Salazar found a dark comedy in the condition of his ship and would have recognised the same spirit on the *Pembroke*, though he would have scoffed at the comparative discomforts. However, in only two-metre swells *Pembroke* pitches and lurches plenty. The fan in my cabin is trying to poison me with diesel fumes and will not be shut off. The strip lights make reading a yellow misery, seeming to close the front of the eye while swelling the back up to your temples. The internet is a disaster: sitting under the router in the corridor at 3 a.m. you are lucky to read one email. (According to the ITF 80 per cent of seafarers and 97 per cent of ratings have no internet access while at sea.) Little Richard, the junior steward, sixteen at the outside by his appearance, dutifully sprays the cabins with God knows what toxin, daily. I am becoming embarrassed about eating the Eternal Salad at lunch and dinner: I know the little choir of vegetables so well it is like mistreating a friend. The bed contrives to rack my shoulders into yelping knots. The sheets, pillowcases and duvet are a bouquet of old sweats. The Queen of the Netherlands seems gaily amused by your career choice as you hunch, oppressed by her Thatcherite hairstyle, contemplating another frankfurter, and suspicious of Mark's overkindness, which you feel must be replaced, when your back is turned, with ludic mockery. The wide gap between the containers and the bridge means we travel with a permanent hurricane audio effect. And it is all for naught, according to the one email I was able to open today: shipping rates have fallen to $790 a container, which is less than the cost of carrying them. Maersk, CMA and MSC plan to take ships out of commission – 30 per cent already are – and hike the charges. One *Gerd* would do away with the need for *Pembroke* and *Palermo* at a stroke and make the run faster. The wide spaces on the deck speak literal volumes: I can see room for fifty more containers from my window. The *Pembroke* is due in dry dock a year from next month. It will be interesting to know if she makes it back to sea.

At around 1300 the waves climb quickly, eager as early guests to a party. Three metres, John reckons, and several times in the next hour they are big enough to stop her with a thump. We reduce revs and speed from 85 and 18 knots down to 83 and 16. By 2 p.m. the guests, in pyramidal lumps, have found friends. Hanging their arms round one another's shoulders they now form ranks hundreds of metres long, some self-effacing, sliding by, while others make a point which sends lucent turquoise-white spray up high on either side, lending butterfly wings to the bow. Apart from our impacts there is almost no white water, just these dark-crested creatures furrowing in front of the rain showers. It is strange how warm it is: we are to turn south towards ice. My head feels gummy and sneezy, nose running.

At four we turn into the waves. She rides much better now, and faster by the feel and the noise. There is a higher, running whine from the machinery and a sub-whistle from the draughts, just short of a note, which sighs in tandem with the pitching, as if the wind blows us along to the end of a breath which catches as she digs in. John comes down at the end of his watch, lists the inaccuracies in *Diamonds*

Are Forever and *The Towering Inferno* and offers a *Dead Calm* DVD. He says there is one millisecond when you can see that much of Nicole Kidman's arse. He has taped his air vent over with a bin bag.

The Captain stands his watch in clean uniform, whistling Leonard Cohen's 'Famous Blue Raincoat'. It is still a shock to hear whistling at sea. The Dutch and the Danes have different superstitions, evidently.

'Now we are in the eye of the storm,' he says. 'You can see here: the barometric graph falls steeply, then bumps, and now runs level. But there are two systems coming together.'

The air is a peculiar blue. Waves no longer march out of the mist but seem to spring out of the green-grey like sudden ideas. It is twelve degrees outside with little wind, just these well-up swells.

The Captain's hands run like large crabs across the chart table. 'I have calculated we can stand six-metre waves. We won't make any speed but the vessel can stand it.'

He marks our position with a pencil stroke: just west of the Azores but twelve degrees north of them; our present heading takes us into the Labrador Basin passing north of the Flemish Cap.

John's air-vent-blocking contraption now piles uselessly on the floor. He has discarded his shirt and sprawls on his bunk reading a maritime newspaper. He is quite a sight.

There is the merest yellowing of the sky around 1500, at 1740, sundown, there is an eerie clear. Suddenly the horizon ahead jumps back a dozen miles below clouds spun from pearly air. There are white-blue and black-blue distances

around us crossed with lines of darkness, behind is a dimly
luminous aquamarine. We are sailing across the Atlantic's
dark pupil, surrounded by its iris. Pieter comes up to join
the Captain and they both stand, gazing across the eye,
weather-worried. Pieter balances easily, hands folded behind
his back. So many, many seas he has travelled, down in the
engine room. Morning and evening conferences on the
bridge are almost all he glimpses of them. Our lives are in
his hands more than anyone's: it is the howling, hungry and
tireless engine that is the main miracle out here, from which
all else hangs. His contemplation is moving to witness, as
though you see a man looking at his life.

There is a lot of lurching and thumping after dinner but
you can sleep through it. Mark, the steward, was right. He
said fatigue was the key.

CHAPTER 19

Storm

E rwin has all the bridge lights on, as it is 6 a.m., and therefore morning, though it is still entirely dark outside.

'Lovely day, Erwin! Thank you!'

'Yes, yes, very nice. But it can't be guaranteed later on . . .'

Day does not so much break as night lightens. I dismantle my air vent and stuff it with my overall. Success! The diesel draught abates. We are on the edge of the depression. The barometer has fallen to 978, stormy weather, but the brute is to the south of us. There are eleven-metre waves on our original course. Chicoy had thirty-degree rolls on Christmas Day four years ago.

'I was scared, really I was scared, but the Captain stood with his arms on the back of the pilot's chair. Everything's falling around the bridge. He didn't look round. He just said, "Second Mate, something is moving. Fix it." Something moving – fix it! I look at him and think OK, maybe not so bad . . .'

He says the first day of pitching makes him feel dizzy but once he has slept on it he is better. He is generously talkative today and he briefs me on the lashing business. The (un)lashing bonus is three hundred dollars and the midnight to 4 a.m. watch earn it exhausted, as they start unlashing at 8.30. It will be done in the St Lawrence so that if something goes wrong it will not happen in port where an accident would bring an investigation. Handling the lashing rod – which frees the catches at the corners of the containers – is hard and dangerous because the rod is long and very heavy. With ice and snow it is more difficult. They will unlash everything except the outside containers. The bonus is paid in cash and worth a lot to a rating whose salary is seven hundred dollars a month. As second mate Chicoy is on three and half thousand a month.

As we talk he calls the bo'sun on the radio: 'Make sure he still on the ship.'

Chicoy has never seen inside a container: 'Maybe plenty girls and drugs!'

I ask him about *Maersk Luz*. 'Maybe you come on board and have enemy,' he says. The rumours report that alcohol was involved. 'Maybe he stabs one and the other cannot get out of the cabin.'

A crewman he knew sided with a bo'sun who had an enemy, and the enemy had a cousin on board. The bo'sun was small and thin. The enemy and his cousin beat him but the bo'sun used his knife.

Chicoy reckons it is better if the captain and the chief engineer are 'white people'. 'Then if chat chat captain does not know anything. If captain Filipino he knows. He hear something. Who tell him? Chat chat . . .' The internet can cause strife, too: 'Someone always say "Who used all the gigs? – You?"'

When a Filipino captain or senior officer has favourites, Chicoy says, the structures fall apart. He sailed on one ship from which the captain disappeared.

'Did someone throw him over the side?'

'Maybe.'

'Which is more dangerous, man or the sea?'

'Man,' says Chicoy, 'because man thinks. If white people shout at Filipino –' he shrugs. 'But if Filipino shouts . . .' he grimaces.

Force eight now; the wind veered in the night and has now backed, more or less abeam, coming at us sideways from the north. We bash through short, punitive seas. There was a strange yellow light in the air before we went into it. Doors are lashed open and there is chatter in the stairwell where Mark and little Richard are mopping the steps. Annabelle is dicing cantaloupes in the galley and the eerie music still plays from the crew's mess. Pieter says he hears voices in it, conversations. I track it down to a screensaver called Waterfall. It never ceases.

The chair slides under me as I write. Jannie has been stripping and cleaning generator cylinders for two days. I have a cold; he does not, though I have been diligent with greens he does not eat. The consensus is that the lurid green minty cherry thing I ate for pudding last night is responsible for the ailment, as no one else touched theirs. Jannie prefers rolling to pitching but currently we are corkscrewing – doing

both at once. An hour ago it was eight degrees outside but
we are currently holding on four and my cabin windows
have steamed up. A hissy rattle of spray-rain fills the air.
Four black fins came plunging in towards the bow; they
must have been dolphins but they looked sinister – perhaps
they were orcas. To think this is only the edge of the storm!
(Thump, groan, roll, thump . . .) I would not go out on
deck for any money. The bo'sun and his party are back
inside. Chicoy knew a bo'sun who was washed off the deck
to his death. It was during that Christmas storm – he went
forward with the captain to see what damage the anchor
had done to the bow while they were rolling thirty degrees.

Now there are long white streaks down the waves which
the Captain says mean force eight or above.

'What are you doing?' Chicoy asked, genuinely perplexed,
as I stared out of the screens and frowned and scribbled
and tried to keep my balance, and the scrawl legible.

'I'm trying to – describe – this! Look at it! How do you
capture this?'

Sometimes in darkness, sometimes in hail, through mist,
rattling rain and footprints of sun, the *Pembroke* tries conclu-
sions with waves. Short, angry punchers; long heaving
monsters; black swells, green roarers . . .

Chicoy laughed.

'Average wave height five metres, with exceptions seven
metres,' the Captain declares. The windward side of the
bridge is a wuthering buffet scored by the bridge screens'
wipers. The faces of the waves are chipped with liquid ridges
and their backs with flying white. Now and then they explode
before we reach them as if a monster is breaching. We are

making seventeen knots but the wind is still rising and backing, coming now from the north-north-west. When the ship misses her footing there is a deep boom in her steel chest and a white curled hand of a billion droplets leaps as high as the foremast and caresses back towards us, whistling and falling as tears on the screens. The containers look as if they are on fire under the gusting spray.

After lunch the gale still roars but the sky clears partially. It is a violent and lovely day now, the sea purple. There are many birds, northern fulmars, kittiwakes bright against the dark water, and I think a great skua. Now it is sunny and rainy with dark-bellied clouds, broken rainbows and ice-blue clears all at once. John stirring his tea with a spoon makes a strangely domestic counterpoint to the billow-bellow gale. Hail comes in rattle blasts and the white streaked foam down the backs of the waves joins with the scars on their faces, forming long straggled lines pointing into the wind's mouth.

You feel much more exhilaration than fear: I see why John likes storms. Fear is quite hard to find in true sea stories, though so many are fearful and fear-filled. Men are not quick to admit it or describe it: to do it justice is to feel it again, and who wants that? Much better to pass on to the happy ending, to the deprecating laugh, as Chicoy did: 'Really I was scared but . . .' Admissions of fear in the Atlantic war are rare. Perhaps it was so ubiquitous it was not worth writing about, while 'talking things through' was not necessarily the habit of the time. An extraordinary exception occurs in the writing of Humphrey Knight, who dramatised an encounter with a psychiatrist after one of the Arctic convoys to Murmansk. These convoys, from Scapa

Flow via Norway's North Cape to Russia, matched and surpassed the Atlantic's horrors. The cold, the seas and the conditions aboard the ships were monstrous, and the convoys were within range of German aircraft most of the way there and back. The psychiatrist asks Knight's narrator how he feels. The narrator can make only non-committal answers, but he tells the reader the truth.

The bewilderment may keep you calm. Even when the fear runs into the joints like hot glue, delaying the reflexes, delaying all save one. The instinct to duck when the dive-bombers scream over the mastheads like express trains with wings. The instinct to plunge deep back into the darkness of your primeval self. The passionate desire to get down into a hole, into the earth (only there is no earth), to take cover. Here is no earth; here is liquid emerald twenty degrees below zero. The feet press into the deck, seeking resilience. Seeking earth which is known to you. No earth here, no earth . . .

You would tear the deck like a dog after a rat. You would throw yourself flat and hide your head in your hands. You would cry for a woman's breast where you could lay your head. You might even think of your mother, for you would cry where once you had sucked life. Life that has brought you here where life and death compare their hideous notes.

Only you don't. You just turn your head from the blast and keep on handing up the shells . . .

At the height of the Battle of the Atlantic, in 1943, more than sixty U-boats were concentrated here, in mid-ocean, ranged in four patrol groups. In March of that year forty of them were directed to attack two laden convoys, eighty ships all heading east, which had come into proximity across a vast area approaching the western end of the Black Hole, where we are now. In the melee of a battle which stretched across days and nights, pitching over hundreds of square miles of ocean, it was not unusual for an escort commander to receive contact reports of half a dozen submarines at a time. Three days of fog and gales ragged the convoys at the outset: what followed was as horror-ridden as any engagement of the Atlantic war. Reading Richard Woodman's accounts of the battle produces a kind of numbed awe, as the mind wonders at the montage of images. A tanker, the *Southern Princess*, blazing so fiercely the heat could be felt on the decks of passing ships, her oil leaving the sea burning where she sank. Men so thick in the water that the lights of their life jackets seemed to a witness 'like a carpet of fireflies'. Torpedoed ships abandoned, their derelict hulks refusing to sink. A ship, the *Elin K*, going down so fast that neither the escort commander nor the rescue ship realised she had been hit. The surface of the sea scattered with the frozen carcasses of Argentinian cattle that washed out in hundreds from a huge hole blown in the side of the Royal Mail cargo liner *Nariva*. The *Coracero* carried the same cargo; one of the hands killed in her engine room was a trimmer named Robert Yates who had gone to sea under the alias J. J. Elder. He was fourteen years old. The *Canadian Star*, hit twice, poised vertically, her bow high in the air for five minutes before she sank. Most of her crew made the boats, but they were overloaded, and the water wild and terribly cold.

The second officer 'had twenty-two men on a ten-man raft, most had to hang over the side . . . We lost six of these fairly quickly; you would see them getting cold, a certain look came into their eyes and then they just gave up.' An army officer who had watched his wife and child flung into the water when another of the boats capsized 'was the first to go'. In these circumstances it was perhaps not surprising that one chief engineer cast off a motor lifeboat and steered clear of his sinking ship, leaving many of his shipmates with no option but to jump. Eighteen of them died of hypothermia, three after they had been pulled from the sea. The chief told a Board of Inquiry, months later, that he had been in a state of terror. No action was taken against him.

The effects of acute tension, fear and worry are related with a coolness typical of the time, by a British submarine commander, William King, DSO, DSC, who captained HM Submarine *Snapper* in the North Atlantic. 'Stress' is the vocabulary of the grandchildren and great-grandchildren of those who fought the war, who seem to have preferred 'strain', but King makes no mention of either.

'I was sitting in the mess waiting for patrol orders when our doctor asked casually, "Let's have a look at your fingernails." Each one showed a series of concentric half-moon ridges from base to tip. "Interesting stigmata," he said. "If you break off patrols for a refit you'll find a gap corresponding to the time spent in harbour. Each ridge is a patrol. They occur in all commanding officers of submarines, in most of their subordinate officers and in a small proportion of responsible ratings – purely psychological."'

The wind blows force nine now, severe gale, and in the sun the waves glow gem-like sapphire and green. It strengthens by the minute, now force ten, storm, and as the waves deepen the sea seems to move with a different rhythm, as if with inclinations and intention. The bright luminescence in the heart of the white when a crest shatters is dazzling, a wild scatter of Poseidon's turquoise hurled into the air. We hold our course on 274 degrees with the sea still building to the north-west: we have to turn across it at some point. Each wave – they are truly mighty now – seems to demand its own description. When we hit them full-on the whole ship shudders, as if winded, and we lose a couple of knots of speed. Because the streaming white lines on the water point back towards the wind, while the waves move forward towards us, the sea seems to travel in two directions at once.

'We are the only assholes out here,' says the Captain.

'What a way to make a living,' John marvels, as we slide into another trough.

At a quarter to four we round Flemish Cap and begin to turn west-south-west to 245 degrees. We are over the Labrador Basin, three kilometres deep. The starboard bow is taking a ferocious pounding as we bear down the world slowly towards Orphan Knoll, which rises to a depth of a kilometre and a half. The Captain calls the chief and they agree to bring the revs down. She lurches heavily, labouring on, pummelled on the windward side where the waves have the measure of the main deck. Vivid blue explosions of foam and solid water come hurling over the rail. Ahead, legs of sunlight break through like searchlights on the roaring sea.

When we cross under one it is so bright that your eyes water and the sea turns obsidian-black.

From the wing I look back at the Captain, alone on his bridge, staring forward. Because he stands his watch in the hours of daylight he has no lookout. And so, alone, he gazes forward, always forward, a solitary figure overseeing his old machine and the violent desolation he has sent her into, watching every blow she deals the sea and every one she takes, lurching down with her, staggering back with her, lurching down, and there is a solitude about him which is emphasised rather than dispersed by his openness in company, and an endurance and absolute toughness about him which is entirely at one with his vessel, though you sense he is tougher than her. He is married but he mentions his wife only once on the voyage. In everything but the sea he is private and held in.

It is too cold to stay long outside.

'This is where they were,' the Captain says, quietly. 'That fishing boat –?' (The fate of the *Andrea Gail* is told in a wonderful book, *The Perfect Storm*, by Sebastian Junger, and a terrible film.) 'They were far out, eh? Very far . . .'

We look at the sea. It is a prospect unutterably bleak and desperate as we move away from the sun patches: grey death everywhere.

'God, Captain. This is the loneliest place I've ever been.'

'Yes,' he says. 'A bad place for anything to happen.'

Captain Koop now sits in his chair, as his ship fights her way through the relentless gale, and talks.

'Have you ever been frightened at sea, Captain?'

'Only once. We were in the Channel. A smoker left his butt in the bin in the harbour control room and went to answer an alarm in the engine room, and went to bed. It was about twelve thirty at night, I woke up and smelt something burning. The alarms went off. I thought this is bullshit, this is not good. I went to the bridge. All the walkie-talkies were on charge in the harbour control room so we had no comms. A crewman appeared, he said the whole main deck is full of smoke, the harbour control room is completely on fire, the computers, everything. The chief officer made an attempt to get an extinguisher on it but he went without breathing apparatus and came back choking. The smoke was full of plastic, poisonous. Now, the Captain has to stay on bridge, and you think, how are the crew going to react? Can they handle this? And they were good. They did the right things and got it under control. It was good. Fire at sea is the worst, in my opinion it is the worst. We put it out and we had a few beers on it afterwards. I didn't call Dover, because if you do that you have all kinds of investigations, troubles – I steered towards shore so if they have to come out or something it's easier. But first you think can we handle this? Apart from that I have never been frightened on this ship.'

'What about storms?'

'Ah! Well, we were fully loaded on one of our first North Atlantic winter crossings and the bow – with thirty thousand tonnes behind it – she crashed into a wave so hard a winch jumped back two feet. We were drydocked and the bow was reinforced, but still – you have to watch her!'

'What do you worry about when you go to bed?'

'The judgement of the officer on watch. You worry he

won't pull back the throttle if she's driving too hard. I sleep very lightly and when I feel it I call the bridge when she's slamming and I say can't you tell this is too hard? Pull back.

'I used to love it,' he says, 'but I love it less now. Everyone of my generation says the same. You arrive and they say the ship is dirty – it's the North Atlantic! If there's damage they say did you take routing from a weather centre? Pfff . . . they have the same information I have but they don't know my ship! I know my ship.

'And you know a sailor is always a second-class person – in the Caribbean we used to say we were students on exchange. Even now you say you are a sailor – "oh, a girl in every port", these old phrases . . . Only the Mission to Seafarers under-stands or cares about us. Nobody else. There used to be seafarers in management but not so much now. My super-visors are in Mumbai and theirs are in Singapore. There have been thousands of redundancies in Copenhagen. So you're emailing people and you don't know if you can trust them. Do they understand, or is it only money to them?'

He has a huge admiration for the Filipinos.

'They are so pennywise, eh? These guys really know the score. They are always talking to each other on email, even on radio if we pass a ship close, saying how much are they paying you? If it's more they're gone. You should see them going through airports. So much stuff! You say how are you going to manage? They say, "Don't worry, we'll help each other." They come on board with nothing. Some of them don't trust banks so they carry their wages home as cash. This can be very dangerous but they know the risks.'

Captain Koop thought for a moment, then he said, 'You know these guys are heroes. It's not just the family they support, it's the whole clan.'

The sea darkened, Erwin came up and it was time for us to go down. 'We're through the worst,' the Captain said. 'And that anticyclone, I used it, eh? Used it to give me a good push this morning.'

It was a sanguine day on the ship, considering the storm. A severe gale, occasional storm force ten and twenty-foot waves, had the following effects: Annabelle produced her best supper yet, soup to start, a fillet of fish in cheese sauce with almonds, and avocado milkshake for dessert. Work continued in the engine room, Pieter commenting that he had to go outside to close a hatch, because it was very cold. Jannie said he did the same as every day. The bo'sun and his gang checked lashings and returned safely. John was moved to get his camera and take a couple of shots of the storm, with the Captain encouraging him and helping him with the door, which was a battle with the wind – 'Yeah, you can take pictures in this!' You only just could, though.

I wake to enraging head-thickness. How is it still happening? I have reinforced the stuffed boiler suit with paper wedges but still the diesel fumes flow. Clock says 0700 so I jump up. Annabelle is frying spam in the galley and Eugene is mopping the bridge. Light on the sea, and the water a colour that makes you feel cold. Erwin talked about his first voyage, on a bulk carrier travelling from Indonesia to New York.

'There was a typhoon in the Indian Ocean. Oh! The waves were sweeping over the deck, the ship was flexing and diving, the hatch covers were under water. I never been

on a bulk carrier before – this was normal but I don't know!
I was very scared and very sick . . .'

Erwin comes from a rice farming family. He has no love
of the city and he plans to get out of seafaring. 'Many
Filipinos do a few years at sea and then find jobs on land.'
He says 90 per cent of his compatriots are Catholic. 'Some
people pray in their cabins, sometimes with a friend, but
we do not pray all together.'

Pieter the chief, the second engineer, the Captain and
Erwin hold a conference on the bridge.

'You're early!' Pieter laughs. 'Time difference messing
you up?'

We retarded another hour last night, so while I am still
in Grytviken's time zone, in line with South Georgia, where
we were yesterday, everyone else is in Nuuk's time zone, in
line with Greenland.

Outside it snows horizontally and hail spatters against the
screens. The gale is supposed to be slackening but it is not.
Northern fulmars and shearwaters ride along with us on the
windward side, balancing the powers of the gale, the four-
metre waves and the smash-back from the ship's side, skiing
along a wind tunnel between chaos and death with perfect,
nonchalant control. There must be an ideal air current
between the ship and the wind because they stick as closely
to us as they dare. We are doing fifteen and a half knots and
when they fire themselves ahead of us and curve around the
bow they must be adding five knots to that easily. They twist
away for their lives as the rebounding waves erupt and claw
after them; sometimes they fly under the very grasp of the
falling water, like surfers shooting out of a tube.

We are now at the same latitude as Cape Bonavista, Newfoundland, and definitely feeling the beginnings of the swell on the Grand Banks. We hit a thunderous wave and the ship shakes from side to side as well as lengthways. Chicoy clicks and hums away his frustration. He and John are at daggers drawn. Chicoy is not yet adept and John is unforgiving. The latest spat revolves around an updated radio signals book which John admits they do not use in any case. When should they send the reminder email? Chicoy had not noticed they had received the wrong updates, John spotted it, and now Chicoy is anxious to send the reminder, which John thinks unnecessary. John checks the log.

'South-west nine! That's never south-west nine!'

'It was stronger earlier,' I protest.

'Twelve o'clock it says here – I've just come up. He writes a load of shit. I give up. I *give* up . . .'

Chicoy goes down to the galley where he restores his humour and standing by telling jokes to Annabelle and Richard. The galley is a crucial place, the Captain says. 'If something is going on I rely on the cook to tell me. The cook is the conduit between the Captain and the crew; the cook always knows everything.'

Annabelle has a calm smile and a workmanlike sense of purpose. She is never idle: a seafarer like any other, her demeanour says, and a good one. She speaks little but the men talk more easily around her, bouncing jokes off her, seeking her approval in glances, making her laugh and using the atmosphere she creates as an opportunity to be 'themselves' – the selves we are in the presence of women being distinct from the mantle we assume with men. Annabelle seems to have mastered a sisterly aura which makes us relax around her. Men's shoulders drop and they allow themselves to moan about things, you can tell, though the conversations are in Tagalog. Most of the laughter on the ship comes from the galley when Annabelle is working.

Mark, the steward, is talkative, as ever. I am warming to him: I think my suspicions of his friendliness were mean-spirited. He is halfway through a nine-month contract and hoping to add a one-month extension. He will cross and recross this ocean throughout. His last job was a car carrier sailing between Japan and South America: twenty-eight days each way.

'I have two children with two women!' he says, laughing with more self-consciousness than mirth. 'Sometimes I gave money to the first one but that is all in the past now.'

I look at him again. He used to send money to the mother of his first child but he no longer does? Why not? What does that mean? I want to ask but it would be presumptuous. ('Who is looking after your family?' Never. I am not a judge.) But I speculate. 'That's all in the past now . . .' Something happened, clearly, and whoever she is no longer has a claim on him, he feels. I wonder if whatever it was has some bearing on his eagerness to please; he seems to carry a wound somehow, whether done to him or inflicted by him I cannot tell.

He serves me bacon, eggs and salt soup. 'White people only stay for three months,' he says. 'Is there news about the weather?'

'The Captain says the whole North Atlantic is eight-metre waves.'

'Oh no!'

During a visit to the engine room an alarm sounds. Orange warning lights flash. You wonder if the CO_2 suppressors are about to go off and kill you. Pieter comes flying by and ghosts up five ladders in two blinks. It turns out to be a boiler problem – for some reason it is not heating the fuel sufficiently. The electrician is on the case with a spanner, his teeth clenched. Pieter says the second engineer switched the steam off before he cut in the other boiler. The second engineer looks embarrassed while black smoke-like steam wreaths the electrician. Pieter mulls on the perpetual motion of the engine. 'That's the thing with engineering, you can start again. It is not like man, or nature. Everything can be replaced.'

In the bo'sun's passage, running the length of the ship, Bobby Sitones, an ordinary seaman, leans on his mop and grins. His working environment today is a concertina of iron loopholes, between which are drums of toxins, all echoing with the moan, clash and wail of the containers above.

In the early afternoon the waves diminish and the fog closes in. To the south of us the warm Gulf Stream is meeting the frigid Labrador Current, running down from the north, their confluence producing a vapour that hides everything beyond the foremast. Through it the swells come again; long, low beasts, purple-faced and swollen with age, driving up from the south. We see a whale that way, blowing and swimming north towards us.

'Well, he's not a northern right whale, I can tell you that,' the Captain asserts. 'They're not here now.' The whale disappears astern and the Captain lectures on navigation before GPS.

'We shot the sun at nine, at noon and at three, and we shot the stars when they came out. We called it nautical twilight, when the sun has gone but while there is still enough light to see the horizon. You need the horizon and the first stars. In perfect conditions you shoot a star ahead, to the flank and behind. Then you get the logarithms from the almanac. If you were good you could get a position in twenty minutes.'

He breaks out the almanac and displays the ranks of tiny numbers which fill every millimetre of the A4 pages.

'When we got calculators with log buttons it was easier. We had an old Decca Navigator, radio direction finder, but we didn't trust it. It was more wrong than right. Then we got a radar but the Captain didn't trust that. We were shooting the stars even in the English Channel! When we couldn't see anything it was down to dead reckoning. When we went to South America we steered for the Azores. When we saw Mount Pico we said, Yes! Now we know where we are – OK!'

A ship appears on the AIS: the *Anvil* is somewhere to the south of us, near the Terre Nova oil and gas field.

'This is a terrible place,' the Captain says. 'Always waves and storms. Truly terrible. You need a psychologist if you stay there.'

The wind drops to the point that we can go outside. The sea temperature is minus one and the air is two degrees. Towards dusk there is a lightening, a single gold bar on the horizon, pale and dead ahead, as though we steered for the end of the ocean. The Captain produces the chart of a formidably desolate and fractured coast.

'You must be mad to live here,' he says. Sable Island to the south of us is known for its currents, sandbars, cross-seas and multiple wrecks as 'the graveyard of the Atlantic'. Its thin grin of dunes, marram grass and pounding surf supports a population of wild horses descended from ship-wrecked Shetland ponies. In 1598 a French marquis, Troilus de Mesgouez, had sixty convicts transported there. Within five years forty-nine were dead. The plight of the surviving eleven so impressed King Henri IV that he pardoned their crimes and paid compensation for their suffering. Miquelon Island, to our north, was assigned to France by the Treaty of Utrecht in 1713 and is still marked French on the chart. French fishermen no longer exercise the right to land and cure their catch there, but they did in the eighteenth century, when it was said that the cod ran so thick in these waters that they slowed the passage of ships.

The wind drops as we cross the one-hundred-fathom line, for a short while the wuthering relents. The constant, echoing rushes and whistling growls are the hallmark of this strange voyage, along with the ghostly piano, the diesel, the pitching and slamming and the Eternal Salad.

CHAPTER 20

The Hold

Wake at five – our clocks have moved again – to dolphin cloud, a wind bitter to listen to and a shuddering sea. In these waters the North Atlantic convoys formed for the easterly run to Britain, while arriving ships dispersed to St John's, Halifax and New York. Leif Ericsson came here around 1001, according to the sagas, followed nearly five hundred years later by the Venetian Giovanni Caboto, known in England as John Cabot, who sailed from Bristol in 1497. No one knows where Cabot landed (the Canadian and UK governments have settled on Cape Bonavista, where there is a plaque) but there are four accounts of what he saw, three written by people Cabot talked to when he returned. The most vivid comes from a letter apparently by a Bristolian who signed himself 'John Day', which scholars now believe was a nom de plume for a London merchant named Hugh Say, writing, it is near certain, to Christopher Columbus. The thrill of first contact, or almost first contact, is palpable. The 'he' of Say's letter is Cabot, the 'master' Columbus, and the events take place in a very different season, midsummer, 24 June.

He landed at only one spot of the mainland, near the place where land was first sighted, and they disembarked there with a crucifix and raised banners with the arms of the Holy Father and those of the King of England, my master; and they found tall trees of the kind masts are made, and other smaller trees, and the country is very rich in grass. In that particular spot, as I told your Lordship, they found a trail that went inland, they saw a site where a fire had been made, they saw manure of animals which they thought to be farm animals, and they saw a stick half a yard long pierced at both ends, carved and painted with brazil, and by such signs they believe the land to be inhabited. Since he was with just a few people, he did not dare advance inland beyond the shooting distance of a cross-bow, and after taking in fresh water he returned to his ship. All along the coast they found many fish like those which in Iceland are dried in the open and sold in England and other countries, and these fish are called in English 'stockfish'; and thus following the shore they saw two forms running on land one after the other, but they could not tell if they were human beings or animals; and it seemed to them that there were fields where they thought might also be villages, and they saw a forest whose foliage looked beautiful . . .

Through a mottled sky of mauve and grey comes our first contact, a Canadian accent over the radio, a coastguard, brusque in static. We are south of the Avalon Peninsula, surely ironically named, below Placentia Bay. In the night we cut inside the Virgin Rocks, turning with the elbow of the wide channel into the Gulf of St Lawrence. South of us are the Grand Banks, and their former bounty is everywhere on the chart: Halibut Channel, Haddock Channel, Whale Bank, St Pierre Bank. These were once the richest fishing grounds in the world, before the stocks collapsed around 1990. There are no birds, no signs of life.

'Another day in paradise,' Erwin smiles.

You hope to smell something in the wind, now we are closing with the land, ozone or salt or something, but the wind smells like cold steel. A fire alarm goes off but it is nothing special, though you look at the freshening gale and the indifference of the sea with fresh eyes, for a few minutes, while it rings.

At coffee the Captain reveals the ice route we have been sent – rather further north than he was hoping. Afterwards I destroy my careful lagging of the air vent, extract my boiler suit and follow the deck crew forward to the cargo hold. You have to be nippy to catch them as they move quickly along the filthy deck, doused with spray and within the waves' grasp, even on the leeward side. We climb a short ladder to a passage between the containers. We pick our way between whining reefers, greasy iron protrusions and bundles of lashing rods. A hatch cover stands open, a ladder below descends vertically into the gloom – or as vertically as the rolling allows.

First we descend three storeys, changing ladders carefully, stepping around a hole in the floor. Behind you, as you climb, is nothing – empty gaps dropping to darkness. The rungs of the ladders are diamond-shaped in cross section, flaky and stinking acidly, like leaking batteries. We climb down two more ladders and move sideways, then two more down. I must be the only idiot to have done this without gloves. You hang on grimly as the rolls pull you away from the ladder. The smells are an evil concoction of metallic, rusty and chemical-fishy.

At the bottom a doorway leads into a cavern four containers wide, three long and seven high, but we are not surrounded by containers. On either side, before, behind and in the gloom high above, are container-sized tanks of sodium-methylate solution, liquid acid and toxic organo-phosphates. Everything is marked with hazard and pollutant symbols. You have to shut your imagination away. If anything leaks, falls or bursts here, anything at all . . .

In one corner Jannie is working with a shrieking angle-grinder, producing showers of sparks, reeks of hot steel and smoke. He is balanced on his haunches. The floor is an inch deep in water which sloshes from side to side and tilts with the motion of the ship. You are grateful for the islands of rust on the deck because there are no hand-holds and the metal is slippy. You are carefully not thinking of the thousands of gallons of acids and toxins around you. Jannie goes on grinding at a rusty hatch cover, the steel screaming. We should be wearing respirators; the air is foul. Your senses are assaulted by the dripping decks, the rusting ladders, the vertical drops, the cut-away holes in the walkways, the lurch and slide, the stink and prickle in your nose, the peril, the scale, the darkness and the toxic slop washing around your boots. Outside is the mouth of the Laurentian Channel, into which we pitch and slam quite hard. Force seven has swelled to eight and the waves are twenty feet high. Jannie carries on, wreathed with smoke, steel-howl and sparks, for all the world like the devil's apprentice doing DIY in hell, with the angle-grinder's flex trailing away through the water. Now he pauses. There is a light in the hole below him, then a voice.

The hatch cover in the floor leads to a half-height passageway, a ballast tank, from which Erwin emerges, his work jacket streaked with black oil. Even a man accustomed to all this shakes his head. 'Horrible down there, horrible,' he says. He has been checking the hull. One of the waves has left its mark on one of the hull's plates, battering a dent into steel designed to take fifteen tonnes of pressure per square metre; it probably dents at double that. When Jannie has done what he can the hatch is replaced and bolted down and we retreat, wincing and gripping up all the ladders and through the hatch, stumbling back down the deck.

Just after noon we glimpse a lump of Newfoundland, the island of St Pierre: grey-yellow rock, high cliffs and banking hills patched with snow appear briefly in the distance. Leif Ericsson may have thought it relatively tropical but it looks bleak to me. The wind has strengthened and the foremast describes churning, crushed ovals. There are one or two northern fulmars and a very small auk, black, white and fluttering, barely blackbird-sized. We dive and climb quite dramatically, punching up container-high spray.

John spots the bo'sun going forward.

'He shouldn't be on deck,' he says, 'not in this.' He seems aggrieved. 'Perhaps he doesn't know it's got worse.'

'Can't you tell him?'

'How can I? They haven't got a radio.'

At that the radio crackles: the bo'sun reporting in.

'You are welcome to go out,' says the Captain. 'You have signed your indemnity.'

The working party are picking their ways between the containers collecting torn shreds of plastic, the blasted remains of the tarpaulin which covered the tractor on the bow. The tractor is a shining green and orange machine attached by pipes and joints to a precision air seeder. We wonder at it: can it be destined for the grain prairies? Surely Canada has its own tractors? Its German manufacturer says it will plant and deliver seasonal yields over 1,500 hectares. We dig fragments of its tarpaulin out of corners and gaps between the containers, unable to face the freezing spray with open eyes as it pours across the ship. The working party are done up in bulky jackets and balaclavas, their brown faces as pale as they will ever be. 'Like nice weather?' shouts Sumy. We bend and pick and pluck, everything around us hard, cold, filthy and catching, lurching in motion with the ship.

The Captain is tense. He needs fifteen and half knots but we can only make fourteen in this, a sea as bad as anything we have had: massive, confused, lugubriously hostile, with waves breaking in blue and white calderas to a near horizon smoked with rain.

In mid-afternoon the sun comes out and the wind blows ever stronger – force nine coming from dead ahead, six-metre waves and the sea furious, Atlantic-black. Beyond the rain to the north are the Blue Hills of Couteau. The rolling and pitching must have paused at some point in the last four days but I cannot remember when. When the propeller is yanked up towards the surface it loses its grip on the

water and cavitates, threshing in foam or air, which causes
deep rumble-shakes. They rattle up your spine. Using the
stairs is never less than interesting; you manoeuvre yourself
with your arms as much as your legs.

We see our first ship, *Flevob*, emerging like a ghost
through the sleety clouded air. *Flevob* is a Dutch freighter,
smaller than us, 120 metres, belonging to the Wagenborg
Line. She rolls heavily and quickly.

'They carry everything,' says the Captain. 'They go
through the locks up to the Great Lakes – wherever the
cargo is they go. Coal, iron ore, wheat, paper, newsprint –
this is what you get from Canada.'

A crew of twelve, he guesses, and she is toppling from
side to side, spray flying around her so that she seems
wreathed in her own mist. She steams past us into the worst
weather map the Captain has seen of the Atlantic.

'What a brave little ship!'

'Yes,' the Captain laughs. 'Yes. We complain but . . .'
Then another thought: 'They probably have beer on board.'

The sky ahead of us opens to an icy clear, fog-white
on the horizon rises to soft horizontal knives of cloud,
then palest blue, then harder blue, luminous. It suggests
an eternal tranquillity but we batter and wallop towards
it, the gale's noise never relenting, only adding or
subtracting a whistle in two parts, one like a child blowing
a recorder as hard as possible, the other like a devil sucking
its teeth.

The chart tells a frank story of Newfoundland. Working
eastwards from a point due north of our position are Grey
River, Bear Head, at the mouth of White Bear Bay, Bay de

Loup, Six Mile Hill, Bread and Cheese Hill, Muddy Hole
Point, Grand Bruit (we know the feeling) and the Highlands
of Grand Bruit, where someone saw five deer at a brook
and called it Cinq Cerf Brook. You wonder who Rose
Blanche was, but, ship or woman, she must have known and
feared Pointe Enrage at the entrance to Cabot Strait. Basque
fishermen came here in the early sixteenth century; they
are commemorated in the names of a port and a traffic
control scheme.

During the Captain's watch the wind changes again,
dropping as we steer into it towards a high clear, most
beautiful. The chief comes up and a new moon comes out,
fabulous glowing silver with one planet attendant. I go out
on the bitter bridge wing and show it fifty pence, make a
wish and consign the coin to the Cabot Strait. It feels right
and exhilarating.

Supper begins with green-lipped mussels, from New
Zealand, Jannie says. 'They stay alive quite a long time
before you have to fridge them.' There is no calculating the
nautical miles the mussels have done but it cannot be much
less than two months by sea from New Zealand to Antwerp.
The mussels now seem to dare me to eat them. The green
lips grin: Have we come all this way for nothing, Nancy?
Jannie, oblivious to my communion with the shellfish, talks
about making his own vodka, which his wife turns into Tia
Maria.

'That was a hell of a job in the hold,' I say, swallowing
a morsel.

'Ja. Shit tool, cheap rubbish, wouldn't bore out the bolts,'
he growls, and gurns at the memory of the smell of the

dangerous cargo, while I grimace at the gassy taste of the green-lip.

Before sleep I go out to the bridge wing. The lights of Basque Harbour and Pointe Enrage make clusters of white and orange, a tiny broken necklace in the wilderness. The stars are in their utmost profusion: there is the Milky Way, the Plough, the planets, strange satellite flashes very high up and a plane heading for New York much lower. But there are nets of further stars between those you normally see; heavens within heavens. You can scarcely believe the night's darkness could contain so much tiny light. The crescent moon turns gold. I sleep and dream of ice clunking against the hull, and think I hear it, and wake to a changed sea.

CHAPTER 21

Ice

A t 0600, in mist, the *Maersk Pembroke* is twelve miles
south of the Île d'Anticosti and bearing into the Gulf
of St Lawrence, the world's largest estuary. Anticosti is
home to a thousand moose, many bald eagles and a great
many white-tailed deer, which ate the island's black bears
to extinction, both species sharing a taste for berries. The
island is said to be ringed with over four hundred ship-
wrecks; weather like this must have done for many of them.
You can see nothing in the icy murk of dawn. Without radar
our first intimation of danger might well be the mariner's
death-knell, waves breaking on rocks, too close to be avoided.
Daylight reveals a narrow, vague field of vision beyond the
ship's rail.

There are streaks in the water like foam made solid, which
lengthen, stretch and harden into broken white slabs, heaving
with the waves. The wind is from the north-east now and
the sea more ice than not. Visibility is shrunk to barely four
hundred yards ahead and though we are doing eighteen knots
we barely seem to move. The ice deadens the motion of the

sea, crushing its vigour and will. Broken frozen sheets form perfect, rocking mosaics. Larger chunks have snowy edges and dark centres, like the tastebuds of giant and freezing tongues. We pass in and out of the white fields and our passage seems very quiet, as if we are trying not to be noticed. There are no waves now and the air is full of tiny snowflakes. By seven the snow is sticking, whitening the containers. The slicks in the sea are called grease ice, or grey water. The occasional crystalline fins, little crests, are brush ice and the suckers are pancake ice, according to the almanac.

As we reach the longitude of the tip of Anticosti, Cap aux Anglais, the engine stops. The wind is back up to gale force as we drift, blown sideways through a black and white sea, barely wallowing despite the storm; the Cap shelters us from the worst of it and the ice keeps the swells down. Off this cape on 13 August 1535 a world-changing conversation took place between the French explorer Jacques Cartier and two Iroquoians whom Cartier had kidnapped the year before, during his first voyage, when he had explored the eastern half of the gulf.

'It was told us by the two savages that to the south of it [Anticosti, which Cartier named Assomption] lay the route from Honguedo where we had seized them . . . and that two days journey from this cape and island began the Kingdom of the Saguenay, on the north shore as one made one's way towards this Canada. The two savages assured us that this was the way to the mouth of the great river of Hochelaga and the route towards Canada.'

The 'savages' assured Cartier that it was possible to travel so far up the Hochelaga 'that they had never heard of anyone reaching the head of it'. Cartier found the river and followed it to the site of what is now Montreal, then a huge Iroquoian settlement, where rapids were all that prevented his further progress to China, he believed. He claimed the Gulf, the St Lawrence and the hinterland for France. Nothing remained of the St Lawrence Iroquoians seventy-five years later, when Cartier's successor, Samuel de Champlain, arrived and founded Quebec. Their disappearance remains a mystery. We are drifting in the Honguedo Strait – their only memorial is its name, taken from their language.

In the engine room Pieter directs the changing of a leaking damper on a fuel-injection unit and comes up smiling: 'Easy! Getting the tools out and putting them away again took more time than the repair.'

We emerge from shelter into an evil wind which blows straight down our back from the Labrador coast, driving blizzards across the black water, whipping up waves which curl and crackle with ice chunks, tearing the tarpaulin off a container below the bridge to reveal a blue seed drill. Sumy, the bo'sun, took advantage of the stop to unlash the anchors and returned safely.

'In this he wouldn't even have two minutes if he fell,' the Captain says. The decks are almost unusable, with pitiless blasts of snow and freezing spray hosing the starboard side, but there are two men down there, prodding at the winch which is meant to lower the gangway. They are oval-shaped in their padded overalls and hoods and they wear safety goggles, so they can just about see out. I manage three minutes on the leeward side. It is horrible.

Nestor, the electrician, descends from the monkey deck, the highest point on the ship, where he has been checking the radar.

'Is OK,' he says, his nerve as cool as the sea. 'Shit bad weather, eh?'

Now and then there is a clatter-clang like dropped metal as ice falls from the superstructure to the deck. Milky slicks of ice combine until entire quadrants are white, an aqueous Arctic, heaving with the motion of slow rollers. Slabs bigger than dinner tables scrape down the hull with a grating rumble. It seems extraordinary that the men working on the winch out there are not polar explorers but seafarers from the tropics.

'We'll all be out in it tomorrow, unlashing,' John says, glumly.

Hectares of sea are patched and marbled, rocking white in a grey-blue murk, as the ship climbs waves iced like snowdrifts, and falls into valleys crazed as if with opaque glass. It all seems dream-like, as though we are halfway between life and something else, in a place where nothing is quite solid or quite liquid, as if our steel ship has left behind all certainty of form and element, pushing herself on by the conviction of habit, the only sure thing left in a universe paling away. The impression that we have sailed into a zone of white erasure doubles with the appearance of a ghost ship, a bulker, which emerges from the freezing mist a mile and a half away. You cannot believe there are men aboard her. The wind comes back up, hurling snow-spray. The ice blanket slows the waves until they are white dunes rolling.

Perhaps I have been missing his irony, or perhaps he no longer feels a need to impress, and no doubt 'What a great job!' can be said the same way and mean different things on different days, perhaps it is all of these, and the psychological desolation of the dismal, borderless ice fields, listless on the black water, but John is very melancholy today.

'Would you leave this, if you could?'

'Oh aye, I would have left twenty years ago. I applied for a job as a fireman but I wasn't fit enough. I was supposed to join the family pilot business – we had a business, river pilots on the Tyne. My grandfather was killed in the war. Climbing on to a ship all blacked out he slipped – crushed between the ship and the pilot cutter. Then the government said anyone could be pilots and we lost the business.

'My first voyage was in 1979. Bahrain. We were in an accident in a bus and we missed the ship. Chased it for six hours in a launch – chasing this tanker! When I got on I said to the captain, what's my station in an emergency? He said don't worry about it tonight. So I went to bed and then the fire alarm goes off – fire in the engine room, on a tanker.'

'But you still wanted to do it?'

'Oh aye. It stopped being fun ten years ago. We used to have women officers and cadets – that's all gone. You think I want to stand and count boxes coming off and on? The companies don't like English officers. Too expensive. If I could get a job on shore I would . . .'

After bemoaning bad captains (killjoys, authoritarians and brutes), John contrasts them with one Captain Robinson, a New Zealander who played music on the bridge, whose wife made smoothies and who used the engineers' passage for ten-pin bowling.

'He'd come up in the middle of your watch and say I've scored this much – you have a go, and he'd take your watch for you!'

Everyone seems to be waiting to get off, except perhaps the Captain. Clearly the Gulf of St Lawrence in February is not the place to look for enthusiasm in seafarers, but the feeling that we are the only ones 'stupid enough to be here' is palpable and often repeated. We take comfort from the sight of other ships, as if they are proof that this bitter, lonely and profitless thing we are doing is something which needs to be done. The two ghost ships we have seen only serve to confirm our quixotic quest. If they were there at all they were both going the other way.

A walk around the deck reveals six inches of snow on the lee side. Nestor is checking reefers: he visits 209 of them twice a day. Vegetables from Poland and Belgium, pork from the Netherlands, Tunisian octopus, Irish meat for Jamaica, Uruguayan beef (well-travelled), juice concentrate from Argentina (also crossing the Atlantic twice on its way to Canada), German cherries, Polish fish, a mass of 'food-stuff' from northern Europe, as well as mystifying 'coffee extracts' sent from India to Costa Rica all depend on Nestor if they are not to melt, though the thought of anything melting out here seems ludicrous. Nestor climbs a ladder in the open bay forward of the bridge in horizontal snow. Thirty seconds' exposure of your hands is too much. A circuit-breaker on one of the refrigerated containers has tripped. At the top of his ladder, thirty feet up, Nestor leans sideways perilously, catching the inspection cover as the wind plucks at it. For a second the forces are in terrifying balance, then Nestor pulls it back, makes an adjustment and descends. He has been at sea seventeen years. With luck the next trip will be his last.

'My family have moved to Toronto. If I qualify for residence, and if my wife does – she's a nurse – if we pass all the tests, including language, it will all be worth it. Children get free school, free health care.'

If the dream comes true then the couple's labour will change the future of all their descendants decisively: they will be Canadians, not Filipinos. Seventeen years of voyages, all those reefers, all those days and nights will have turned the globe.

John is back from his supper and listening to his compilation: the same every time, which starts with the bars with which Universal Pictures begin their films, and progresses to Queen, Robert Plant and Dire Straits.

Our evening clear, which is traditional now, shows a dark bruise-blue sky and the lights of Baie Corneau and the Betsiamites Indian Reserve. We have turned into the mouth of the St Lawrence River; the southern shore is hidden in cloud. The river here is a steep-shelving gorge, giant and deep, which is good, as we are sailing across an explosives dumping ground. We have a rendezvous with Escoumines pilots at midnight.

Supper, after a muted start, turns into an excellent evening. First Pieter and the Captain describe Antwerp on the cusp of containerisation.

'Ships went right into the Scheldebank,' says the Captain. 'We tied up in the centre of the city. We unloaded tobacco, beef and coffee – the Antwerp stevedores were the fastest in Europe.'

'There was always something going on,' says Pieter, 'until the first containers came.'

'We used to lash them to the deck any way,' the Captain laughs. 'And the decks then were covered in bitumen to protect the steel, which was not so good in the Persian Gulf. We stuffed the cargo into the containers on board, at first.'

From Antwerp we travel to Central America, Pieter recalling two cadets persuading a watchman to report an illness, as it was the only way they could get a launch to take them ashore in British Honduras, now Belize. One of them immediately met a girl he knew on the dock.

'Ah, sometimes they travelled with you!' says the Captain.

This leads to memories of Colombia. Jannie takes over. An Indonesian he knew attempted to befriend another man's girlfriend in Colombia and was consequently shot in the arm. In hospital he sprayed urine around the ward: 'Maybe he was angry, or maybe just excited. The next day a taxi driver comes to the ship, says this man owes him money. The captain says "You take him then!" The guy came back later, said his drink was spiked.'

Now we are in Jamaica, Kingston, a dangerous and popular port. Assuming a deep voice Jannie says, 'Black stone, black stone, make chikki-chikki all night!' He repeats this with relish and emphasis.

'What is this black stone?'

'Ach, you rub it under your hat,' Jannie says, pointing to his crotch.

The ship has a tilt to her now, wind-heeled, and our little blue foremast light is on again. There is quite a large town on the southern shore, New Brunswick. I try to imagine what they do in New Brunswick on a February night. Bars, DVDs, suppers, studying, dating, putting children to bed and reading to them, watching the news – the same as everywhere else in the Western world, perhaps, but it all seems remote, unlikely and isolated from the perspective of the *Pembroke*; from the shore we are just three lights passing, far out in the darkness.

The bridge after supper is fun, now: we become a happy Filipino ship, energised by the proximity of land and the prospect of unlashing, activity and landfall. Chicoy is in his chair, someone is on the phone calling home: you can hear a woman's voice on the line, compressed and eager. Sumy, the bo'sun, is supervising Mark, the steward, who is practising his steering. Mark does not want to stay a steward but so far his advancement is limited to occasional night driving. He has been on two ships before this one; a bulker and a ro-ro. He liked the latter because all the accommodation was on one deck: 'No stairs!

'On first ship I was so homesick, so homesick, I hit myself here, here.' He mimes punching the side of his head. 'I hit myself until I bleed. I said to the Captain I am so homesick I hurt myself but maybe I hurt someone else?'

The Captain sent him home, where he became a salesman. But he was not successful so a friend helped him find another ship. Mark talks about doing another twenty years at sea.

'We sacrifice ourselves,' he says.

We discuss books and cheap razors: he wants to know which are the best and interrogates me closely, with his mobile face near mine and his fragile eyes beseeching.

'Well,' I manage, never having thought about it, 'I am quite a fan of Wilkinson's Sword.'

'Wilkinson's Sword? OK! These I will get in Montreal and sell them at home. If only I could grow a beard like yours,' he says, wistfully. 'I wish I could have that beard.'

'No you don't! When you have to shave it is a complete pain in the ass.'

'I think anyone who can have one does not want it, and anyone who can't does,' he says.

By 0445 we are steering for the leading lights of Saint-Michelle-de-Bellechasse with two pilots aboard. Their French is too quick and Québécois for me. We trundle through thick and shattered ice. The wind is very bitter and the Île d'Orléans glows blue with snow. Now we can see the lights of Quebec City ahead. It looks as though it will be a lovely day, but cold, cruelly cold, for handling lashing rods. We pass a ship in the channel, all blacked out, her men working her through the darkness like an echo of war. We go quickly towards a freezing clear sky where the stars are fading. We are close to the shore of the island now and it is strange to see normal things: trees, houses, a street, all so domestic and yet remarkable, after all the ocean. There is a church, a garbage truck and tall pylons: is this life, then? A world of mundane miraculous things? The channel narrows and spurs of ice reach towards us. We are about to start breaking a passage through it. Now sheets seven inches thick snap and rock in the greenish river.

Just before sunrise on a Sunday morning Quebec City stands brave on its bluff, Cap Diamant, between air and water of luminous blue. What a defiant, magnificent outpost it is, with its back to the Laurentian Mountains which roll away under skies of shivered, snow-pregnant cloud. The spires and turrets of the Château Frontenac hotel – part baronial, part Gotham, part French fantasy – are harmonious with the skyscrapers, the French apartments and grand houses on the river, with a rampart of grain silos and the few moored ships, as if a single glance over the ice floes encompasses a way and a means of surviving, living and prospering here, at the mouth of the wild remote. The Quebec pilots are jolly and macho.

'This is the best day this week, Capitaine. Sun today, snow tomorrow, snow for the rest of the week. You were delayed, eh?'

'Two days of strikes,' says the Captain. 'They cost this ship three hundred thousand dollars.'

Maple leaves and fleurs-de-lis look brightly assertive in the frigid wind. We pass the Plains of Abraham, now a park, where James Wolfe died in 1759, and then the cliff he had climbed, leading his troops in the storming of Quebec. A British defence of the city in the winter of 1775 ended the northward advance of American revolutionaries, eventually determining the separation of Canada from the United States. The Americans found the ground so hard they could not entrench their cannons, while the defenders had five months' supplies behind the walls. No army could fight this cold. A moment or two on the bridge wing has you crying freezing tears; the cold burns through all the bulk of my jacket and sweaters in an instant.

The sun rises and a goods train keeps pace with us along the ridge of Sainte-Foy. It has four engines, dragging trucks with wheat symbols; we pull ahead before it crosses the bridge at Cap Rouge. It is rousing to see the Canadian Pacific Railway in operation from our ship, in this pre-dawn blue. Through the efforts of the railwaymen and the seafarers was all this made possible, from the lamp posts down to the paperweights in the big houses overlooking the water. One imagines, battered though we are, that our ship greatly adds to their view. The St Lawrence here is more a seaway than a river, fierce rather than pretty. The ground is low-rising to spinneys of bare trees. The great north tolerates this little cling of habitation, but no more than that. An arctic essence seems in only temporary abeyance, as if a really strong ice-gust could render it pristine.

'Yes! Make some money!' says Annabelle, and snaps more instructions at Richard. How he handles a rod will be interesting. There is great excitement in the galley and throughout the ship: everyone is going unlashing. As well as her usual work, putting away breakfast and prepping lunch, Annabelle is also making extra meals for the pilots and clearing decks for business. Nestor pads off to do his first reefer round.

At 0830 precisely a line of swaddled figures set off down the starboard side. The sun brightens the battered primary colours of the containers and icicles glint on the hatches, handrails and ladders. The lashing rods are zinc-coloured and unforgiving, criss-crossing the ends of the boxes. The tension in each must be broken with a sharp lunge and heave of the clawed wrench. The cold cuts through gloves as the crew crane their necks back, arms up, wrestling with the long bars. The long bars, ten metres of unwieldy metal with hinged bolts at the tip, secure the second layer of containers. These bolts must be broken from their iced sockets. Wincing and straining, the men jerk at them until there is a crack, ice falls and the bolts are loose. Sometimes they leave the bars hanging and work on along the bay. The teams are split into pairs and almost nothing is said. The sounds are the clash of bars, the crack of spanners and the shuffle of feet in the snow.

On the windward side – and the St Lawrence snakes slowly, changing the angle of the wind's eye, exposing us all, turn by turn – the conditions are cruel. Your cheeks freeze painfully and you are aware of liquid running down your face, from your nose, mouth or eyes you cannot tell. Six hours of this they estimate, at fifty dollars an hour. Ships pass, a bird flaps on a floe and the bow wave sets off a clinking of broken ice. It is a sparkling and bitter day, this day to make money. Annabelle is hard at it, wrapped in a heavy-duty orange jacket and a yellow helmet. Everyone is wearing as much as possible, overalls, balaclavas, goggles, hard hats and scarves.

The emptying out of the ship's interior and the scattered profusion of the crew in the bays is like a sudden disclosure, a thin swarm of men and one woman working in plain sight, where they are usually hidden away. They have no attention for anything but the threat, weight and resistance of the rods and bars. At ten they come back in, puffing and blowing:

imperturbable Nestor, little Richard dishevelled, John poking his tongue out.

'How heavy those long bars are!' he pants. 'And we've got the long ones. Everyone else has the short ones.'

Luckily he also has Jannie, who seems much less bothered. In fact other bays, and smaller men, also had the long bars. There is a definite impression in his smiling face that John is more fond of his grievance than stung. Trying it, though, you understand the difficulty. The long bar is a horrible thing to manoeuvre; thirty feet of steel weighing eighty pounds. Starting in the middle and taking the weight of one lying flat, a moderately strong man can raise it to waist height without difficulty. After that it must be manipulated by pivoting or heaving it beyond the border of control. Pushing it up needs two of you.

'Ja, heavy bastard,' Jannie expectorates.

On the way back they will do all this in reverse: lashing is therefore worse than unlashing, as they will be erecting rather than dismantling with gravity's help. The only thing they will be spared is the mechanism of the locking pin. At each corner of the containers a steel cable with a toggle on the end must be jerked free. Releasing the second layer is easy, the third not so hard, but layers four and five require a kind of aerial fishing with a very long pole. Next, all the hatch covers must be freed in the same way.

The aerial toggle-fishing is not so bad if you are tall: Chicoy lets me use his hook and it is no trouble. But Chicoy is barely three-quarters my height, so he balances on bundles of lashing rods. The temptation is to sidle sideways, eyes on the target, but this is a mistake as none of the walkways are free from hatch covers, bars, protruberances and cables. High-voltage wires go into the reefers and vile smells come out. Malevolent gases vent from the engine room and stink rises from the cargo holds. There are steel stills to catch your shins and low plates to hit your head. As in the hold you are grateful for the pitted and rusty decks because everywhere is iced.

At Lac St Pierre the horizon drops back, opening up twenty miles of water; the southern half is frozen and the northern is a deep and glittering blue. A wooded shore and pale lilac ground lifts to far hills and you have no conception of Canada's great lakes until you see one too small to qualify. A small bulker curves ahead of us up the channel and there is a buzz of snowmobiles on the frozen white. The glare is spotted and dotted with the huts of ice fishermen.

'Oh yes,' says our pilot, his Québécois accent growling through his beard, 'you cannot complain. You 'ave a stove and some wood, you drill an 'ole . . .'

I bet they do well for sustenance and refreshment, too. The huge space of the lake, making miniature the ships, is an uplift, a sudden welcome from the wild. As the afternoon unrolls at the pace of the speed limit, ten knots, we pass frozen marshes, deserted bird sanctuaries, snow and etchings of woods. There is beauty in the naked birches and pale bronze reeds, but it is a beauty of emptiness, of space, where the earth seems little more than a rind of frozen sky.

As the channel squeezes in and the inhabited banks return, lights come on behind windows, timer-tripped residues of life. There is just enough breeze, this ghostly mid-winter, for the bridge to whistle its storm song softly. As the sun gutters orange a mountain rises over the frozen plains. This mountain has skyscrapers attendant, poking angular heads above the trees, some of them winking: Montreal.

We nose in past oil refineries and power lines, pylons and warning lights, reds, greens and cities of sodium orange reminiscent of Antwerp, as though we have circled a world, not crossed one. It is Sunday night so I sit at the bar with Jannie and demolish a burger which is served with a paper Filipino flag flying from the bun. Jannie has sympathetic, pale blue eyes in a pallid and hard-lived face, tough and enduring; he is gentle and often amused. He married at twenty-four and his wife sailed with him for the first three years. They brought their son on board when he was three; when he turned fifteen Jannie added a week to the boy's holidays and took him to the East.

'There were lots of children on board in those days, and wives – it was great, great fun . . .'

Jannie has an endearing way of collapsing his expression into hopeless despair at his past exploits: 'Fifteen beers every night – achhh . . .'

His grandfather sailed with the Dutch East India Company. 'His first trip was a year and a half at sea.' Jannie's father did a few months at sea, but for the son: 'One minute sitting in a classroom, next minute sitting on a ship. When you are falling forwards you must be working. When you are falling backwards you must be sleeping, and if you are not falling you are at home.'

He is on the *Pembroke* until May. Each time he is in Rotterdam his wife will drive to see him. Their twenty-five-year-old son is still at home, too: Jannie makes shooing motions, laughing. In six years' time, after thirty-eight years, Jannie's sea days will be done.

'And then what will you do?'

'Retire. Don't know. Take it easy. Make vodka, do the garden . . .'

The *Pembroke* ends her voyage in the same haphazard style with which she arrived in Antwerp. Someone has disconnected the bow thruster for maintenance and forgotten to plug it in again: Pieter puts it right while the Captain tries not to fume on the bridge. The tug comes out on schedule but there is no Chicoy to receive it. There is a swearing pause and they make it fast. We come to a dead stop and the younger of our two pilots takes over.

He issues orders to the tug, commands to Eugene at the helm for main engine and rudder (helming is the only part of his job that Eugene enjoys) and instructions to Erwin for the thruster. The young pilot balances the effect of the wind and the strength of the current, spinning us so that *Pembroke* rests facing her next port, bringing us alongside slowly and perfectly, making allowances for a gangway which is not quite where it should be (lowered too far down) and a general feeling that no one else is going to show any initiative. The Captain is not sure of our berth, between the two vans, he thinks, so that is where we go, and here we are, snow thick on the ground, the St Lawrence deadly black, the stevedores ambling like orange bears and down-town Montreal glittering upriver.

'Do you have time for much maintenance, Captain?' the young pilot asks, with great tact.

'No, we are in the Atlantic, difficult for the crew. And supplies take months to get.'

All the life of Montreal is just there but we cannot leave the ship because immigration is not working tonight. There will be no unloading until 8 a.m. and the internet is down. Jannie is disappointed to learn we lack clean linen. 'Two weeks in my sheets already and there are no others,' he frowns. Our families do not know we have arrived safely: perhaps it was ever the sailor's condition to feel forgotten, but the men trading this ancient, semi-defunct route really do feel themselves beyond the world's bother. At least we have arrived safely, though. Jannie recalls a trip across the Bay of Biscay last November.

'At 3.30 in the morning the general alarm went. Think oh God, what's this? I got out of bed, get in an overall, went up. Two ships had collided. Waves were six metres. We went to help but an American ship was closer. You couldn't lower lifeboats it was too dangerous, so we put nets ready over the side. The Americans got everybody, everybody survived, but we saw the ship go down. There's lots of traffic there, everyone in lanes – somebody must have fallen asleep . . .'

Before bed I watch a crane operator, presumably training or practising, miss a box four times before giving up.

CHAPTER 22

Landfall

I wake in panic: why have we stopped? I stumble to the window: where are we? The Netherlands? It looks like the Netherlands, but is the river entirely frozen? Is that ship stuck in it?

'I thought I was still dreaming.'

'It's because you are up early,' Jannie says. The bridge is locked, the deck doors are locked, the internet is down, so no booking a hotel for tomorrow night. There is a telephone call.

'Immigration you go now,' says Chicoy's voice. It is not entirely clear what this means but I descend hopefully to the harbour control room. The Captain is radiating charm at two enormous and heavily padded immigration officers. One has a wire in his ear; the other smiles and says little.

'It is his fault we have storms,' the Captain says, introducing me.

'You said it was Annabelle's fault before.'

'Yes, maybe both of you.'

The officers muster a laugh and issue a visa.

Annabelle is in a smart leather jacket and pink baseball cap, Richard and Alberto, an ordinary seaman, are also nattily dressed in denim with accessories (Alberto uses a checked handkerchief to wipe snow out of his eyes), and I am letting us down in a dumpy green coat which is warm if not at all trendy. I am about to see a seafarer's version of Canada: we are going shopping. A security van takes us through the container wilderness to a gate where guards call us a taxi and tell us where to find it. Richard shivers and Annabelle sets a rapid pace. Our Montreal, under a cement sky, is dismal suburbs, flyovers, banks of dirty snow and slushing traffic.

We arrive at the Galeries d'Anjou, a retail park and mall. Richard investigates cameras in Best Buy. He wants an SLR, and declares these a hundred dollars cheaper than in the Philippines. 'Maybe next time,' he says, wistfully. At three hundred dollars they cost half his monthly salary. We go to Zeller through heavy snowfall. Two Filipinos from another ship pass us, nodding. Zeller is first a cut-rate clothes shop, then a mall, then a giant retail bunker with no obvious end. Annabelle says it is very small, compared to one at home, the Mall of Asia: 'They have firework displays every week.'

Richard, Annabelle and Alberto buy crisps, sweets and ice cream. We sit in a consumption space and gaze at the shops. Scarab, Subway, Chez La Famille Burger, Thai Express, Suki Yaki, Franx Supreme, Kojax Souflaki, Cultures and SAQ Wine. People sit at tables on red plastic chairs, eating and staring. I find it confusing and discombobulating. Where are we? Only the Banque de Montreal gives a hint.

'So this is Canada!'

Alberto laughs. Men like him carry most of the contents of most of the shops. Like their compatriots in LA, the first thing they do, given the brief freedom of the city, is to look for fragments of their cargo which they can afford. In Melville's day the crew of a whaling ship would have shares, or fractions of shares, in the profit of the voyage. No crew agency would contemplate giving their contract labourers anything like a share in the great Maersk corporation: Alberto would laugh at the idea.

Traffic and snow fill the horizon outside as a digger works over a torn patch of mud and ice. Annabelle leads us to a bus; twenty minutes later we arrive at a metro station where we discover we must make a huge horseshoe, from St Michel to Assomption, in order to return to the ship. Richard talks a little about his career.

Richard could sit in any class of sixteen-year-olds and not be thought the eldest. When you have talked to him you would put his age at twenty-one or -two – it seemed rude to ask him directly; he is so small. Richard is a steward: he washes up, cleans cabins and mops floors.

'My last ship? Was Saudi Arabia.'

'Did you like Saudi Arabia?'

'Gulf. Cannot get off ship.'

'What?'

'Offshore! Cannot leave ship one year.'

'Richard, sorry, are you telling me you were on a ship for an entire year and you never set foot on land? You never got off?'

'Never! Aramco. Offshore.'

'But – for God's sake . . .'

'Ha ha!'

'I don't believe it! What was that like? What did you do?'

'Very bad. Very hot there. Small crew – seventeen. Like prison. Watch TV. Like prison . . .'

Far from being rendered insane or unstable by the sacrifice of a year of his life at its most expansive stage (he must have been eighteen or nineteen) for a wage a European waiter would sniff at, Richard meets your eyes with the steadiest gaze. Travelling on the metro, his hands deep in his pockets, his hat pulled down, Richard looks entirely insouciant, though he has never set foot in this country before. Posing for a photograph, his legs move a little way apart, his chin lifts, his elbows drift outwards, hands still in pockets, and he gazes at the camera with that precise calibration hip-hoppers deploy, at once mocking the camera's interest and taking full advantage of it. His preparation for his year's sentence in the Gulf was some weeks' training in stewardship. But no training on earth could have produced this enduring, good-humoured young man: his character and his job did that, as he served for a year in a floating cell block reeking of petrol under the broiling sun, with other men who showed him, by example, what it takes.

The metro is a kaleidoscope of aftershaves and perfumes; the faces, the voices and languages are beguiling and strange after the ship and the Atlantic air. We arrive at Assomption and wait for the bus. It is cold, bleak and miserable, though the evening paper trumpets Snow At Last! There is plenty. Alberto says his last ship went to Australia and various Asian ports.

'Redback spiders in the hold. Poisonous. Lots of them, lots.'

He mimes going through the holds shooting invisible spiders – around, above and below – with some sort of spider spray. With all the ladders and drips, the heat, the holes in the floor and the 'many, many' spiders he makes it seem like a kind of *Call of Duty*, fought with an aerosol instead of a gun.

Shore leave for seafarers is a lot of waiting, confusion over public transport and rapid glimpses of the indelicate parts of town. We take the bus to a supermarket where Annabelle leads an exhilarating burst of shopping. The trolley rapidly fills to the top and beyond with carrots, spinach, cabbage, pasta, cleaning materials, fish and more vegetables. The budget was $120 Canadian and the bill is $125, and the cashier will not take US fifty-dollar bills (our only currency); furthermore, the cashier says, the US bill is $137. Richard and Alberto are worried about how the Captain will react to the overspend but Annabelle is unhesitating. We pool our money and make the target. In a hurry now, because it is 1810 and the Captain expects to eat at 1830, we grab a taxi.

'Who are they?' asks the driver, looking at his passengers in his mirror. 'What do they do?'

'They are seafarers,' I say. 'They're off a cargo ship.'

'But – but –' he looks at me, 'they are children!'

We help the driver find the right entrance to the port, then sit, itching as the minutes pass, as an interminable goods train clanks from right to left, pauses, and clanks back from left to right. We abandon the taxi and charge over a footbridge, lugging the shopping. A friendly guard takes ages to verify our IDs: the others are extremely patient while I try not to jump up and down. The guard tells us not to attempt to walk through the containers to the ship because we will be fined if we are caught. The security van takes an age to arrive. We make it back; Annabelle hurls herself around the kitchen and I go up to stall the Captain, finding him in his cabin, putting on his shirt. I further delay him, Jannie and Pieter in the bar. We descend at ten to seven. Richard serves chicken soup, followed by tuna steaks (new) with crinkled chips (new), spinach (new) and carrots. Richard does not understand Jannie's request for mayo, so ignores it, and he clangs two dishes together. The Captain jumps like a man with bad nerves, exaggerating, and turns an interrogative glare on the boy. Richard stills him with a cool glance. Semolina and cherry pudding finish the evening, Annabelle having produced a three-course meal in eighteen minutes.

Pieter, the chief engineer, and I sit in the bar afterwards, not drinking the evening away. He lives in Thailand.

'Oh really? Lucky you!'

'Not really – it's too hot, much too hot. And loud! It was worse a few years ago when all the motorbikes were two-stroke. Terrible. But now more of them are four-stroke so it's a bit better, at least.'

'How did you come to move there?'

'I met someone,' he shrugs. 'And that's it. When you meet the person, you know. And we have a son, so . . .'

He flies between his family in Thailand, his mother in the Netherlands and the ship. I feel a shock of recognition.

I too met someone and knew I had 'met the person'. I too divide my time between her, in one country, my family in another, and my work, frequently in other places. But I have not learned to smile at this strange, diffuse and too-travelled existence the way Pieter does. His grin has an extraordinary goodness in it, a slant of pure forgiveness such as you might hope to find in a truly holy man. Perhaps it comes from a long time ago, from forgiving himself and them, when the Dutch navy rejected a brilliant seaman and a natural engineer because he was 'not assertive enough'. Neither of us are cynical and drunken, which one of Joni Mitchell's characters claimed was the fate of men like us, but we are both romantics of the second stage. (Romantics take a long time to grow up; the lucky ones, perhaps, never do.) Instead of staring down bottles in a dark café, as Joni had it, we sit in the bare and cosy bar agreeing that in order to improve the lot of the world's seafarers, without whom the world as we know it would end in hunger, mass shortage and general confusion, the Filipinos must be paid more, the crew should have the right to know what is in the containers ('I risked my life to move a box to Montreal' not being as good for status or self-worth as the reality), and they should bring back beer.

'Then maybe people would want to go to sea again, and they could pay them even less!' Pieter cries.

Tuesday 28 February

We are unloading for a second day. Only fifteen containers will stay on for Halifax; everything else is going. Box by box

Pembroke–Sydney's scarred grey decks emerge. Occasionally a container sticks and a stumpy figure trudges across the hatch covers and fishes for a toggle with a long hook. Bit by bit the deck clears, three hundred metres of it, then the hatch covers are lifted off and seven storeys of containers are plucked out of her guts. She rises and rises in the water, the gangway slopes steeper by the minute.

The surveyor is aboard, a Newfoundlander called Dan. His boots, hard hat, jacket and head torch are immaculate. Everything looks like the perfect tool for the job and there is no excess about him. You know he has charmed seafarers many times when he shows us a photo on his phone of a sign for a town called Dildo. He works for a company called ABB which offers a ship inspection service.

'It's voluntary for the shipowners. 'Course, if we pass the ship Maersk get lower insurance rates, but Maersk pays us – so no conflict of interest there at all!'

'Can you stop a ship from sailing?'

'Yes I can, but it's bad for everyone. Bad for us, because someone would have inspected it a year before, so what did they miss? Bad for the crew, bad for the owner, bad for the captain . . . So it's not a tool I use lightly. Do I ever? Sure.'

'For what sort of things?'

'A crack in the main deck! If a ship's about to break in half it's not going to sail. I had one, there was a problem with the life rafts, and I'm not sure if the guy was joking, that's the scary thing, but I said to him there's a problem with the life rafts and he said so what? It's only fifteen Chinese! Loads more where they came from!'

'How's this ship?'

'OK. Old, but OK. Built in Germany, eh? Well, at least it's not Chinese!'

'What's wrong with them?'

'The welding. The steel. The maintenance . . .'

Pieter looks reflective. You can see he is enjoying going over his charge with an expert, but he regrets that she is no longer beautiful. And she smells – the stink of the hold is coming off our overalls. There is a fuel leak after coffee, and in early afternoon a fire alarm of mysterious provenance.

After lunch I pack, feeling I can delay no longer. The fire alarm goes again as I am taking my leave with warm, quick handshakes. I find Pieter in the CO2 room, the safe room (in the event of North Atlantic pirates), and thank him for his kindness.

'No, no,' he protests. Then, 'I'm afraid we are rather busy now, it's not really a good time . . .'

'I know, the ship's on fire, right?'

'Sort of,' he laughs, and glides down the ladder to his engine room, his feet barely touching each step as he controls the slide with his hands. It is a trick I have watched him doing every evening on the way down to dinner. I bet he is an excellent dancer.

In the galley Annabelle, Mark, Richard and I pose and take photographs of each other. Richard gives me a complicated handshake. There is a turmoil of seafarers in the crew mess, where David from the Seaman's Mission is helping Alberto fill in forms to send money home.

'It used to be really simple,' David sighs. He is a tall, neat man in respectable clothes which suggest a tiny salary. 'But since the whole security thing it's much more

complicated. They're worried about money-laundering.
Like anyone's going to launder two hundred dollars . . .'

Chicoy comes in, sporting an extraordinary vertical
haircut.

'Who cuts it?'

'We do!'

'Is there someone aboard who is particularly good at it?'

'Not on this ship – some ships yes . . .'

This explains the second engineer's busby, the number of
close-crops, and Book's bullet-look. When Cabot made his
second, successful voyage he had a barber with him. (He
turned back the first time, having found nothing but sea and
bad weather.) Scholars assume this gentleman was aboard as
a surgeon, but who is to say that Cabot, a Venetian after all,
did not believe that seafaring should be done with style?

On deck Ordinary Seamen Bobby Sitones and Wallace
Yambao are on watch. No one knows what they are guarding,
as the containers continue their cascade. German aircraft,
spacecraft and parts thereof fly by unsuspected. The Captain
was right about the cheese: we have brought twenty tonnes
from Norway. Four tonnes of flower bulbs from the
Netherlands we might have predicted, but only an eccentric
would have guessed twenty-seven tonnes of Dutch cocoa
powder for Chile, or five tonnes of Polish grass and moss,
or three hundred and fifty tonnes of Tanzanian seaweed,
fertiliser for the prairies. Fifty tonnes of Czech candy have
reached their destination, but twelve tonnes of Iranian dates
are going on to Colombia.

To survive the winter Canada requires Indian spices,
twenty-five tonnes of Greek wine, Danish yeast, British malt,

Latvian clothing, six hundred tonnes of Belgian beer, a hundred tonnes of Irish alcohol, Estonian chemicals, German tools, thirty-four tonnes of Belgian chocolate, twenty-four tonnes of Sri Lankan tea bags, Indian seeds, Polish glue, Hungarian tyres, tinned vegetables from Spain, Russian plywood, British sanitary towels, Dutch medicine, Swedish paper – you can see why these things are shipped across the Atlantic in the cold midwinter. But why ninety tonnes of Argentinian milk, and why send it via Europe? Who plans to do what with two tonnes of used machinery from Congo? What is the second-hand vehicle, weighing almost two tonnes, from Sierra Leone – a diamond dealer's Mercedes? What is so desirable, in this land of forests, about the three hundred tonnes of sawn timber from Germany, and the eighty more from Russia? (The wood in three containers from the Ivory Coast will not grow in Canada, presumably.)

In Chile someone is waiting for eighteen tonnes of Saudi Arabian carpets. Four tonnes of Polish 'personal care products' are on their way to Cuba. The Dominican Republic has been producing tobacco for five hundred years but it needs seventeen tonnes of tobacco accessories from the Netherlands, where a Scandinavian firm owns a factory producing Dominican cigars. British industry is not quite dead, exporting plastic and machinery to Chile, one container of manufactured articles to El Salvador and twenty-eight tonnes of synthetic resin to Colombia, though this triumph is rather overshadowed by the three thousand tonnes of similar resins that Saudi is sending to South America. As we sat in the dry museum of our bar we had no idea we carried almost two thousand tonnes of booze, half of it Dutch and German beer. Britain's contribution, one container for Panama, is listed as 'alcoholic beverage': surely Scotch. The mystery tractor is going to Peru.

'Got to be strong,' says Wallace. It is achingly cold out here, and all he and Bobby are doing is watching the gangway. Another container off, and another, and another. Another voyage gone, another to come; another month gone; another to come, and another, and another . . . We say goodbye and Bobby and Wallace wave me off, Wallace offering a brave thumbs-up.

The way back to the other world is patrolled by container trucks, roaring and snorting smoke and impatience. A Haitian taxi driver takes me to the metro. The last I see of the *Pembroke–Sydney* is her bridge, and dirty flags flying bravely above the smoke stack, just another grimy ship in a bleak container yard somewhere far away.

Wednesday 29 February

She will be on her way to Halifax now. With a bit of help from the current, despite the speed limit, she will be well into the semi-wilds of Quebec. They will have been lashing all this morning, in this hard cold. I hope Jannie's back is OK – it was hurting him after unlashing. Twenty past four: Captain Koop will be on his bridge, Pieter in the engine control room and John will be listening to the music of his youth. Annabelle and Mark will be resting, counting down to their next shift. Many of the crew will be on or in their beds, watching DVDs, sleeping or trying to get an internet connection. And the ship will be doing what she does, what she has always done and what she will do until the day comes when someone who has never seen her, and never heard her storm songs, and certainly never smelled her, decides she has done enough. All my clothes, even those just washed, stink of her. I woke this morning without a thick and throbbing head for the first time in a fortnight. I barely knew her. But I saw her darkness; I felt her loneliness and her obscurity. I will always be able to hear the moans and whistles of her stairwell, her ghost music, the muted and ceaseless piano of her theme tune, and the enduring, resisting stoicism of the men who sing and hum her on.

CHAPTER 23

Signing Off

That night the sights of Montreal, the live music in bars, the presence of women, the choice of food and wine and beer were surprisingly scant compensation for the comradeship of the seafarers. I felt like an odd ghost, something like Coleridge's Ancient Mariner: I wanted to take someone by the arm and say, listen, there is a ship at sea tonight, and this is who is on board, and this is what their lives are like, and without them none of this world you call normal could exist . . . The months afterwards were strange. I missed my ships and my friends. One image from Montreal kept coming back. As we hurried back on board that night, with supper to cook, we saw Mark making his way through the containers, striding to his few hours of shore leave. He looked tremendously neat and preoccupied. Perhaps he was going to buy cheap razors and other goods to sell at home. The others laughed, for there was always something slightly off-centre about Mark, about his near-obsequious friendliness and his eagerness to please. You did not have to know his story of punching himself in desperation to divine that he is a man who suffers isolation; he is a nation of one. But I remember him with great admiration. He has as much strength, playing the cheery servant fadelessly, as any man I have known.

Inner strength is the secret of seafaring. Men like Pieter, Jannie, Sorin, Joel, Rohan and the Captains Koop and Larsen must make almost ideal husbands and fathers, though they are so often absent from their families. I did not see them with their wives and children, but I saw them. Their stories have one thing in common: they all begin with wishes. But a wish is not a cautious thing, certainly not when a young man makes it. All these men made the same one, when they were too young to know better. They wished to go to sea. They came to know the imperturbable embrace of the oceans, and the relentless and perilous demands of ships. The life changed and changes under them; in most cases it became and continues to become harder and more demanding; its cushions – in leisure, comforts and pay – all continue to shrink. Their greatness – and it is a greatness – is that they have all fulfilled the demands of another old saw: you made your bed, now you must lie on it. And they do, with great grace – even when it is rocking, reeling and trying to throw them off. On the ships I began to understand that lying on the bed you made is perhaps the condition of adult life.

In recent months Chris has been promoted to chief officer and acquired two fine swallow tattoos, one colourful bird on each shoulder. The old sailors believed that wearing them meant swallows would carry their souls home if they were to die at sea. Joel is now a third engineer and the company is keen he sit the exams for second. He writes from the *Gjertrud Maersk*, which he calls an 'old turtle', saying he is in a warship-and-pirate-infested area known to the crew as the Hardship Pay Area. He signs off his all emails with 'It's me!! Joel'.

As for the ships, you can sometimes find them on a website which tracks their AIS transponder signals, but its coverage only extends a few nautical miles from land. Searching for *Gerd Maersk* and *Maersk Pembroke* returns the same message: 'Out of Range'. They are working their way across waters far from the world we know. Their futures are more uncertain now than at any time since they were launched. Stringent EU financial regulations (demanding banks hold cash, rather than other people's debt) mean ship funding is withering: Commerzbank, the world's second biggest provider of ship finance, has shut down its twenty-billion-euro shipping fund and now owns a fleet of foreclosed vessels. Cutting costs, the industry increasingly employs riding gangs, non-seafarers whose pay and situation are covered by no agreements, who provide cheap labour, cargo handling and maintenance. In their pursuit of declining profits many shipowners are shameless in rolling back what-ever progress has been made in the working and living conditions of sailors. Recent reports by inspectors who detain vessels in the United Kingdom's ports could have been written fifty or a hundred years ago.

'The crew accommodation was no longer provided with heating; there were insufficient fruit and vegetables on board . . . There were insufficient life rafts, the sanitary water system was inoperative and there was no fresh-running water. There were no nautical publications and charts were incomplete for the operational area . . . The ship was dangerously unsafe as the engine room bilge wells were full of thick black oil . . . There was insufficient diesel fuel on board for the voyage . . .'

None of this improves the likelihood of fair pay for Filipino seafarers, though the discrimination with which the shipping world treats them is a moral disgrace, but it does explain why the men I met did not complain. A company like Maersk may be content to run ships not covered by international labour agreements, but their conditions are not like those described above.

'Have you seen a great freighter slide by in the bay on a dreamy afternoon and as you stretch your eyes along the iron serpentine length in search of people, seamen, ghosts who must be operating this dreaming vessel so softly parting harbor waters off its steel-shin bow with snout pointed to the Four Winds of the World you see nothing, not one soul?'

So asks Jack Kerouac in his essay 'Slobs of the Kitchen Sea'. And so had I looked, and so not seen. I looked at the long tankers hiding from Celtic storms in St Bride's Bay, at the horizon-bound ships making for the Atlantic out of the Severn Sea, at low slim rectangles on the skyline off the shores of Africa, at the giant and dirty sky-shrinking bulkers streaming up the Bosphorus past the Golden Horn. I see them now more keenly, sometimes from the air, towing their arrowhead wakes, or anchored in the bays of Trieste and Naples, on misty seas evaporating in salt hazes, where great blocks are freighters waiting – their wipers, oilers, engineers, electricians, stewards, officers, chiefs and captains invisible. But when I think of the freighters now I see their swept corridors and the red-lit decks at night. I smell the cooking and the diesel, and up on the bridge I picture the watchman, and the officer making tiny pencil marks on a square metre denoting thousands of miles of sea.

I thought I went to sea to find out about ships and oceans, but though I saw something of these I saw much more of men. The sea gathers congregations of men, from the oldest, the Archer, glimpsed across five millennia, to the youngest, Richard, born barely twenty years ago. It lights up men in terror like Humphrey Knight at his anti-aircraft gun, and Captain Rugiati, hiding under his bed, and men in extremity like the oiled survivor. The ocean offers up heroes of their time like Captain Loxley, going down with his ship on a blessing and a cigarette, and puts the passenger in the hands of the ordinary, enduring, extraordinary men who worked and sailed the ships I travelled on, as I looked at them and marvelled.

Their lives are not like ours. While what it means to be a man and what is asked of a man evolves on land, the sea asks only one question, the same it has always asked. Can you face yourself – and me?

The *Maersk Luz* sails from Singapore, across the southern Indian Ocean, around the Cape of Good Hope and up through the South Atlantic to ports on the eastern seaboard of South America. With slow steaming – extremely slow steaming sometimes – to save fuel and cut losses, she can be out of sight of land for two months at a stretch. Erwin and Chicoy talked about what can happen to a man on a ship if another takes a dislike to him; about weeks or months or a year of bullying; quarrels relating to feuds at home; trouble with women ashore; men ganging up on a victim, and taking it and taking it until you can take no more. They do not talk about facing yourself, in your cabin, at work, over the meal, in your cabin, at work, over the meal, again and again and again, facing yourself as you lose faith in yourself, and the messages from home get worse. The painter with the knife could not take it. No one knows how many, like him, snap.

The seafarers taught me a great deal, and though I will no doubt forget much of their practical knowledge, I came to feel that the lesson of the sea is that this earth is a ship, and all of us are sailors – wipers, oilers, engineers and captains all at once. I will not forget the ways in which the good ones are gentle with each other and mighty with themselves. I am writing this in the days just before my partner gives birth to our first child: crossing oceans suddenly seems an uncomplicated business, the sea a straightforward place, and being responsible for yourself alone a wonderfully clear task. I know I am not a good sailor in many ways. I am more excited and scared now than at the approach of any storm, and more apprehensive about my inner strength than I have ever been. But I find myself recalling something Captain Koop said, one evening in the Atlantic. He was talking about teaching junior officers to cope with the fishing fleets of the eastern seas, as they guided the *Sydney* through the darkness towards squadrons of bobbing fire: 'I always said don't panic, don't try to see them all at once. Bring the radar in close. Deal with what is in front of the ship. Let the fishing boats come to you.'

A Note on Sources

This book is informed by a variety of writings but it is particularly indebted for its accounts of the Atlantic war to Richard Woodman's *The Real Cruel Sea: The Merchant Navy in the Battle of the Atlantic 1939–43,* published by John Murray, London 2004.

Any reader wishing to know the fullest available account of that conflict will find Mr Woodman's superb history as engrossing as the story it tells is extraordinary.

Among many volumes and websites consulted in the course of the research I would recommend the following especially, and would like to acknowledge the debt I owe their authors' scholarship – in every case greater than my own, to which any errors in the text are wholly attributable.

Joseph Conrad: The Major Phase, Jacques Berthoud, Cambridge University Press, Cambridge 1978

Four Captains, Captain George Clark, Brown, Son and Ferguson, Glasgow 1975

The Nigger of the 'Narcissus': A Tale of the Sea, Joseph Conrad, Doubleday Page and Co., London 1897

The principall navigations, voiages, and discoveries of the English nation, Richard Hakluyt, London 1589; published for the Hakluyt Society and the Peabody Museum of Salem at the University Press, 1965

The Perfect Storm – A True Story of Men Against the Sea, Sebastian Junger, Norton, New York 1997

A Book of Sea Journeys, Ludovic Kennedy, Collins, London 1981

Lonesome Traveler, Jack Kerouac, McGraw Hill, New York 1960

The Golden Book of the Dutch Navigators, Hendrik Willem Van Loon, The Century Co., New York 1916

The Cruel Sea, Nicholas Monserrat, Penguin, London, 1951

The Hairy Ape, Eugene O'Neill, New York 1922

Argonauts of the North Sea – a Social Maritime Archaeology for the 2nd Millennium BC, Robert Van de Noort, Proceedings of the Prehistoric Society 72, 2006, pp. 267–287

Coleridge's Notebooks: A Selection, edited by Seamus Perry, OUP, Oxford 2002

Before the Bells Have Faded: The Sinking of HMS Formidable, Mark Potts and Tony Marks, Naval and Military Press, Uckfield, 2009

The War at Sea, 1939–1945: An Anthology of Personal Experience, selected and edited by John Winton, Hutchinson, London 1967

Acknowledgements

M y first requests went to Michael Christian Storgaard at Maersk Lines in Copenhagen and were then handled with infinite patience by Claire Sneddon in the company's London office. I am entirely indebted to these two for their kindness and pains, and would like to thank the company for its hospitality and cooperation.

To Captains Henrik Larsen and Petrus Koop, and to their officers and crews, particularly Sorin Simonov, Chris Nielsen, Joel Embuscado, Shubd Prashant, John Holmshaw, Pieter Mulder, Erwin Callarman, Johannes Edelman, Anabelle Salazar, Mark Gigremosa and Richard Duller, as well as to those who preferred not to be named (and to those whose frankness led me to disguise them) I can only offer my deepest thanks and these pages, in gratitude and admiration.

Without the encouragement and support of Zoe Waldie at Rogers, Coleridge and White and Clara Farmer of Chatto & Windus this book would not have been written or published. Thank you both: all your writers are utterly blessed in your backing and empowerment, and none more than I. Special thanks to Mohsen Shah, Lexie Hamblin for your great kindness and pains. Susannah Otter's phenomenal eye and brain were huge boons to the manuscript, and Lisa Gooding is the best publicist any writer could hope for: thank you both.

I have been hugely lucky in the kindness and skill of Victoria Murray-Browne and Alison Rae at Vintage Books, and the world of objects is much indebted to James Jones who designed the stunning cover. Thank you.

John Clare gave the book a going-over at a crucial stage, and saved it from multiple failings. Thank you, Dad.

Among friends too kind and too numerous to mention Roger Couhig, Merlin and Anna-Rose Hughes, James and Elizabeth Mann, Alison 'Tig' Finch, Julian May, Mohit Bakaya, Sally Baker, Sarah Dunant, Niall Griffiths, Anne Garwood, Ben Hardiman, Caroline Flinders, Candace Cade, Richard Coles, Suella Darkins, Rob Ketteridge, Jeremy Grange, Elizabeth Passey, Rupert Crisswell, Jody Trick, Anna Gavalda, Sian Walker, Scott Tetlow, Robin Tetlow-Shooter, Gail Marsh, Jenny Shooter, Mike White, Richard Davidson-Houston, Chris Kenyon, Toby Lynas, Graham da Gama Howells, Mary Generelli, Robin Jenkins, Robert Macfarlane, Jane Matthews, Allegra McIlroy, Jan Morris, Jim Perrin, Stephen Fleming and Diarmaid Gallagher contributed especially (and in some cases unwittingly) to the life of this book and the sustaining of its author. Thank you, you rockers-on.

Thank you, my dear family: Sally, Alexander, Meghan Best and John Clare, for your love and care – and for the inspiration to write and travel. And thank you, dearest Rebecca and Aubrey, for gifts beyond all words.